THE

RIVERSIDE

GUIDE

TO

Writing

INSTRUCTOR'S RESOURCE MANUAL:

THE RIVERSIDE GUIDE TO *Writing*

DOUGLAS HUNT
University of Missouri

CAROLYN PERRY
University of Missouri

HOUGHTON MIFFLIN COMPANY   BOSTON

Dallas   Geneva, Illinois   Palo Alto   Princeton, New Jersey

Printed in the U.S.A.

ISBN: 0-395-57276-2

ABCDEFGHIJ-CS-99876543210

Contents

Preface

To begin with an oversimplification, composition textbooks may be built on one of two philosophical models. They may treat writing as a field separated from the center of the curriculum, a matter of specialized skills and knowledge, rather like trigonometry. Or they may treat writing as a more broadly defined mental discipline, something allied to the core of a liberal education. *The Riverside Guide to Writing* takes the broad view. It assumes that the composition class is, so to speak, an introduction in miniature to college level reading, writing, and thinking.

There are practical reasons to view the composition class in this broad way. In an era of academic specialization, it has become one of the few common experiences of all students. On most college campuses, we can't count on all students having taken a sociology course or a geography course or a philosophy course, but we can count on their having taken composition. If there are general aims of a college education, they may fall between chairs unless they are addressed in that composition class. And since composition classes are ordinarily taken early in students' academic careers, they provide us with an excellent opportunity to give a preview of the patterns of thought and discourse that hold the curriculum together. Without such a preview, students may never see the patterns.

Of course, making the composition class a preview of the college curriculum is an ambitious undertaking, not to be undertaken lightly or without the support of colleagues. The aim of this manual is to provide some of the necessary support. The bulk of the manual comprises chapter-by-chapter advice and comment—the sort of thing we would want to talk with you about if we could meet you in your office or in the faculty lounge. There are also sample syllabi for courses with various emphases and courses that fit into various curricular structures (semester system, quarter system, single-term course, two-term course). "A Note to New Instructors" provides advice for those who have not taught composition before, but it may also be of interest to experienced instructors who are eager (as we are) to learn how other committed writing teachers conduct their business.

Many parts of *The Riverside Guide,* including many of the exercises, have been "class tested" for years, but we owe a special thanks to the first class to use the book in its entirety—a composition class at the University of Missouri in the spring semester of 1990. Their insights and advice were heartening and chastening. They showed what *The Riverside Guide* could contribute to a writing class, and also encouraged us to make some corrections and improvements. We want to acknowledge the particular contributions of the following students, whose essays we have included in the "Package of Student Essays."

Bret Alsop	Drew Dunning
Matthew Bailey	Brian Kimzey
Stephen Best	Jenny Smith
Steve Beane	Amy Willis
Mike Brady	Dena Vann
Kim Cox	Marian Zellner

Classes that used the text in subsequent semesters also made significant contributions to it, but this first group of freshman pioneers must be credited with pointing out the worst of the ruts and potholes.

Finally, we should say a word about pronouns. On subsequent pages "I"s in the *Purpose, Overview, The Chapter Step-by-Step,* and *The Assignments* sections generally refer to Doug Hunt. "I"s in the *End-of-Chapter Readings* sections generally refer to Carolyn Perry. To avoid sounding like a corporate entity, we have both allowed ourselves frequent use of the pronoun "I" when we were talking about personal experiences or insight.

Doug Hunt
Carolyn Perry

INSTRUCTOR'S RESOURCE MANUAL:

THE
RIVERSIDE
GUIDE
TO
Writing

Suggested Course Plans

The Riverside Guide is designed to serve courses with a range of objectives and formats. On the following pages you will find several semester and quarter plans for courses that emphasize, variously, personal experience writing, argumentation, research, and literature-based essays. Each syllabus is organized around a series of writing assignments. We have also suggested chapter assignments, exercises, and readings that aim to prepare students thoroughly for the writing they will be asked to do.

Although you may vary the length of the assignments, by *Essay* we mean a paper of 750 to 1250 words (3–5 pages) and by *Microtheme*, one of no more than 250 words. Microthemes are useful because they allow for flexibility within the syllabus; depending on the performance level of your students, you may make these short papers as formal as the essays, or as informal as an in-class writing. *Exercises* work well both in class, particularly through small group discussion, or as out-of-class writing assignments.

While you may wish to use one of these syllabi directly, you may find them helpful in choosing appropriate exercises and readings or in setting a workable pace for the writing assignments. Variations on the included syllabi can be made by keeping the parts of the book in mind. The first two chapters lay the groundwork for any course and work well as semester or quarter-openers. The rest of Part I (Chapters 3 and 4) take up personal experience writing; Part II, then introduces students to argumentation. Within Part III, Chapters 8 through 10 can either be taught as an extension of argumentation (with less emphasis put on research) or as a basis for research projects (and be taught with the research chapters, 11 and 12).

In our experience, the chapters in Part IV fit most smoothly into a course if each one is sandwiched between two of the earlier chapters, during those weeks when students are putting most of their time into the writing assignments.

4

One Semester Course:
Exposition and Argumentation

Week 1:   Introduction to the course
Chapter 1

Week 2:   Chapter 1 Readings: Didion, White, Angelou
Assign Essay 1: Chapter 1, Assignment 1 *or* 4

Week 3:   Chapter 2; Exercises 1 and 2
Microtheme 1 Due: Chapter 2, Assignment 1
Workshop for Essay 1

Week 4:   Chapter 2 Readings: Dillard and White
Essay 1 Due

Week 5:   Chapter 3; Exercises 1–4 *or* 5–8, and 9–10
Assign Essay 2: Chapter 3, Assignment 3

Week 6:   Chapter 3 Readings: Orwell, Twain, Angelou
Microtheme 2 Due: Chapter 3, Assignment 1

Week 7:   Workshop for Essay 2
Chapter 5

Week 8:   Chapter 5 Readings: Twain
Chapter 13; Exercises 1 and 4
Essay 2 Due

Week 9:   Chapter 6; Exercises 1–3
Assign Essay 3: Chapter 6, Assignment 2

Week 10:   Microtheme 3 Due: Chapter 5, Exercise 1
Chapter 6 Readings: McCarthy, O'Brien, and Will

Week 11:   Chapter 14
Workshop for Essay 3

Week 12:   Essay 3 Due
Chapter 7; Exercises 1 and 2
Assign Essay 4: Chapter 7, Assignments 2–7

Week 13:   Chapter 7 Readings: Miller and Brownmiller
Microtheme 4: Chapter 7, Assignment 1
Chapter 15; Exercises 1–4

Week 14:   Workshop for Essay 4
Chapter 16; Exercises 1–3

Week 15:   Essay 4 Due

We have found that our classes include many students who have difficulty with argumentation, so we have allowed several weeks for Chapters 6 and 7 and have limited the number of essay assignments to four. If your students are particularly good at writing argument papers, you may quicken the pace and add either Chapter 8, 9, or 10, all of which build on Part II.

* * * * *

One Semester Course:
Composition and Literature

Week 1:   Introduction to the course
            Chapter 1

Week 2:   Chapter 1 Readings: White and Angelou
            Chapter 10 Readings: Brooks and Browning
            Assign Essay 1: Chapter 1, Assignment 2

Week 3:   Chapter 2; Exercises 1 and 2
            Workshop for Essay 1

Week 4:   Chapter 2 Readings: Dillard and White
            Assign Essay 2: Chapter 3, Assignment 2
            Essay 1 Due

Week 5:   Chapter 3; Exercises 1–4 *or* 5–8, and 9–10
            Chapter 10 Readings: Canin and Bambara
            Workshop for Essay 2

Week 6:   Chapter 3 Readings: Twain
            Essay 2 Due
            Chapter 14

Week 7:   Chapter 4; Exercises 1–4
            Assign Essay 3: Chapter 4, Assignment 6
            Microtheme 1 Due: Chapter 4, Exercise 6 *or* 7
            Chapter 10 Readings: Robinson and Oates

Week 8:   Chapter 4 Readings: Orwell and White
            Workshop for Essay 3

Week 9:   Chapter 9; Exercises 3 and 4
            Essay 3 Due

Week 10:   Chapter 9 Readings: Dillard Reviews and Will
            Microtheme 2 Due: Chapter 9, Assignment 2
            Assign Essay 4: Chapter 9, Assignment 4

Week 11:   Chapter 15; Exercises 1–4
            Workshop for Essay 4

Week 12:   Chapter 10; Exercises 3 and 4
            Assign Essay 5: Chapter 10, Assignment 3
            Essay 4 Due

Week 13:   Chapter 10 Readings: Munro, Miller, and Woodard
            Microtheme 3 Due: Chapter 10, Assignment 1

Week 14:   Chapter 16; Exercises 1–3
            Workshop for Essay 5

Week 15:   Essay 5 Due

By combining composition and literature, this course allows you to study literary texts, criticism of literature and other art forms, and non-fiction prose by both novelists and essayists.

*   *   *   *   *

Two Semester Course
First Semester: Exposition and Research

Week 1:   Introduction to the course
            Chapter 1

Week 2:   Chapter 1 Readings: Didion, White, Angelou
            Assign Essay 1: Chapter 1, Assignment 2

Week 3:   Chapter 2; Exercises 1 and 2
            Workshop for Essay 1

Week 4:   Essay 1 Due
            Chapter 2 Readings: White and Dillard

Week 5:   Chapter 3; Exercises 1–4 *or* 5–8, and 9–10
            Assign Essay 2: Chapter 3, Assignment 3

Week 6:   Chapter 3 Readings: Orwell, Twain, and Angelou
            Microtheme 1 Due: Chapter 3, Assignment 1
            Workshop for Essay 2

Week 7:   Chapter 4; Exercises 1–4, 9–10
            Essay 2 Due

Week 8:   Chapter 4 Readings: T.H. White, Johnson, and Didion
            Assign Essay 3: Chapter 4, Assignment 5

Week 9:   Chapter 14
            Workshop for Essay 3

Week 10:   Chapter 8; Exercises 2 and 4
            Essay 3 Due
            Assign Research Paper

Week 11:   Chapter 8 Readings: Miranda, White, and Thomas
            Microtheme 2 Due: Chapter 8, Assignment 1

Week 12:   Chapter 11
            Microtheme 3 Due: Chapter 2, Assignments 1 and 2
            First Workshop for Research Paper

Week 13:   Chapter 12
            Conferences

Week 14:   Conferences
            Final Workshop for Research Paper

Week 15:   Research Paper Due

Because this course builds toward research, you may wish to refer to Chapter 11 ("Some Advice on Research") early on, such as in Week 8 while your students are working on the interview-based assignment.

Our assumption here is that you will *not* be assigning a major research project of the sort sometimes called a "term paper" and properly (we believe) belonging to advanced classes. Such projects require several weeks of work by students and, in our experience, work best when classes are small enough to allow several conferences with each student. See this manual's comments on Chapter 12 for a discussion of the logistics of the term paper.

A short paper involving limited research (perhaps a 1000–1500 word essay with a half-dozen sources) can, however, be managed in about three weeks.

*   *   *   *   *

Two Semester Course
Second Semester: Argumentation

Week 1:   Introduction to Course
           Review of Chapter 1

Week 2:   Chapter 1 Readings: Tuchman and Dillard
           Microtheme 1 Due: Chapter 1, Assignment 4
           Chapter 5

Week 3:   Chapter 5 Readings: Twain
           Assign Essay 1: Chapter 6, Assignment 1

Week 4:   Chapter 6; Exercises 1–3
           Microtheme 2 Due: Chapter 6, Assignment 4

Week 5:   Chapter 6 Readings: McCarthy, O'Brien, and Will
           Microtheme 3 Due: Chapter 5, Exercise 1

Week 6:   Workshop for Essay 1
           Chapter 7; Exercises 1 and 2

Week 7:   Essay 1 Due
           Assign Essay 2: Chapter 7, Assignment 8
           Chapter 7 Readings: Miller and Brownmiller

Week 8:   Microtheme 3 Due: Chapter 7, Assignment 1
           Workshop for Essay 2

Week 9:   Chapter 9; Exercises 1–4
           Essay 2 Due
           Assign Essay 3: Chapter 9, Assignment 4 *or* 5

Week 10:   Chapter 9 Readings: Dillard Reviews, Santoro, and Will
           Microtheme 4 Due: Chapter 9, Assignment 2

Week 11:   Workshop for Essay 3
           Chapter 15; Exercises 1–4

Week 12:   Essay 3 Due
           Chapter 10; Exercises 1–4
           Assign Essay 4: Chapter 10, Assignment 3

Week 13:   Readings for Chapter 10: Browning, Bambara, and Miller

Week 14:   Chapter 16; Exercises 1–3
           Microtheme 5 Due: Chapter 10, Assignment 1

Week 15:   Essay 4 Due

This half of the course is designed for students who have already had considerable experience writing. The initial argument chapters are covered thoroughly, but the application of argumentation to evaluation and writing about literature are of equal weight. In addition, this half builds well on the first in that it allows you to include research skills in all of the essay assignments.

*   *   *   *   *

One Quarter Course:
Exposition and Argumentation

Week 1:   Introduction to the course
          Chapter 1

Week 2:   Chapter 1 Readings: Didion, White, Angelou
          Assign Essay 1: Chapter 1, Assignment 1
          Microtheme 1 Due: Chapter 2, Assignment 1

Week 3:   Chapter 2; Exercises 1 and 2
          Workshop for Essay 1
          Chapter 2 Readings: Dillard and White

Week 4:   Essay 1 Due
          Chapter 5

Week 5:   Chapter 5 Reading: Twain
          Chapter 6; Exercises 1–3
          Assign Essay 2: Chapter 6, Assignment 2

Week 6:   Chapter 6 Readings: O'Brien and Will
          Microtheme 2 Due: Chapter 5, Exercise 1
          Workshop for Essay 2

Week 7:   Chapter 7; Exercises 1 and 2
          Essay 2 Due
          Assign Essay 3: Chapter 7, Assignments 2–7

Week 8:   Chapter 7 Readings: Hitt and Lewis
          Microtheme 3 Due: Chapter 7, Assignment 1
          Chapter 14

Week 9:   Workshop for Essay 3
          Chapter 15, Exercises 1–4

Week 10: Chapter 16; Exercises 1–3
          Essay 3 Due

With so few weeks to master argumentation, this course is designed to introduce students to the rationale behind *The Riverside Guide* through one essay built on personal experience, and then dive immediately into Part II of the book. Because the style chapters come so late in the course, you may wish to spend the last three weeks focusing on revision of all the essays.

*   *   *   *   *

Two Quarter Course
First Quarter: Exposition

Week 1:   Introduction to the course
           Chapter 1

Week 2:   Chapter 1 Readings: Didion, White, Angelou
           Assign Essay 1: Chapter 1, Assignment 1 *or* 4

Week 3:   Microtheme 1 Due: Chapter 1, Assignment 4
           Chapter 2; Exercises 1 and 2

Week 4:   Chapter 2 Readings: White and Dillard
           Workshop for Essay 1

Week 5:   Essay 1 Due
           Chapter 3; Exercises 1–4 *or* 5–8, and 9–10
           Chapter 3 Readings: Orwell, Twain, and Angelou
           Assign Essay 2: Chapter 3, Assignment 3

Week 6:   Chapter 14
           Workshop for Essay 2

Week 7:   Essay 2 Due
           Chapter 4; Exercises 1–4, 9–10
           Microtheme 2 Due: Chapter 4, Assignment 1

Week 8:   Chapter 4 Readings: E.B. White, Johnson, and Didion
           Assign Essay 3: Chapter 4, Assignment 5

Week 9:   Chapter 15
           Workshop for Essay 3

Week 10:   Chapter 16; Exercises 1–3
           Essay 3 Due

We have not included Chapters 11 and 12 in this syllabus because it is notoriously difficult to include a significant research paper in a quarter-system course—unless one term is specifically designated for such a course.

*   *   *   *   *

Two Quarter Course
Second Quarter: Argumentation

Week 1: Introduction to Course
Review of Chapter 1

Week 2: Chapter 1 Readings: Tuchman and Dillard
Microtheme 1 Due: Chapter 1, Assignment 2

Week 3: Chapter 5
Chapter 5 Readings: Twain
Assign Essay 1: Chapter 6, Assignment 1

Week 4: Chapter 6; Exercises 1–3
Microtheme 2 Due: Chapter 5, Exercise 1
Workshop for Essay 1

Week 5: Chapter 6 Readings: McCarthy, O'Brien, and Will
Essay 1 Due

Week 6: Chapter 7; Exercises 1 and 2
Assign Essay 2: Chapter 7, Assignments 2–7
Microtheme 3 Due: Chapter 7, Assignment 1

Week 7: Chapter 7 Readings: Miller and Brownmiller
Workshop for Essay 2

Week 8: Chapter 8; Exercises 1 and 4
Essay 2 Due
Assign Essay 3: Chapter 8, Assignment 4

Week 9: Chapter 8 Readings: Miranda, White, and Thomas
Workshop for Essay 3

Week 10: Essay 3 Due

This syllabus is intended for students who, having completed the first half of the course, are prepared for more intensive writing. Therefore, in addition to the three argument chapters, we have included the application of argument to proposals (Chapter 8). You may find it best to drop this last chapter in order to give your students more time with 6 and 7; if so, consider changing Microtheme 1 into an essay assignment.

*   *   *   *   *

A Note to New Teachers

Watching Robin Williams' performance in *The Dead Poet's Society* convinced me there will never be a movie about a great composition teacher. Literature teachers sometimes accomplish a great deal by flamboyance, by occupying center stage, by winning an admiration from young people that amounts to hero-worship. But the composition class (in my experience, at least) does not thrive when it is centered on the teacher. In composition, it is the students' performance that counts. Ideally, the instructor works in the margin, so to speak, not at the center of attention. The great composition teacher is a coach, not a star athlete.

In many classes, instructors (inspiring or otherwise) dispense knowledge and students receive it. Ideally, they receive it tentatively, with critical faculties fully alert, but after twelve or thirteen years in our educational system, too many undergraduates have been schooled into passivity. To a distressing degree, they see college as a series of spiral notebooks filled with transcribed lectures. If composition teachers walk home at the end of the day with shoulders sagging, it is largely because they have struggled all day to reverse the effects of an educational system that treats students as consumers of knowledge and opinions. In the composition classroom an instructor must turn the tables and make the students producers—must convince students that they have something worthwhile to say.

Some Practical Hints

1. *Stress your role as a coach.*

An instructor can no more teach a student how to write than a coach can teach a player how to shoot a jump shot or a piano teacher lecture a student through a difficult passage. When the student must perform, the teacher's work is largely to respond to and correct what the student does on his or her own initiative. It is probably best to explain this situation to your students at the outset, and to tell them that the business of this course will be *their* drafting and revision of

13

essays. You can and will help with this drafting and revising process: by assigning and reviewing reading that prepares students to draft particular kinds of papers, by orchestrating peer review sessions, by commenting on drafts, etc. But nothing you can do changes the fact that success or failure on essays is ultimately the writer's responsibility. And, as a practical matter, the way everyone learns to write is by writing and revising with a *personal* commitment to do the job right. When students understand your view of their situation, most will respond positively, pleased (at some level) to take some responsibility for their own education.

Chapter 2 of *The Riverside Guide* attempts to underscore the student's responsibility and the instructor's role as a coach/editor—an "intermediate" audience that helps students learn to write for various "ultimate" audiences.

2.   *Make use of peer editorial groups if you can.*

With each passing year, I become more convinced of the practical advantages of establishing editorial groups in the class and relying on them heavily, not only to comment on drafts of essays, but to brainstorm, to discuss readings, and to collaborate on exercises designed to prepare students to write particular assignments.

Without peer groups, students often write and speak with the narrow aim of pleasing the teacher, and so indirectly learn the rhetoric of dissembling and petty deception. One result is that they produce essays that are grotesque parodies of "what the teacher wants to hear." In my first year of teaching, I apparently looked like someone who wanted to hear about parties "characterized by a congenial atmosphere that is conducive to intimate interpersonal relationships," about "daffodils dancing lazily on sweet breezes in the shimmering sunshine of a hazy summer day," and about embarrassing sexual experiences. I don't think that the students who wrote these papers were conscious of dishonesty, but they had been put in the false position of looking for a way to please a single reader about whom they knew little.

The most practical way out of this situation is to broaden the audience, to create a "public" for the student writer, and editorial groups can do precisely that. Like most composition teachers, I have used such groups in a variety of forms over the years. My present preference is to divide the class frequently (at least once each week) into very small groups—three or four students each—to work exercises or criticize each others' work. The memberships of the groups change from time to time, so that students get a chance to widen their circle of acquaintances and also broaden their view of their audience.

When the groups are to review drafts, I have each student bring the original copy plus a copy for each of the other people in the group. A group of three students can typically discuss everyone's draft of a short essay (500 words) in one fifty-minute session. Longer essays may require two days. Unless the physical circumstances make it impossible, I insist that the author read the original aloud while the other students in the group make notes and comments on the copies. Reading aloud solves many problems of voice: few students would want to read the sentence about parties "characterized by a congenial atmosphere" aloud in front of their fellow students.

The first two or three times that you use editorial groups in class, you will want to provide a structure that gets the group going and keeps it on task. I usually give each group a checklist or agenda to work from and tell the groups that one member (arbitrarily, for the first session, the one born furthest from the classroom) should be in charge of keeping the group's attention on the agenda. Another member (the one born nearest the classroom) should serve as timekeeper, making sure that every essay gets equal attention. At the end of Chapter 2, you will find a peer-review checklist that can serve as an agenda. At the end of chapters 3, 4, 6, 7, 8, 9, and 10, you will find additional questions for peer review that are appropriate to the particular assignments featured in those chapters.

Group work bears unexpected fruit. When I began to use peer editing groups to supplement my own commentary, the quantity and quality of the feedback the writers got improved significantly, and the students seemed much more engaged with the class. Most of the editorial groups worked very hard for the whole of every class hour, and I often noticed that when the class broke up, there would be a flurried exchange of phone numbers and some appointments made to meet outside of class to look at subsequent revisions.

Since that time, I've encouraged the peripheral class, the class of phone calls and meetings at the student union, in every way I can. In the first week of class, I make it very clear to students that I will not grade their papers relative to each other's, but relative to fixed standards. If everybody writes well, works hard, and solicits help from classmates as necessary, we could conceivably have a class of all A's and B's. If they don't, we could have a class of D's and F's. I pass around a sheet of paper on which students can put their phone numbers if they don't mind being called by other students in the class, and I duplicate the sheet so that everyone will have a copy. I put my own home phone on the sheet, but with a request that students not call me with a problem until they have called at least one of their classmates.

Some of you will be reluctant to give out your home number, and understandably so. But it has worked well for me. I've done some of my best teaching with a dishtowel in my hands. Because students call after they have consulted one or two classmates about their problem, they tend to be fairly focused and articulate about their dilemmas. "Julie says that the introduction still leaves my framework too unclear. What do you think?" "Ray looked at this last night and thought that one of my sentences could mean two different things, but I don't see it. Can I read it to you?"

Editorial groups are not a panacea, and some instructors who try them tell me frankly that they found them to be disastrous. They may have given up too soon: the first two or three sessions tend to be a bit uncomfortable and unproductive because the students are not used to each other and not quite ready to talk frankly. I encourage new teachers to experiment with group work and, if they have trouble, to talk with a colleague whose groups seem to succeed.

3. *Begin the semester with a short moratorium on grades.*

Few of your students will be experienced writers, and many will begin the semester with more anxiety than they can put to productive use. As Mina Shaughnessy noted in her ground-breaking study *Errors and Expectations* (1977), the least secure of your writers will see their prose as "a line that moves haltingly across the page, exposing as it goes all that the writer doesn't know, then passing into the hands of a stranger who reads it with a lawyer's eyes, searching out flaws." If you assign a fully graded, major essay at the beginning of the semester and return a well-deserved salvo of C's, D's and F's, you may scare such students out of their wits, killing their desire to take chances with their writing and their willingness to invest their egos in it. This is not to say that you should avoid all writing assignments in the early days of a term. On the contrary, you need to get students started quickly. But you might start with an ungraded draft that you comment on as encouragingly as possible, and you might consider assigning only "satisfactories" and "unsatisfactories" on the first essay of the semester. If you feel you need to assign a full grade to the first essay, you might consider making its weight in the final grade calculation rather light, thus indicating that you have anticipated a rough start for some students and that you expect they will improve as time passes.

Some instructors, wanting to be encouraging in the early part of the semester, simply grade generously—giving B's to papers that might receive C's or D's at the semester's end. This can be a dangerous policy, since a student whose work remains at the same level will see his grade sink steadily as the term progresses, a dismal situation, and one that tends to produce grade protests.

The early-semester moratorium (or honeymoon) can't be continued too long. At my university, students need to have a graded paper under their belts by the fourth week (before the add/drop deadline) so that they can take stock of their situation and make adjustments accordingly.

4.   Explain your standards as a grader.

Students sometimes get tangled in the ambiguities of a course where the instructor is both a coach and a judge. While the paper is in progress, the instructor is an ally—almost a lawyer for the defense—accentuating the positive and extenuating the negative, looking through the murkiness of what a draft actually *is* to see what it *might* be. When the paper is completed, the instructor must leave this personal involvement behind and read on behalf of the "ultimate" audience discussed in Chapter 2—the audience of strangers.

Students need to understand this peculiar situation. One way to clarify it is to give them a written set of the standards you set for final drafts. The set below is appropriate for most of the assignments in *The Riverside Guide*, but see the cautions that follow it:

Typical Characteristics of the A Paper

Both the subject of the paper and the framework of interpretation are always clear. The careful reader can discern the purpose behind every paragraph and sentence.

The paper seems at every point well suited for the intended audience.

The paper is well organized, and the organization does not seem mechanical or awkward.

The sentences are varied in length and structure according to the writer's meaning and emphasis.

The word choice is almost uniformly good. Words are chosen for precise denotation, connotation, and tone.

In grammar, mechanics, and usage, the paper is correct except for excusable errors of inadvertence and violations of extremely technical rules.

Typical Characteristics of the B Paper

The subject and the interpretive framework are always clear. The careful reader may have some difficulty seeing the pertinence of a brief passage here and there.

Except for rare lapses, the paper is well suited for the intended audience.

The organization is correct, but transitions are sometimes strained.

Each paragraph has its own framework, subject, and details.

The sentences are usually varied in length and structure according to the writer's meaning and emphasis.

The word choice is generally correct. The writer has gone beyond the automatic word to find one more precise and effective.

The paper is generally correct in grammar, mechanics, and usage, though there are some problems with complex grammar and punctuation traps.

Typical Characteristics of the C Paper

Though the reader can name the subject and framework of the paper, the paper does not seem consistent or forceful in its interpretation. Readers may feel that they are hearing conventional ideas about a conventional subject, or they may feel they are reading the work of someone who has not thought his or her way to a clear view of the subject.

The organization is acceptable, though some parts may be slightly awry. The essay has a clear thesis or principle of organization, but parts of the paper seem to be in revolt or on vacation.

The paragraphs have their own frameworks and subjects, though the quality of the supporting details is sometimes disappointing.

There are very few errors in sentence structure, but the sentences are not varied.

The word choice is generally correct, but the range of words is limited; therefore, the diction is sometimes imprecise and monotonous.

Though the paper contains few major errors, there are mistakes in niceties of spelling, grammar, punctuation, and mechanics.

Typical Characteristics of the D Paper

Only in a few places can the reader detect the writer's framework. As a result, the paper seems an unfocused exercise rather than an interesting essay. The writer does little to engage the audience.

Some principle of organization is apparent, but it isn't successfully followed.

The paragraphing is rational, but the body paragraphs are underdeveloped. They may be made up of a series of generalizations without details or of details that seem to have no controlling idea or framework.

Errors in sentence structure are frequent enough to distract the reader, but are not pervasive.

Words are occasionally misused. Attempts to go beyond everyday vocabulary go awry.

The sentences conform well enough to the grammar of English as spoken by educated (but not fussy) people. They often fail to conform to the conventions of written English.

Typical Characteristics of the F Paper

The paper seems to be a mechanical exercise without a significant framework and without a realistic sense of audience.

There is no apparent principle of organization.

There is no apparent rationale for the paragraphing.

There are frequent sentence structure errors of a kind that would make most educated readers suspect that the author has little education.

Words that should be within the range of almost all college students are misused and confused.

Some errors indicate a failure to understand the basic grammar of the sentence. Simple words are frequently misspelled.

I think it is dangerous to use a list like this as if it were a contract. Student papers will usually mix characteristics from two or more grade levels: a paper that has the focus and organization of A work may contain sentence-level errors that make it look like D work. For about a year, early in my career, I tried to assign percentages to the various aspects of the essay, but this proved cumbersome and futile: the whole effect of the paper is what counts, and I kept having to alter my ratings of the various features to justify my grade for the whole.

I tell my students that my set of standards—like the U.S. Constitution—must be interpreted with some flexibility in order to preserve the spirit rather than the letter of the law.

5.   *Remind your students that you grade by merits rather than demerits.*

Students may imagine that their essays start off in some Platonic heaven as A's and then fall, error by error, to a lower grade. This view partly explains their tendency to complain that they get C's, even though "hardly anything is marked wrong." You can save your students some confusion if you tell them that a blank page starts out as a zero and works its way up to a certain level more by a display of strengths than by an avoidance of faults.

I used to explain this distinction to students via a sports metaphor. Writing a paper is not like playing golf, where your main job is to keep the ball safely in the fairway, avoid the rough and the traps, and keep your score *low*. It is more like softball, where you swing at the ball lustily and try to put some points on the scoreboard. My golfing students complained that I had misunderstood their game.

6. *Be clear about how you distinguish between what is said and how it is said.*

I sometimes hear a teacher tell students that they will be graded entirely on form because composition is the study of *how* to write rather than *what* to write. This is a perfectly sensible position, but one almost certain to be misunderstood. The teacher probably means, "Don't worry about whether I agree with the position you take in a paper. The final issue in this course is not whether your position is right or wrong, but whether you can articulate a position and present it persuasively." What some students will hear is, "I don't care what you say so long as you spell and punctuate correctly." Even if you make yourself generally clear on this slippery form/content distinction, you may need to add a couple of warnings: first, that essays involving required reading must show an understanding of that reading; second, that some topics invite bad writing. I doubt that I have a half-dozen students a year who could write A papers on abortion or religious conversion, topics that offer the writer an armor of impenetrable clichés to "think" and "write" with. If you attack the armor, your students will probably feel that they are being attacked somewhere near their souls. Therefore, you will probably want to discourage students from writing on topics about which they cannot be reasonable.

The five-part heuristic at the end of Chapter 5 can be a help to you in dealing with the problem of clichéd thinking. I don't allow students to write argumentative essays until they have successfully completed this heuristic or something like it, and so have shown themselves capable of seeing their subject in more than one framework.

7. *Take a sensible stance on error.*

Composition teachers are divided on the issue of how to deal with errors in grammar, spelling, and usage. A classic statement of the "liberal" position can be found in Mina Shaughnessy's *Errors and Expectations*, which questions the value of that persnicketiness people have come to associate with English teachers:

> This emphasis upon propriety in the interest not of communication but of status has narrowed and debased the teaching of writing, encouraging at least two tendencies in teachers—a tendency to view the work of their students microscopically, with an eye for forms but with little interest in what was being said, and a tendency to develop a repugnance for error that has made erring students feel like pariahs and allowed teachers of mediocre talents too many easy victories.

The "conservative" position is vigorously argued by journalism professors on our campus who wonder what the hell we composition instructors can be doing in our composition classes, since we have clearly left to them the job of telling juniors and seniors what sentences are, and explaining why these formless things they are writing don't fill the bill. It is more thoughtfully argued by a linguist in our department who marks every error he sees on every paper, on the theory that the only way to make students aware of the conventions of written prose is to make them aware of their habitual deviations from the admittedly artificial standard.

Sympathy with both positions has led me to take a position of uneasy moderation. I tell my students that error is a serious problem, but that the time for them to systematically focus their attention on it is late in the composing process. (In Chapter 2 of *The Riverside Guide* I point out that the mind's capacity for focused attention is small, and that most of us are unable to think simultaneously about our ideas and the letters we are putting on the page.) I *never* use a student paper as the butt of a usage lesson, though I occasionally point to bad sentences in papers that are generally strong. On drafts and final papers, I mark all errors that draw attention to themselves. If the final copy has so many errors that the paper must be graded down severely for them, I offer students a chance to correct and resubmit—taking, as a result, the point deduction I always make for late papers.

At one point in my career, I made it my practice to mark the first ten errors in a paper only, and then to draw a line across the page indicating that I could read no further until I got a cleaner draft. There are advantages to this procedure, and I think I would recommend it for some classes. I no longer use it myself because I'm uneasy with the tone it sets and because its emphasis on counting errors makes some students over-cautious. A student once told me that she avoided putting a quotation into her essay because she was afraid she would make a punctuation error if she did.

If you decide you are going to mark all errors, you'll still want to avoid being overbearing. When I worked in our university's writing lab, I frequently saw papers red-penciled sentence by sentence until they were written in the teacher's style. The student would write "Johnson was a proud man," and the teacher would change "proud man" to "arrogant person." The student couldn't understand why the change was an improvement and was forced to conclude either that the teacher was playing the petty tyrant or that the whole business of prose style was cloaked in mysteries he or she could never penetrate. If you are confident about your ear and are teaching very good students, you may find it worthwhile to attack sentences that are clear, economical, and unesthetic. But with average undergraduates, you will probably want to restrain yourself. When you find a sentence that *you* wouldn't have written because it sounds too much like *Time* magazine or *National Geographic*, lift up your pencil and let it go. Don't consider a variation from your style an error.

8. Use conference time wisely.

Most composition teachers post office hours and encourage at least some of their students to come in for individual conferences. I find that I need to post an hour a week per fifteen or twenty students and tell students whose schedules conflict with mine that I can arrange special appointments. Individual conferences are probably most beneficial to your best students and your worst. Some of the most enthusiastic will come in as often as they can because they really do want to talk about their writing. Count your blessings and spend what time with them you can. Some of your weakest students will have to be encouraged to come in. I often arrange a conference with a student when I return a paper with a disappointing grade. The conference allows me to point out all the things he or she did well and to suggest some steps that may strengthen the next paper. I always arrange a conference when I find myself tempted to write an end comment accusing a student of plagiarism, laziness, insincerity, or some other heinous crime. Such accusations, reduced to writing, quickly build a barrier between student and teacher. But the plagiarist sometimes comes to the conference with a disarming confession, and the "lazy" student may turn out to have a learning disability or a family problem.

As a teaching tool, the conference has the advantage of allowing instruction tailored to the individual student, and I have sometimes set up a series of conferences for students who needed special instruction in grammar or punctuation. But preparing individualized instruction is very time-consuming, and the new instructor should approach it warily. Actually, it may be best to view the conference more as an opportunity to learn than as an opportunity to teach. Did the last paper go awry because you assigned a topic too far outside this particular student's experience? Do the sentences that so confused you make perfect sense when the student reads them aloud or explains them? Does the absence of examples come from lack of thought or from an assumption that "you already know all that stuff anyway"? Does the weakness of the conclusion indicate an inability to generalize or an inability to stay awake after working the night shift? Showing an interest in these things may improve a student's performance more than making a few more observations on dangling modifiers.

I don't want the preceding paragraph to be misunderstood: conferences should be kept businesslike. Students coming straight from high school may have had very few individual conferences with teachers that were not strictly disciplinary. They may be so befuddled by your kindness and attention that they will misconstrue them. A student who begins to unfold his or her personal life may need to be reminded that your main interest in it is that it not interfere with his or her work. A student who begins to cry (and composition classes can be great provokers of tears) may need a few words of consolation and an invitation to leave for a few minutes to regain enough composure to continue productively.

A final warning about conferences is that you should not overload yourself with them by requiring every student to come in routinely. This practice creates scheduling problems for everyone and often leaves the teacher too exhausted to offer any sensible advice.

9.   Be realistic about your students' interest in their grades.

I have known some idealistic teachers who regarded their students' "obsession" with grades as a disease to be eradicated. Unfortunately, their cure was to refuse to discuss exactly how course grades would be assigned: "You'll hand in papers and talk in class, and in the end I'll know very well who deserves what grade. Don't worry about it." Students who are confident in their abilities and who have no fear of failing out of school or losing scholarships may not be troubled by such a system. But by the end of the semester, others, less able or less confident, may be paralyzed by anxiety. One way to spare them this needless worry and spare yourself several "how am I doing?" conferences is to develop a simple point system for the term and encourage students to total their grades as they go. In freshman classes, I usually assign points for everything I expect students to take seriously. With older and better motivated students I loosen up a bit.

10. *Be realistic about your workload, especially in marking papers.*

Some experts in composition have argued that time spent commenting on papers is essentially wasted. I can't agree. I know that word-for-word the comments conscientious teachers wrote on my papers were the most instructive reading of my college years, if not the most pleasant. And I know that on end-of-semester evaluations, my students almost uniformly suggest that more comments would be useful. I don't deceive myself or my students by claiming that I limit my comments for their sake; I limit them for my own.

One way that I have economized on my grading is to concentrate my attention on drafts, where my comments serve an obviously useful purpose, and spend less time on final essays, where a marking of superficial errors and a brief end comment will suffice. If I don't comment on a draft of an essay, I comment more thoroughly on the final form.

My typical grading process for a draft is to scan a few papers quickly to get a sense of what the range of the essays is likely to be, then to begin grading proper. When I begin to grade, I try to read each paper through once with my pencil idle except to make an occasional mark where I know I will want to return to make a comment. This first reading allows me to see the paper whole, appreciating the good things in it without concentrating on what should be improved. My next reading is for marking and commentary. I use circles and underlines (as noted in the checklist at the end of Chapter 2 of *The Riverside Guide*) and some proofreader's marks. I make brief comments in the margin. Longer comments (perhaps a half dozen per paper) are numbered and put on the backs of pages; a number in the margin shows where they apply. All this commenting naturally distorts my view of the paper, so I give it a quick rereading before I make an end comment and assign a grade. Over the course of the afternoon, fidgeting included, I can get through papers of moderate length (three pages) in about twenty minutes per paper. This means that a set of forty papers (two sections) will take me about 13 hours. Many of my colleagues are faster; some are slower.

Thirteen hours of labor added to a week's other work is quite a strain, and I have learned to keep that fact before me while I am marking. It helps me fight off the guilt when I have to limit my comments on a paper that shows prodigious labor and great potential for improvement. Being frank with your students about the limitations you work under can be a still better salve for your conscience. You can tell them that you will do the best job you can in fifteen or twenty minutes per paper, and that in many cases it won't be enough. Encourage those who want more help to see you during office hours. Remind them that they can make up for some of your shortcomings by commenting carefully on one anothers' drafts during workshops, and spend a class period after each major paper discussing two or three representative papers at length.

11. *Be conscious of the value of your work.*

The extrinsic rewards for teaching composition are not very impressive, as you almost certainly know. If we were looking for money and prestige, most of us who have made a career in composition would be looking elsewhere. But to confuse money and prestige with importance is, of course, a vulgar error.

Composition teachers have an opportunity increasingly rare in American higher education: they can deal directly with students' individual struggle to become reasonable, articulate adults—open-minded without wishy-washiness, and forthright without abrasiveness. We teach smaller-than-average classes, get to know our students individually, and are relatively exempt from the lecturer's tendency to "cover the material" by talking to himself. We get daily glimpses of how our students' minds work, and so we have an extraordinary opportunity to improve and correct not only their prose, but their thinking and their attitudes.

My university used to collect "exit surveys" from students at the end of their college careers. One question asked students to name the worst class they had taken. Our composition course consistently got more votes than any other on this question. But another question asked students to name the best class, and the composition course also got the most votes here. The composition course has a potency about it that—for good or ill—makes it a memorable experience for students. Ten years from now, when the memories of other professors are fading from the minds of your former students, they are likely to remember you for a job well done.

PART I

Writing and Thinking

CHAPTER 1
Writing When Facts Don't Speak for Themselves

Purpose

This chapter, unlike most chapters in *The Riverside Guide to Writing*, is essentially an extended lecture. It is intended to lay the groundwork for the term by weakening one view of a writing class and strengthening another. The view it aims to weaken is one that basically equates writing with the safe and correct recording of an objective reality; the view it aims to strengthen is one that equates writing with the interpretation of reality. To strengthen this view, the chapter preaches a bit about the inevitability of interpretation. Sermonizing is something *The Riverside Guide* generally avoids, but it seems necessary here because so many undergraduates resist interpretation, clinging to a view that things are simply right or wrong and that reasonable people shouldn't disagree. Obviously, this simplistic view of the world hampers students' development as writers. Only when they see that reasonable people can reasonably disagree will they begin to write papers that are persuasive and purposeful.

Overview

Like the other early chapters of *The Riverside Guide*, Chapter 1 includes the chapter proper, a set of assignments, and a set of readings. The whole package may seem bulky, but we assume that most teachers will assign the chapter proper (pages 4–18) one day, then select assignments and readings in ways that suit their syllabi and their fancies. The major parts of the *chapter proper* are

1. the "detour" that discusses four cases in which "truth" is a matter of interpretation.
2. a discussion of the role of *subject* and *framework* in interpretation.
3. analyses of subjects and frameworks in expository passages by Theodore White and a narrative passage by James Weldon Johnson.

27

4. an explanation of the connection between *The Riverside Guide*'s view of interpretation and the traditional composition text's emphasis on thesis statements and details. This section includes analysis of a passage by Barbara Tuchman.

The *assignments* are calculated to reinforce the distinction between the subject of an essay and the framework the writer brings to it. They include an essay that redeems a hackneyed subject by putting it into a fresh framework, a light research essay that analyzes a political cartoonist's interpretation of an event, a similar essay involving a poem on a historical topic, and a summary that stresses interpretation.

The *readings* also stress the importance of the author's framework. In addition to Joan Didion's "Marrying Absurd," which is used as an example in the summary assignment, the readings include:

E. B. White's "Once More to the Lake," which makes the well-worn subject of a summer vacation significant by putting it into the framework of the passing of generations.

Maya Angelou's "My Sojourn in the Lands of My Ancestors," which puts an African journey into a framework concerning the individual's acceptance or rejection by the community.

Barbara Tuchman's "Chivalry," which puts its subject into the framework of the human failure to live up to high ideals.

Annie Dillard's "Singing with the Fundamentalists," which shows fundamentalist students in a new light by reminding the reader of the universal human desire to connect with the cosmos.

The Chapter Step-by-Step

The Detour (pages 4–6)

The key here is to be certain that students understand that the "truth" in each of these examples will be created by interpretation. The order of the examples is not random. Many students are willing to concede that the sort of political question raised in Example 1 may be unresolvable except by debate, fewer students will concede that legal questions (Example 2) ought to be matters of opinion, and fewer still will be inclined to believe that the meaning of scientific evidence (Example 3) is a subject on which reasonable people can disagree. Example 4 ices the cake by suggesting that even photographs are not truly objective. Whom do we trust and why? That is the central question of *The Riverside Guide to Writing*.

A good way to promote class discussion is to ask the following questions about any or all of the examples:

1. Why is it so difficult to establish the truth about this subject?
2. What evidence, if any, could be gathered to make the truth more apparent?

3. If you are not personally able to gather more evidence, how do you decide whom to trust?

4. What difference does it make which version of reality we accept?

Getting students to discuss such questions can help them see what is at stake when they write (or when they read). In discussing Example 1, for instance, they may discover that America's involvement in Vietnam is such a large topic that no one can see it whole and pronounce a definitive judgment on it. This insight will prepare them for a lesson emphasized in Chapter 4: that reporting involves simplification. They may also fall into a productive discussion of the relative reliability of firsthand witnesses like Wheeler versus secondhand witnesses like De Palma (an important distinction in Chapter 6, "Arguing When Facts Are Disputed"). And students may—with some prodding—see that widespread acceptance or rejection of the image of American soldiers as overwhelmingly compassionate and just can affect everything from the psychological well-being of disabled veterans to the likelihood of future military engagements abroad.

"Subject" and "Framework" (pages 7–10)

The notion that good writing comes from the interaction between the sort of mind-stuff we call framework and the sort of world-stuff we call *subject* is basic. Students need to become comfortable with this notion early in the term so that they can see it at work in later chapters (in Chapter 7, for instance, where the framework becomes the "rule" in a lawyerly argument and the subject becomes the "facts").

No terms we could find seem to capture perfectly the distinction between the two parts of an interpretation, and we would encourage you not to insist too strongly on the particular words *framework* and *subject*. In a philosophy class, these terms are likely to be replaced by *concept* and *percept* or by *noumenon* and *phenomenon*. In a science class, the terms *theory* and *data* may be used. In a history class, the professor may talk about *contexts* and *events*. Probably the more ways that students can name the essential dichotomy, the better they will understand it.

The White and Johnson Passages (pages 10–14)

The passages by Theodore White in the section called "Subjects and Frameworks in the Expository Essay" (pages 10–12) are so clear that they may need little discussion. The Johnson excerpt in "Subject and Framework in the Narrative" (pages 12–14) is worth pausing over because students may be in the habit of reading narratives as if they were simply objective reports of what happened. The questions that appear in the margin may make students aware of some of the ways that Johnson turns his report into an interpretation of the event.

In our classes, we have found that it is best not to discuss all of the marginal questions mechanically: the idea is that the students should consider them as they read. However, you may want to ask one or two as a way of probing students' thinking and generating class discussion. The best discussion may be generated by two questions that appear in the middle of page 13:

What ironies do you find in this conversation?

What is the effect of the word *pleaded*?

Both questions point to the very quiet humor that underlies the passage. Johnson obviously enjoys the confusion in status that is created when he stands on his dignity and the conductor, a white man in a position of some authority, must beg him to violate the segregation law by sitting with the insane white man.

Johnson puts the incident into a framework we could name "individual dignity in the face of racial insults." The conductor and some of the passengers would presumably have other stories to tell. An interesting move in class discussion might be to ask your class what framework the conductor, a passenger, or the deputy sheriff might employ. Some of these people would surely have seen this incident as an example of what happens when in their view, Negroes are allowed to rise above their place. The conductor might have seen it as just another example of how every passenger expects to be treated like a prince and has no sympathy with the plight of an honest workman like himself who is only trying to do his job.

Thesis and Details (pages 14–18)

This section revisits and reinforces the framework/subject distinction and introduces a visual image that recurs throughout the text: details of a subject enclosed in the box of a framing idea, sometimes with boxes inside boxes. Crude as this kind of diagram is, we have found it very useful in our campaign to make students see the intellectual activity in an essay. Box diagrams are used extensively in Chapter 13, "Organizing the Expository Essay."

The Tuchman passage is worth a close look because it does so much, both intellectually and stylistically. Correctly or incorrectly, it sets out to portray Shaftesbury as a man driven almost exclusively by religious duty, a man whose acts of compassion are not the product of a naturally warm heart. The first three marginal questions on the passage are intended to help students see the sharpness of Tuchman's portrayal. The next two (about the coal carts and about Dickens) point to the more laudatory aspect of the passage: Tuchman may present Shaftesbury as something of a freak, but she finally emphasizes the great good that his peculiar disposition led him to do. I suspect she cites Dickens because she believes readers will recognize him as a man of a very different type—one whose compassion comes from his heart and his experience rather than from his principles. The endorsement tends to raise even the less-informed reader's estimate of Shaftesbury, however, since Dickens is one of the most famous names of the Victorian period.

An Activity for Class

The admittedly fuzzy notion of *framework* is so crucial to several chapters of *The Riverside Guide* that you may want to reinforce it with a visual lesson. In *Gestalt Psychology*, Wolfgang Köhler uses an illustration like the one reproduced here to demonstrate the way that the mind imposes a pattern on objects of perception.

You can easily draw this simple image on a flip chart or sheet of cardboard. The ideal way to use the image is to reveal it to your class very briefly (for less than a second) and then ask students what they saw. Almost all will tell you that they saw a star. Ask them if there was anything unusual about the star. Ordinarily, if you have flashed the image before them briefly enough, only a few students will have noticed that the lines do not meet at the star's vertexes. The drawing is not actually a complete star, but the viewer has in mind an idea (or gestalt) of a star, and the mind completes the figure, interpreting this set of disjointed lines as a complete image.

The analogy should be fairly clear. The subject about which an essayist writes is essentially disjointed until the writer finds and articulates a framework that converts it to one figure.

A second illustration can be found in the "Perception" article in *Encyclopaedia Britannica* (volume 25, page 475, of the 1990 printing). It is a set of variously shaded rectangles that seem bewildering when viewed up close but which, viewed at a distance, clearly represent the face of Abraham Lincoln. For our classes, we have copied and enlarged this illustration, discussed the way that it works, and then asked a simple question: "What would happen if the illustration were put in a time machine and shown to people who lived two hundred years ago?" Obviously, these viewers couldn't identify Lincoln by name, and because they hadn't been exposed repeatedly to the familiar face in the familiar pose, they would probably take longer to make out *any* face in this collection of rectangles.

Again, the analogy is fairly clear. The rectangles correspond to details of the subject; the idea of Lincoln's face corresponds to the framework. The image is a gestalt, shaped by the viewer's experiences of faces generally and of one face in particular. Without the framework, *which the viewer acquires from experience and carries in his or her mind*, the details have no meaning. Without interpretation, we don't even know what we are looking at.

The Assignments

Assignment 1: Sow's Ears.   The first time we taught this chapter, we gave our students the choice of doing any of the assignments. Under these circumstances, at least, Assignment 1 tended to be something of a trap. The students who chose it were ones who wanted to write just the sort of papers they had succeeded with in high school—sow's ears. Most of these students turned in flowery narratives without a clearly defined framework.

As it turned out, this entrapment was a benefit to the students. In class discussion of the drafts, other students made it clear that they couldn't identify any redeeming framework, and the writers realized that they were going to have to rewrite and get with the program. In the process of rewriting, they clarified their view of what a framework for a paper is.

If you want to avoid the trap, you might consider assigning the variation on the assignment first. After students have studied the way that the professional writers use emotional and intellectual frameworks, they are less likely to write aimless papers.

Assignment 2: Editorial Cartoons.   Students who chose this assignment wrote exciting papers. Some of them got so caught up in their research that they wanted to be excused from the length limitation we had imposed. The greatest difficulty we can imagine your encountering with the assignment may come if several composition sections use it simultaneously and so create a research bottleneck.

There are at least three ways around this problem. One is to use the alternative assignment provided in the booklet of supplemental assignments, one that gives famous works of art in lieu of cartoons. A second possibility is to use the variation given in the text, sending your students out to find contemporary political cartoons. The third is to find one or more cartoons yourself and use what you find as a basis for the assignment.

The typical weakness in student responses to this assignment is a failure to tailor the writing to the audience and purpose. Some bright students want to show that they are master researchers, capable of finding all the facts. Their overdetailed and underexplained drafts can give you a chance to talk about the importance of attending to the audience's expectations and current level of knowledge.

The four cartoons reproduced in the text deal with historical subjects that can be pinpointed rather precisely by the dates below the cartoons: Nixon's preparation for his debate with Kennedy; the Cuban missile crisis, with its "revelation" that Cuba (Castro) was serving as a surrogate for the Soviet Union (Khrushchev); the controversy over U.S. participation (or nonparticipation) in the Moscow

Olympics while Andrei Sakharov and other dissidents were being detained or punished; and the U.S. invasion of Grenada. Students will find adequate sources for any of these by consulting *The New York Times Index* or *Readers' Guide to Periodical Literature*.

Assignment 3: Poems, Historical Subjects, and Frameworks. This is the most difficult assignment of the set because (particularly in the case of the Browning poem) the research task is less sharply focused and because students will be tempted to write literary criticism rather than a straightforward explanation. If you intend to stress literature throughout the semester, you may want to require all students to write on this assignment so that they can get their feet wet immediately. Otherwise, we suggest that you offer it as an option open to students who think they can handle it.

Students who write on "The Chicago Defender Sends a Man to Little Rock" should be able to manage the research by the same route suggested for Assignment 1. Students writing on "My Last Duchess" will follow a different route. If they begin with *Encyclopaedia Britannica*'s micropaedia article on Ferrara or the macropaedia article on Italy, they should soon find that the "nine-hundred-years-old name" must surely be Este, the ruling family in Ferrara throughout the Renaissance. This should lead students to the micropaedia article on the Este family, which will give them a sense of the world of greed, power, and political marriages in which the dukes of Ferrara lived. Apparently, the closest match between the historical dukes and Browning's fictitious one is Alfonso II, who married Lucrezia, daughter of Cosimo de' Medici in 1558 (see Jacob Korg, *Browning and Italy*). But precise historical identification is not the issue. If they read enough material about the Estes or the Medicis, students will get the drift of the period and of the personality type.

Assignment 4: Summaries in Frameworks. More is going on in this assignment than meets the eye. The three types of summary progress from the most dependent on the text to the least dependent. The student who works with more than one of the options will get a sense of how altering the framework can alter the "truth" to be found in a subject. But because all summaries must be attached to the text by a long tether or a short rein, this assignment also gives students experience with the tension between interpretation and fair play.

Option 1, the most traditional summary, requires students to suppress somewhat their egos and opinions, to adopt an *objective tone*. It also requires them to represent the essay adequately by maintaining its *proportions*, allocating space in the summary in a way that corresponds to the relative importance of points made in the original. *Coverage* in such a summary must be complete in the sense that no major points are excluded. Students must also create a *distinction* between the author's ideas and their own: it should be clear to all readers of the "detail/framework" summary that by and large they are reading the opinions of the original author, not the opinions of the summarizer. If you believe that your class needs more guidance in writing the traditional summary than *The Riverside Guide* provides, you may want to state and explain these criteria before students write and then reinforce these guidelines in your critiques of the papers.

Some of our students have responded to Options 2 and 3 with gusto, glad for the opportunity to do with a text something more intriguing and risky than writing the standard summary. The danger, of course, is that the essay being summarized will vanish completely from their papers or will be distorted to the point of misrepresentation. Once again, a large part of the problem comes from the failure to distinguish between ideas that come from the original essay and ideas that belong to the summarizer.

Note: Sample papers and additional assignments are available in the package of supplemental material that accompanies the main text.

End-of-Chapter Readings

JOAN DIDION

Marrying Absurd

Perhaps because she is a Californian and because one of her most remarkable early journalistic pieces ("Slouching Towards Bethlehem") was about the drug culture of the Haight-Ashbury district in the mid-sixties, many people seem to assume that Didion is vaguely countercultural. This is a terribly bad guess. Didion is relatively conservative in her politics and solidly conservative in many of her social attitudes. She is, as the biographical sketch on page 15 indicates, the fifth-generation daughter of one of the earliest families to settle in the Sacramento Valley, and she grew up in a society that was, by American standards, remarkably secure and self-contained. When she looked about her in the mid-sixties and saw how many Americans were rootless and lost, she took an almost anthropological interest in their situation. The key insight in "Slouching Towards Bethlehem," for instance, is that the hippies of Haight-Ashbury couldn't really be called rebels. When Didion talked with them, she found that they had nothing to rebel against. They came from the rootless families of post-war America, nuclear families that pursued financial success here and there across the landscape and felt no attachment to a native place, to previous generations, to customary ways of doing things. In some ways the hippies were not rebelling against culture; they were trying to invent it from scratch.

The same sad sense of culturelessness makes "Marrying Absurd" a remarkable essay. To the student of uprootedness, Las Vegas is, as Didion says, "the most extreme and allegorical of American settlements."

QUESTIONS

1. What conflicting views of the nature of Las Vegas does Didion present in the essay?

The conflict is complex enough that different students may articulate it differently. Most clearly and most importantly, it is a contrast between the notorious decadence of Las Vegas—"bizarre and beautiful in its venality and in its devotion to immediate gratification"—and the "niceness" of the ideal wedding. Didion never lets us forget the gaudiness and sleaziness of the place: "a place the tone of which is set by mobsters and call girls and ladies' room attendants with amyl nitrite poppers in their uniform pockets" (paragraph 2). In fact, you might ask your students to look at the first two paragraphs in isolation for a moment and ask themselves, "What, to this point in the essay, is Didion's attitude toward marriage in Las Vegas?" The answer would surely be that a Las Vegas wedding is simply another manifestation of the place, another case of "venality" and "devotion to immediate gratification."

Just when we seem to see where Didion is going, she wheels around with the "and yet" that begins paragraph 3 and tells us something very surprising: that the wedding chapels are marketing sincerity and "niceness." From that point on, images of Las Vegas venality and nuptial decorum are combined, notably in the last two paragraphs.

The discord created by the combination of decorum and venality provides Didion with a framework for the essay. Or we could say she presents Las Vegas in two frameworks—the "venal" and the "nice."

2.   What are Didion's sources of information?

This question anticipates Chapter 4, "Writing Reports and Observations," and Chapter 11, "Some Advice on Research." One of our goals in *The Riverside Guide* has been to reinforce at every turn the integration of research and writing.

A journalist looking at this essay would see fairly quickly what Didion's modus operandi is. Didion might have had one formal interview, with Justice of the Peace Brennan, though the information about the "peak of operational efficiency" achieved on August 26, 1965, is more likely a bit of library research or accidental reading. The parenthetical detail of the mimeographed bulletins in Harold's Club might come from memory or from library research. But Didion gathers most of her information by simply keeping her eyes and ears open. By eavesdropping, apparently, she obtains the revealing conversations of wedding parties reported in paragraphs 4 and 5. Almost all the information in paragraph 3 comes from signs and other advertising. The information about the signs along the highway from Los Angeles and several other visual details (notably, "one is standing on a highway in the middle of a vast hostile desert looking at an eighty-foot sign which blinks 'STARDUST' or 'CAESAR'S PALACE'") are essentially snapshots from Didion's own journeys to the place.

Perhaps because we live in a period in which information is being reduced to data suitable for electronic manipulation, students sometimes need to be reminded that they can use their own eyes and ears to collect material for their writing.

3.   What is Didion's attitude toward the people she writes about?

The concern here is with tone, another aspect of writing that needs to be discussed early and often in a composition class. In the introduction to *Slouching Towards Bethlehem*, the collection that includes "Marrying Absurd," Didion says that her unprepossessing appearance is a great advantage to her as a reporter: she doesn't look like a threat; she is an enemy in disguise. The first paragraph contains an example of the writerly treachery Didion is talking about: "'I got it down from five to three minutes,' Mr. Brennan said later of his feat. 'I could've married them *en masse,* but they're people, not cattle. People expect more when they get married.'" Didion hardly needs to point out the unintended irony of Brennan's statement. She is ruthless here; she does nothing to make us think Brennan is anything but an opportunist. She carefully notes that he made 528 of those heavy 1965 dollars in three hours.

The harshness of Didion's treatment of Brennan provides a benchmark against which we can measure her treatment of the people who come to Las Vegas to be married. Is she equally ruthless toward them? Toward the couple in the long parenthesis of paragraph 4—the bride with the flame-colored hair and the groom who looks like a mobster—she clearly is. But toward those who come to Las Vegas looking for a "facsimile of proper ritual," her attitude is more difficult to ascertain. These are not opportunists or caricatures; these are grooms who appear in white dinner jackets and with "even an attendant or two," mothers who cry, stepfathers who try gamely to play their role properly. They aren't contemptible; they're sad. I won't claim that Didion can empathize with them: "What people who get married in Las Vegas actually do expect—what, in the largest sense, their 'expectations' are—strikes one as a curious and self-contradictory business" (paragraph 2). The word *curious* tells us a good deal. Didion finds these people alien and sad and saddening. She sounds a little like Dante describing one of the circles of Hell.

E. B. WHITE
Once More to the Lake

"Once More to the Lake" has become a fairly common anthology piece, and it troubles me a little that some people know White exclusively through it. It is certainly a great essay, but to me part of its greatness lies in White's having set aside some of his usual tools. His wit is subdued here; he plays it straight, parodies no one, hardly smiles. Usually, his pieces are quick and light and avoid taking themselves terribly seriously, even when they are on themes that concerned him all his life. Here he sustains one dominant mood, goes for one effect. For most readers the effect is magnificent. A few, no doubt, wish the other White would come back.

The sustained autumnal mood of the essay is of a piece with the essay's framework, which I take to be White's consciousness of the passing of generations and of his own progress toward death. In the headnote, your students will find hints that may help them see this framework. White, now a father, is returning to a lake associated in his mind with his own childhood, his own father, and the death of his parents. It provides a fixed scene in which White has been playing out the ages of man.

Students will find a profile of White on page 59. The several drafts of his comment on the 1969 moon-walk (pages 72–79) give a sense of both the meticulousness of his drafting process and his effort to avoid overwriting.

QUESTIONS

1. Explain what White means in paragraph 4 when he says that he seemed to be living "a dual existence." How is this illusion of a "dual existence" related to the framework of the essay?

Older readers are probably quicker to respond to the psychological impact of this dual existence than are twenty-year-olds, but White should make even your younger students feel the pain of mutability. One of White's existences is what we might naively call his "real life," the life of a forty-one-year-old father on vacation with his son and also on his way, like all fathers, to the grave. The other existence is in memory. Besides White's corporeal existence as a middle-aged man, there is his psychological continuity with the boy who existed thirty years before. Lucille Clifton once wrote a poem about the girl trapped inside her aging body. White gets a double dose of this phenomenon because the lake is largely unchanged and he is with his son, now the same age he was then and so much like him that the boy becomes a sort of phantom limb. Over and over, White has the "creepy sensation" that his son is actually himself.

There is a rather obvious point to make about the two existences: the boy who exists in memory is immortal and ageless; the man changes every day, and every day comes closer to death. These facts underlie the whole essay and rush up to meet us in the final line.

2. Where in the essay does White do a particularly good job of recording details?

This question takes us away from the mortality theme for a moment to look at one of White's unfailing strengths. He has a wonderful eye, and being more inclined here than in most essays to indulge himself in a bit of fine writing, he gives us a series of still lifes:

- In the bottom of the boat he sees "fresh-water leavings and debris—the dead helgramite, the wisps of moss, the rusty discarded fishhook, the dried blood from yesterday's catch" (paragraph 5).

- He looks into the lake and sees a school of minnows swim by, "each minnow with its small individual shadow, doubling the attendance, so clear and sharp in the sunlight" (paragraph 6).

- He passes the unused tennis court and notices that "the tape had loosened along the backline, the alleys were green with plantains and other weeds, and the net (installed in June and removed in September) sagged in the dry noon" (paragraph 7).

But White doesn't restrict his images to the visual; we also get some memorable sounds and smells:

- He remembers the old inboard motors that "all made a sleepy sound across the lake. The one-lungers throbbed and fluttered, and the twin-cylinder ones purred and purred, and that was a quiet sound too. But now the campers all

had outboards. In the daytime, in the hot mornings, these motors made a petu-
lant, irritable sound; at night, in the still evening when the afterglow lit the
water, they whined about one's ears like mosquitoes" (paragraph 10).

- He remembers "how the bedroom smelled of the lumber it was made of and
  of the wet woods whose scent entered through the screen" (paragraph 2).

3. Where in this essay does White risk overwriting? Why does he take the
chance?

In a sense, this whole essay takes that chance. The descriptions listed for Question 2, while they are extraordinarily good, are also, for White, extraordinarily
adjectival—deliberate bits of fine writing. There are other passages that make me
uncomfortable because White seems to be working too hard for his effect:

- "I wondered how time would have marred this unique, this holy spot" (paragraph 2). Two such adjectives, affective and vague, stacked so closely, would
  ordinarily be a magnet for an editor's blue pencil.

- "I remembered being very careful never to rub my paddle against the gunwale
  for fear of disturbing the stillness of the cathedral" (paragraph 2). Is the metaphor *too* dramatic?

- "This seemed an utterly enchanted sea, this lake you could leave to its own
  devices for a few hours and come back to, and find that it had not stirred, this
  constant and trustworthy body of water" (paragraph 6). Students who don't
  catch the contrast to the ocean's tides may be baffled by this passage. Even
  with the contrast in mind, White is almost saying more than the language will
  support.

Why does White, who could be a sharp-eyed critic of his own style and the
style of others, produce these sentences that remind me of freshman honors essays? A part of the answer must be that he is on unusually personal ground, where
the thing itself is worth reporting only as a way of conveying the writer's deep
emotion. White finds the lake a unique and holy spot and risks saying so, trusting
that by the time we have finished reading the essay, we will understand the appropriateness of the adjectives. The lake is constant and trustworthy partly because
it is tideless, but largely because it is a fragment of that unchanging world of
memory, not part of the mutable world of the present. White risks the expansive
adjectives because he trusts that the essay will grow into them—or so I would
guess. But I would warn my students that the risks are serious.

For White, with his superb ear and control of the language, things pan out.
For White, they usually did.

MAYA ANGELOU

My Sojourn in the Lands of My Ancestors

As part of the panel of writers, Angelou will be making regular appearances
throughout *The Riverside Guide*; you may wish to direct your students to the biographical sketch of Angelou (page 132) before they read this essay so that they
get a better sense of how this incident fits in the context of her life. Angelou's essay

should help you reinforce your students' understanding of frameworks and subjects because it is not simply an account of her travels in Africa and not just a story about a few kind people that she met: it is an experience interpreted through a framework, or perhaps we should say through a series of frameworks.

The complexity of belonging is certainly one of the strongest messages that comes through, though we leave the essay not knowing how permanent Angelou's belonging is. Our friend and translator of the Fanti words in this essay, Maxwell Boafo, is a highly educated Ghanaian living among African-Americans in low-income housing in a typical American city and attending a Midwestern university with its share of racial tensions; he understands in part the displacement felt by Angelou as one separated from community. But he is a Ghanaian and will return home, something not quite possible for Angelou in this country. The essay concludes with her reminding us that she is not a Bambara after all, and that community can sometimes be established only by false identity, by passing for a Bambara just as many African-Americans have passed for white. Yet her essay ends not in despair but in a flicker of hope. Belonging briefly—as Angelou did in Africa—may be all we can hope for as we establish ourselves in a community of family, friends, or ancestors. But that we *can* belong makes all the difference in the world.

QUESTIONS

1. What is the essay's largest framework?

Students may suggest several answers, particularly as they are probably still getting used to thinking in terms of frameworks. Racism, what it means to be a foreigner, the influence of the past on the present—any answer on this level should be encouraged since all refer to a "greater truth" that serves as a means of interpreting "smaller truths," or the specific subjects within the essay. But in the introduction, Angelou explains that while in Ghana, she "became a hunter for that elusive and much longed-for place the heart could call home." Perhaps the framework that is most inclusive is that of "community." While frameworks often take the form of a thesis statement (as in Chapter 1's flag-burning arguments), they also can be a single concept implying a less-defined thesis statement; if we had to name a thesis for Angelou's essay, it might be something like "all people are defined by their inclusion in or exclusion from a community" or (more emotionally) "exclusion from the community is one of life's great sorrows and inclusion is one of its great joys." At this stage, it is most important that students think of framework as a *means of interpretation* and not worry so much about naming the framework with a false precision. If your students seem dissatisfied, you might return with them to page 10 of the chapter to review the list of terms that we can identify with framework and subject.

"Community" works well as a framework for this essay because it encompasses the many identifications Angelou makes with various groups of people throughout the essay. Within this frame, we find the community of Africans, who all "belonged somewhere, to some clan"; the community of slaves held in the Cape Coast Castle (who exist, of course, first in the past but who come to life again as Angelou re-creates them in her imagination); the community implied by the spirituals Angelou identifies with, linking her to the slaves in America; the African-American community of Angelou's childhood in Stamps, Arkansas; the community established by family in Egypt; the community of African-American friends in Ghana; and finally the community of Dunkwa. Our understanding of the essay comes from Angelou's position within or outside of each of these communities.

2. How does Angelou present herself and her personal life, and how does this presentation shape our understanding of the essay?

You might begin by encouraging students to list everything they know about Angelou; besides defining her unique position as a black American woman living in Africa (never the Bambara she lets the Dunkwa people believe she is), such a list should also emphasize how personal the essay is. You might also take a few minutes to consider the introduction separately, for by adding it, Angelou may have given us clues to the framework she had in mind while writing the essay. The introduction reveals that Angelou not only found herself in a strange country but that she had lost the community of family with the breakup of her marriage. Although White Americans may tend to think that African-Americans would feel at home in Africa, Angelou shows how she and her American friends are at least as isolated there as in America; her experience makes her feel closer to her "unknown relatives," the slaves, as she relates to the pain and hope of their spirituals. And yet her isolation in Africa is more poignant precisely because she is in the land of her ancestors, feeling the need to belong even if that means "passing" for a native.

Consider also Angelou's careful use of details to emphasize the framework of her personal experience. The introduction juxtaposes the pain and isolation she has experienced after leaving her husband and being rejected by the Ghanaians with "the delicious and rare occasions when [she was] accepted." Both her pain and joy find expression in spirituals sung by her forebears. Then, at the beginning of the essay itself, she focuses again on her loneliness: driving alone she watches people singing and shouting together from the crowded trucks, and alone she views Cape Coast Castle and attempts to understand the experiences of her ancestors. The details reinforce the bleak picture: dungeons with cold, wet walls; the cries of the dead; the ghosts that linger with her; the defeated bodies of the captured. We cannot help but feel her depression, and therefore we are set up to feel the impact of her joy over her sense of belonging in Dunkwa. By framing the story so personally, Angelou is able to emphasize the emotional need for community that may hit home where logical arguments against racism or prejudice—or even in favor of community—could not.

The details of Angelou's life and experiences also blend together the many communities identified in her essay. She was married to an African who has devoted his life to fighting for a community of blacks nearly as oppressed as the Cape Coast slaves. When she arrives at Dunkwa she finds the streets filled with vendors selling Pond's cold cream as well as Killi Willis, and her visit with Patience and Kwame reminds her of gatherings in her childhood home in Stamps, Arkansas. Most of the conversation revolves around Angelou's identity as the people find a way to remove the "stranger" label she gave herself and to make her a part of the family. The children call her "Auntie Bambara," which defines her position well: as part of the family, yet as an outsider at the same time (Ghanaians use *Bambara* to refer to any stranger whom they presume to be from Liberia, though the word refers specifically to a particular Liberian tribe). Angelou keeps the essay's framework constantly before us by playing the various communities off one another while reminding us of her precarious position within them.

3. The essay seems to reach a turning point when Angelou recognizes that the neighbors' bringing food to assist the Dunkwa family with their guest parallels her experience in Stamps. She writes: "I felt the distance narrow between my past and present." What past and present is Angelou referring to, and how does this concept relate to the framework of community?

I think Angelou wants us to think of two of her pasts. She means primarily her *personal* past, her growing up in Stamps. But at the same time she may mean her *ancestral* past. Recognizing the community's custom of providing meals for strangers connects the moment with the South but also makes clear to her that she understands her African hosts and is thoroughly accepted by them. This understanding and acceptance seem at least temporarily and emotionally to bridge the gap between Angelou, American descendant of slaves, and her African forebears.

4. What does the presence of Cape Coast Castle contribute to the essay?

If we remove all the references to the slave-holding forts from the essay, we still have an account of Angelou's search for community in Africa, and the story on one level remains complete. But the slave castle introduces another framework through which to read the essay. The entire issue of slavery that the castle represents is crucial to Angelou's experience, for without slavery, she would not be experiencing the loss of community forced on her by the movement of Africans to America; therefore she has no choice but to be tied personally to the slave community. But why does she have to stop and be "plunged . . . back into the eternal melodrama"? Angelou seems to feel that in order to become part of the African community, she must somehow be reconciled with the spirits of the Africans forced into slavery and to America. She felt "pangs of self-pity and a sorrow for [her] unknown relatives"—relatives separated, as she was, from all other Africans. It is worth noting that Angelou focuses on the fact that the slaves were "sold by sisters, stolen by brothers" as much as on their being "bought by strangers, enslaved by the greedy." Angelou seems to believe that coming to terms with this ghostly community is just as important as fitting in with the living community in Dunkwa.

BARBARA TUCHMAN
Chivalry

For most students, the selection by Tuchman is probably the most difficult in Chapter 1 because it deals with a relatively unfamiliar topic, uses some unfamiliar words, and is about five thousand words long. A careful reading may well require a half-hour of the average undergraduate's concentrated attention.

Its difficulty is one reason for the essay's inclusion, since it approximates the level of difficulty students may encounter in an economics textbook, let's say, or in the sources they would use for a research paper. Therefore, if you take seriously the idea that your course is preparing students for work in other classes, you might want to consider assigning this selection for a detail/framework summary.

If you do so, we recommend that you give students an opportunity to critique and discuss each other's drafts, either in small groups or with the whole class commenting on examples. Students tend to think of summaries as things that are simply right or wrong and that require simple reading, not interpretation of a work. Comparing summaries of a passage as thick with details as Tuchman's will reveal that different readers gain different impressions of what the author's framework is and what details are important. Some students will be convinced in the process of discussion that although they have read every word and summarized the details that they read with some accuracy, they have actually missed the point. This may be a step toward seeing the forest despite the trees.

QUESTIONS

1. Into what framework does Tuchman fit the details of her discussion of chivalry?

If your students have trouble with this question, you might point them to such statements as the following:

- "That it [chivalry] was about four parts in five illusion made it no less governing for all that" (paragraph 1).

- "Gain was not recognized by chivalry, but it was present at tournaments" (paragraph 11).

- "It [courtly love] remained artificial, a literary convention, a fantasy (like modern pornography) more for purposes of discussion than for everyday practice" (paragraph 19).

- "If the fiction of chivalry molded outward behavior to some extent, it did not, any more than other models that man has made for himself, transform human nature" (paragraph 24).

The first and last of these statements, taken together, form a fairly clear statement of Tuchman's thesis. Her discussion of chivalry is essentially a debunking, and her repeated pattern of development is first to show us some chivalric ideal, then to contrast the reality. Chivalry is treated as yet another example of the human capacity for self-delusion.

The debunking has its limits, however; Tuchman does not dismiss the code as entirely deluded or hypocritical. See the final sentence: "Yet, if the code was but a veneer over violence, greed, and sensuality, it was nevertheless an ideal, as Christianity was an ideal, toward which man's reach, as usual, exceeded his grasp."

2.   What does Tuchman do to make her discussion of chivalry interesting to and comprehensible by readers who know very little about medieval history?

Some of your students will think, and may have the courage to say, that Tuchman does not make the subject interesting to or comprehensible by *them*. But the book was a best seller, and even students who don't find it to be their particular cup of tea may be able to appreciate objectively the strategies that an expert (relatively speaking) uses in writing for nonexperts.

Perhaps the most obvious strategy is translation. Tuchman frequently uses a foreign phrase that gives us the feeling of being in touch with the words of her primary sources, but she finds unobtrusive ways to provide a translation for those who don't know Latin or French. See paragraph 10:

> "Originating in France and referred to by others as 'French combat' (*conflictus Gallicus*), tournaments . . ."

> "Becoming more regulated and mannered, they took two forms: jousts by individuals, and melees by groups of up to forty on a side, either *à plaisance* with blunted weapons or *à outrance* with no restraints . . ."

The translation is not always from language to language. It is sometimes from culture to culture, and these translations can be pointed and controversial. In paragraph 19, for instance, she compares the adulterous fantasies of medieval courtly love to the fantasies of modern pornography; they are similar in that they exist "more for purposes of discussion than for everyday practice." In paragraph 6, she compares the universal brotherhood of medieval knights to the universal bond among workers that exists in Marxist theory. Tuchman's tendency to translate aspects of medieval culture into things she imagines her modern readers to be more familiar with produces a rather comic image in paragraph 3, where the knight's eighteen-foot lance is said to be "half the length of an average telephone pole." The anachronisms produced by Tuchman's comparisons sometimes clarify her subject and sometimes seem intended to shock or amuse.

As valuable as translation for the general reader is Tuchman's in-text identification of medieval people, particularly the people she uses as sources. In paragraph 1, for example, she quotes Ramon Lull, a name few of her readers will recognize, in a way that establishes his identity and his credentials: "Chivalry's famous celebrator Ramon Lull, a contemporary of St. Louis, could now state . . ." We can tell very accurately what her assumptions are in such a passage. If she thought her readers knew who Lull was, she would simply write, "Ramon Lull could now state . . ." If she *didn't* think her readers knew who St. Louis was, she wouldn't use him as a point of reference. In paragraph 21, she treats La Tour Landry as she had Lull: "La Tour Landry himself, a seigneur of substance who fought in many campaigns . . ." Not every figure is identified, of course, and you might invite your students to list names that are complete ciphers to them; discussing these references will prepare students to think about the state of the reader's knowledge when they write their own essays.

A third strategy used by Tuchman is to minimize her use of abstractions and generalizations and present instead people and actions. Even readers who find history boring will tend to react to and remember the image of Don Pero Niño fighting with a bolt from a crossbow embedded in his nose.

3.   What kind of sources does Tuchman use, and how confident does she seem to be about their reliability?

There is no great mystery about this question. It merely draws students' attention to the fact that Tuchman gets back to primary sources when she can—to the "companion and biographer of Don Pero Niño" or to the troubadour who wrote the *Châtelain de Coucy.* The original sources are more colorful in this case, and as a general rule they are more credible: every court prefers eyewitness testimony.

On the other hand, original sources can be biased, as Tuchman warns in paragraph 22, where the historian Froissart is dismissed as unreliable on the story of Edward III's rape of the Countess of Salisbury because he was patronized by Edward's wife. At times, however, Tuchman seems to accept uncritically whatever information will make the best story. The "companion and biographer of Don Pero Niño" reminds me of the companion and biographer of Paul Bunyan.

ANNIE DILLARD
Singing with the Fundamentalists

This essay involves a radical shift in frameworks. Early in her essay, Dillard gives us a glimpse of the fundamentalists as they are seen by most members of the academic community (and by most of Dillard's own friends). This perspective, this framework, reduces them to members of the right-wing lunatic fringe. In some ways, Dillard's essay reads like a thought experiment: What if we rejected this way of viewing the fundamentalists? Is there another framework in which they would fit better? Dillard makes the case that there is, that these students are involved in the universal human quest to find a spiritual connection with the universe, and that their involvement with the quest makes them—if anything—less odd, less "out of it" than the professors who look down from their office windows on the singers below.

QUESTIONS

1.   What images stand out in your memory after you have read this essay, and what do these images seem to mean to Dillard? Do they mean the same thing to you?

There may be more agreement about what the dominant images are than about what they mean. The three images that strike me most strongly are the "five still men" in the science building (paragraphs 28–31), the rubber gloves in the fountain (paragraphs 33–34, and returned to in the essay's final sentence), and the upraised hands of the singing students (paragraphs 36–41).

None of these images is overtly interpreted, and I think none has a didactic intention. These are things that Dillard saw, and she has some of the same problems knowing what to make of them that we have. But by her diction and by the details she chooses to note, we can understand where the images seem to be leading her. Dillard says that the first of "five still men" (there are actually four, by the way) "is drawn to look, as I was drawn to come" (paragraph 29). She emphasizes the way that the men stand isolated in their offices with their doors closed, invisible to each other, opening their windows to let the singing in. One has to feel that the men long for something their cubicled lives in the science building (she chooses to name the building) are not providing them. Nowhere does she state that this image encapsulates our longing for the spiritual, but she has made me feel that it does.

The rubber gloves in the fountain are presented very modestly at first: they remind her of the cardboard hands stuck in the back windows of cars, and they are a "good prank" since the maintenance crew will be slow to remove them. But by planting the thought that cardboard hands that say *hola* may be addressing "a little wave to the universe at large" and by comparing this wave to the radio signals we send to outer space, Dillard raises the ante. Her image begins to "mean" our longing for something beyond this life, our longing for God.

Similarly, those upraised hands of the students grow larger in meaning as they are discussed. They gather some of their significance by association with the rubber gloves, of course. But Dillard starts her discussion of them on a note of irritation: the gesture imitates one learned on television; it is bogus, junk (see paragraph 40). But, as Dillard says earlier, "each [student] has a private relationship with 'the Lord' and will put up with a lot of junk for it" (paragraph 15). Embarrassing as she finds the gesture, it is part of the "broad current" she mentions in the last paragraph. The palms "raised . . . as if to feel or receive a blessing or energy from above" (paragraph 37) are in the final paragraph compared to a radio astronomer's radar cups, a startling metaphor that reminds us that the longing to be connected with something larger than ourselves is not a peculiarity of the fundamentalists but a universal drive.

Whether I or any other reader is on Dillard's wavelength in interpreting these images is impossible to say. All the problems associated with the intentional fallacy in poetry or fiction are equally applicable to the essay. Nonetheless, when we read an essay, we instinctively want a conversation with the author, which means that we want to think of the writer as another mind working on ours. I find Dillard works very successfully on mine. The upraised hands, for instance, I would have been inclined to dismiss as merely embarrassing, pure hokum, but she has persuaded me to see them otherwise. The framework has shifted.

2. How does Dillard deal with the stereotype many people have of fundamentalists?

Perhaps we should stop here to think for a moment about the relationship between Dillard and fundamentalists generally. Though deeply religious in her way, she is not a fundamentalist. She was raised Presbyterian, which means that she is considerably more "high church" than the student fundamentalists with whom she sings, and who are, in turn, considerably more high church than the Midwestern "Community of Praise" people whom the students emulate with the hand-raising gesture. In addition, Dillard is a part of America's academic culture, which is not often sympathetic to fundamentalism. So we might begin by noting that Dillard is not dealing with "her" people in this essay: "My colleagues and students here, and my friends everywhere, dislike and fear Christian fundamentalists" (paragraph 3).

She seems to assume that her readers' backgrounds and attitudes are similar to her own, and her first description of the fundamentalists acknowledges a shared hostility by detailing the stereotype:

> You may never have met such people, but you've heard what they do: they pile up money, vote in blocs, and elect right-wing crazies; they censor books; they carry handguns; they fight fluoride in the drinking water . . .(paragraph 3)

Notice the pronoun *you*, in close conjunction to references to "my friends" in the same paragraph. In effect, she makes us her friends, and she hints almost immediately that our attitude toward fundamentalists may be ignorant prejudice. (In paragraph 7, she will parody this prejudice: "no animal sacrifices, no lynchings, no collection plate for Jesse Helms, no seizures, snake handling, healing, or glossolalia.")

Later in the essay, she carefully undoes the stereotype. She emphasizes, for example, the diversity of the students, showing that they are no monolithic bloc of crazies: notice the details of physical appearance and the assumptions Dillard draws from them in paragraph 5. In paragraphs 16–21, Dillard assembles a wide variety of evidence to counter the stereotype, starting with her own recollection of talks she has had with the students and her impression that they are a varied group, if anything a bit further left than most of their classmates and a bit more capable of abstract thought. She adds information from an Arbitron rating and an academic study to show that the solid fundamentalist right is partly a media fantasy. She analyzes the content of *Eternity: The Evangelical Monthly* and shows that its readers "are not book-burners" and that the editors seem to share the views of the American Civil Liberties Union. And she ends this section of the essay with a fairly nasty jab at the simple-mindedness and hypocrisy of professors who promulgate the stereotype. This sizable collection of evidence deserves to be looked at very closely in class—twice: the first time through, it can serve as an example of carefully gathered information used to counteract a widespread bias; the second time through you may want students to examine the evidence carefully to see whether it is reliable. Would everyone who examined *Eternity* draw the same conclusions Dillard does? Such an analysis might be an interesting assignment.

Beyond assembling evidence, Dillard does a remarkable job of shifting our sympathies by putting fundamentalism in the larger context of all religious longing, including some scientific longing that might recoil before the name of religion (see comments on imagery under Question 1). The more carefully we read the essay, the more we think of the fundamentalists as a splinter group of "us" instead of a herd of "them."

3. How does Dillard organize her essay?

Dillard makes particularly good use of a pattern of organization like that used in E. B. White's "Once More to the Lake" and Maya Angelou's "My Sojourn in the Lands of My Ancestors." The pattern is so frequently used and so effective that I'm surprised by how little textbooks have to say about it. The writer builds the essay on a narrative (in Dillard's case, the history of her involvement with the fundamentalists) but interrupts the narrative periodically for exposition, argumentation, or background information. The interruptions can be short (like paragraphs 3, 11, or 37) or long (like paragraphs 16–21), but we always return to the narrative. The interrupters are like commercials in television programs: they may be the most important thing, but they are nominally subordinate. Notice that this pattern of organization is the converse of the commonly discussed pattern that introduces narrative examples inside an expository essay.

4. Does Dillard like singing with the fundamentalists?

This question is a trap of sorts, since Dillard's response is neither simple like nor simple dislike. If your students give the question much thought they will realize that, like the documentary she praises in paragraph 37, her essay is a "good and complex" treatment of the subject. She is, of course, more sympathetic with the fundamentalist students than she is with their too-hasty detractors, but she is quite willing to let her mixed emotions about the singers show. The leaders of the singing group are not presented sympathetically (see, for example, paragraph 14), she is never quite reconciled to the hand-raising gesture (although she understands its significance), and she clearly despises the songs she sings. At the end of paragraph 9, she says that the lyrics come from "the same people who put out lyrical Christian greeting cards and bookmarks"; in paragraph 11, she speculates on the relationship between the introduction of such songs in Catholic churches and the decline in membership; in paragraph 14, she characterizes a verse as "singularly monotonous"; in paragraph 23, she heaps scorn on a song that talks about love as "a bond that can't be broken"; and in paragraph 26, she lumps the songs under a single adjective, "vapid."

Since Dillard has made it clear that her preference is for the "good and complex" treatment, we can see that her singing really is evidence of how much junk she is willing to put up with for the sake of her private relationship not only with God but with the body of believers.

CHAPTER 2

Writing as a Process of Understanding

Purpose

Like Chapter 1, Chapter 2 endeavors to weaken one view of writing and strengthen another. The view it aims to weaken is one many of us had as undergraduates: that thinking is one thing and writing quite another. The chapter attempts to show students that—for very practical reasons—writing is a great aid to thought and that the person who attempts to think an essay out completely before putting words on the page is likely to run aground. Students who read the chapter can hardly miss the point that experienced writers make time their ally by taking an essay through a series of drafts, a process that allows them to concentrate on a few issues at a time.

Overview

The *chapter proper* divides into two major parts: from page 50 through the middle of page 58, the concern is primarily with the psychology of the writer; thereafter, the concern is with the psychology of the reader as it affects the writer. Because the chapter is not a quick read, you may want to assign it by halves. In the first half, the principal parts are

1. a discussion of the "fogginess" created by our limited working memories and of how the drafting and redrafting process helps us deal with this fogginess.
2. an annotated example of a passage taken through multiple revisions to work the fogginess out.
3. a discussion of writer's block, with a recommendation that the blocked writer learn to trust the revision process.

The second part of the chapter includes

1. a rationale for delaying consideration of the audience and using such techniques as free-writing.
2. a distinction between the intermediate audience (such as a teacher or peer reviewer) and the ultimate audience.
3. a discussion of things to consider about the ultimate audience.
4. an overview of the writing process.
5. a peer-review checklist.

The *assignments* following the chapter proper do not produce finished essays but encourage students to experiment with or investigate their own writing process. You may therefore want students to continue to work on assignments from Chapter 1 while they read and discuss Chapter 2.

The *readings* at the chapter's end should reinforce the chapter's message that the process of writing is largely a process of revising:

"Erase Your Tracks" is Annie Dillard's impressionistic description of the writing process, emphasizing above all a willingness to let things go, discarding if necessary the very parts of an essay that seemed at first to be nearest its heart.

E. B. White's six drafts of the "moon-walk" paragraph are an objective demonstration of this sort of radical revision.

The Chapter Step-by-Step

Fogginess (pages 50–53)

Students have told me repeatedly, in their behavior and their words, that they think of writing as a matter of talent—some have it, some don't. There is surely an ounce of truth in this position, but there is also a pound of falsehood. The aim in this section is to present a more democratic view of the writing process.

The cornerstone of the discussion is foggy-headedness, a quality that even the most modest student can claim to have as much of as the next person. If we can convince students that *everyone* is congenitally foggy and that writing is a way of coping with this fog, then we may set them on the road to writing essays that are enlightening for themselves as well as for the reader. The campaign of persuasion here includes Dashiell Hammett's discussion of the Dain Curse (which most of us will read with a shock of recognition) and a summary of related work on memory done by cognitive psychologists. The text then gives the most elementary reason for seeing writing as a way out of the fog: that writing expands working memory.

Exercise 1: A Test of Working Memory (page 53). This exercise demonstrates the power of writing on thinking and will also create a few minutes of furious activity in the classroom. You'll probably want to give students no more than five minutes of actual working time so that the activity won't drag. Taking time to ask students for some of their more ingenious unconventional uses will give the exercise a sense of closure and get students comfortable talking in class. If you think students may come to class with their lists already made, try a switch by giving these instructions:

> Think of eight consumer products invented in the last two centuries. List the products in alphabetical order. For each product, list two prior inventions that paved the way—as, for example, the camera and the lightbulb paved the way for the photocopier.

Or develop a comparable exercise of your own.

Multiple Drafts of the "Dain Curse" Passage (pages 53–56)

The section headed "Writing and Thinking in Stages" is as honest an account of my own revision process as I can give and still hold my head up in public. I've been surprised at the tonic effect such an account has had on my own composition classes: students are delighted and relieved to learn that their teachers also struggle when they write. If you have time and facilities, you may want to show students some of your own messy drafts to give them a sense that there is nothing wrong (and everything right) with darkening a few pages on the way to an improved passage.

The section headed "The Advantage of Revision: Mental Reprocessing" merely nails down the point that revision takes the fog out of both the writer and the passage. It also contains a gem of a quotation from Martin Joos.

Writer's Block (pages 56–58)

The most severely blocked writers I have known are ones who have not learned to trust the process of drafting and revising, and so insist on "getting it figured out" before they write "it" down. "It," of course, wriggles around in their heads and resists assuming a definite form. The message of this section is that the best way to avoid writer's block is to draft material in a form that is clearly not final. The method of persuasion includes references to the drafting practices of four of *The Riverside Guide*'s featured writers.

Exercise 2: Rules for Writers (page 58). This exercise bore unexpected fruit when I first used it in class. Its intention was primarily to smoke out rules that are too rigid and prescriptive to be imposed early in the writing process. As it turned out, the exercise smoked out rules that would hamstring writers at any stage of the process and it led to a lively exchange about the nature of "good" writing.

Front Areas and Back Areas: Delaying Consideration of Audience (pages 58–60)

This short section serves as a transition from the early writing-as-thinking-for-one's-own-sake half of the chapter to the later writing-as-thinking-for-the-reader's-sake half. It merely reinforces a point Peter Elbow often makes: that there is nothing wrong with consciously holding the awareness of audience at bay during the early stages of drafting.

Intermediate and Ultimate Audiences (pages 60–62)

This section is important largely because it helps sort out the politics of the writing class. Sometimes students see themselves as condemned to play the writing game on the teacher's field and according to the teacher's capricious rules. Sometimes, alas, they are right. I have found it very useful in my own classes to define my role as analogous to the editor's role and to say that my students' job is not to write something that will please *me*. Instead, *our* job is to work together toward writing essays that would please (or interest or challenge) another and wider audience.

Exercise 3: Visualizing an Audience (pages 61–62).   This exercise makes its point with an almost theatrical flourish, requiring students to use their imagination to construct a precise picture of the range of their ultimate audience for an upcoming paper. In my own classes, I have sometimes *assigned* an audience containing a half-dozen members described in detail. An interesting follow-up on the exercise might be to create from your students' visualizations a written description of some members of the ultimate audience for the upcoming paper.

Considering the Audience (pages 62–64)

I confess to feeling as I wrote this section that I was belaboring the obvious, but I have been impressed over the years by how confused some students are when they first attempt to "consider" an audience. I therefore devoted a couple of pages to three key considerations: the readers' expectations, their knowledge, and their opinions. You may find that this section is a good point of reference when you comment on papers: "Remember that some religious conservatives reading this paper may be offended. Can you find common ground with them? See pages 62–64 of your text"—that sort of thing.

The Overview of the Writing Process (pages 64–65)

This section serves as a summary of the chapter and reminds students that their attention may be focused somewhat differently at various stages of drafting and revising.

The Peer-Review Checklist (pages 65–66)

This checklist will be referred to repeatedly in chapters that follow. It is based on one given to me by Dorothy Haecker, a philosophy professor on my campus and the most successful user of peer review I have ever seen in action.

I like Dorothy's scheme very much, but should say that she has at this point gone on to another, which she thinks is more successful still. She has her students buy three highlighters of different colors and then has them mark each other's essays according to a scheme like the following:

• Mark in green every sentence or passage that strikes you as giving a key insight or advancing the argument to a new idea.

- Mark in blue each passage that strikes you as giving clear and substantial support to a statement marked in green.

- Mark in pink each passage that strikes you as cluttered, irrelevant, or unclear.

- *Do not* expect to mark every sentence. There will ordinarily be some sentences that you don't feel belong in green, blue, or pink.

Dorothy then has the peer reviewers (four for each essay) turn the paper over and write a brief note on the single most important point for the author to consider in revising the essay. Her scheme is excellent because it engages the peer reviewers and produces clear visual feedback. The student leaves class with four copies of his or her paper and can see at a glance where reviewers agree and disagree on greenness, blueness, and redness. I did not mention this scheme in the book because I doubted that all instructors would want to send their students to the bookstore for highlighters, but you might want to consider doing so.

The Assignments

The assignments for Chapter 2 are little more than exercises. My own practice is not to treat them as major papers but to have students read and discuss Chapter 2 while they continue to work on assignments for Chapter 1.

Assignment 1: Free-writing and Looping. The free-writing and looping exercise hardly needs additional comment, except to say that unless you are dealing with an exceptionally motivated class, you will probably want to use this activity as an in-class writing assignment rather than an out-of-class one. Until people are used to free-writing, they do best with a timekeeper and slave driver who will keep them on task.

Assignment 2: Listing. This too may be a better in-class assignment than an out-of-class one. If you are comfortable with the sort of free-form idea mapping shown on page 68, you might demonstrate it in class. The best way to manage such a demonstration is to lead the class in a brainstorming session for a hypothetical essay. This might be done in conjunction with the E. B. White drafts of the "Moon-Walk" paragraph: you and your class could outline an essay answering the question "How and why did White's paragraph change as it went through revision?" Major divisions might be tone, content, and fine points of wording. Or they might be (more mechanically, but in this case productively) changes in the beginning, the middle, and the end.

Assignment 3: Analysis of Your Own Revision Process. Writing this analysis can be a consciousness-raising experience for students, but the logistics involved can be difficult. Unless you have told students well in advance that they need to do so, most will not have saved preliminary drafts. My practice is to announce at the beginning of the semester that students should, for the first few weeks at least, keep every scrap of every draft.

If students follow this instruction, they have material to help with this assignment. If they do not follow it, they are forced to make up preliminary drafts and supposed reasons for changes. It may be that this bogus procedure is as instructive as the honest one: it forces students to imagine what a good revision process should have been like.

Another alternative is for students to locate a revisable passage in a paper that has already been submitted, revise the passage, and then write an account of their revision process.

End-of-Chapter Readings

ANNIE DILLARD

Erase Your Tracks

Three interesting reviews of *The Writing Life* can be found on pages 354–357 of *The Riverside Guide*. In one, Sara Maitland, speaking as another professional writer and as someone who generally admires Dillard's work, confesses that the book "irritates" her because she finds it "overwritten, self-important, and, therefore, unrevealing." In the second, Michael Edens calls it "thin and fragmented, and self-pitying." Neither Maitland nor Edens seems to find writing quite the agonizing experience that Dillard makes it out to be.

In the third review, B. Jill Carroll says that the book is "full of penetrating metaphors, lucid stories about sacrifice and struggle and keen bits of humor." Carroll's review makes a couple of points worth noting: first, Dillard's book is about what it *feels* like to be a writer; second, Dillard is by nature a mystic, a seeker of perfection. The book gives an account of what writing feels like when it is undertaken with total abandon, total commitment.

I mention these reviews because I think they give you a sense of the perils and promise of teaching this selection. The prose is very high-octane: it leads naturally to a discussion of the advantages and disadvantages of a flamboyant style. The account of the writing process as a relentless pursuit of perfection might at first seem irrelevant to the mundane business of producing college essays, but undergraduates are not always the cynical shirkers they are made out to be. They often approach their writing with an idealism that parallels Dillard's, and they find it both reassuring and inspiring that a writer of her caliber struggles as she does.

QUESTIONS

1. Dillard says that "it is the beginning of a work that the writer throws away" (paragraph 8). Why is it that beginnings must so often be discarded?

In the context of the essay, it should be clear that by "beginning," Dillard does not necessarily mean "introduction." She means "the original key passage, the passage on which the rest was to hang" (paragraph 6).

Given Dillard's view of the writing process, we would expect the writer to reject precisely this passage. For her, writing is "an epistemological tool" (paragraph 3). As writers work, *they ought* to be making new discoveries that make their old understanding of the subject outmoded. Keeping the "original key passage" would be attempting to put new wine into old wineskins.

Dillard's position is extreme, of course. (She has been praised for many things, but not for moderation.) Even the most intense and committed writer must sometimes start with a good idea and find that it holds up fine, particularly in a short work. And since your students will be writing short essays rather than books, they ought to be assured that their beginnings have a fair chance of survival. But students need to know that the chance is *only* fair. Reading the Dillard selection will, I hope, make them more willing to change their minds as they write and change their prose to reflect their new thinking.

2.   How credible do you find Dillard's guess that full-time writers average less than one page of usable writing per day?

It appears from paragraphs 14–16 that Dillard is extrapolating partly from her knowledge that an unnamed American writer produced "a dozen major books over six decades" and partly from the fact that the remarkably prolific Thomas Mann produced his body of writing by averaging a page per day. She surely has other examples in mind, and in a sense what she is saying is both indisputable and useful. *Writing takes time*, surprising amounts of it if one is to do a good job, and Dillard does us a favor by making this point with such emphasis.

She does some damage to her credibility, however, when she says such things as "out of a human population on earth of four and a half billion, perhaps twenty people can write a book in a year" (paragraph 15). Has she never heard of Barbara Cartland? Agatha Christie? Louis L'Amour? I'll wager that a half-day of serious research (the time required to write one-tenth of a page, according to Dillard) could produce a long list of writers who have produced more than ten books in a decade. Not masterpieces, perhaps, but books.

Nonetheless, I hope students will take the point that good writing grows out of time and effort as well as out of talent, and that they will succeed in it only if they allow the time and put forth the effort.

3.   Dillard is known for her energetic use of metaphor and analogy. What striking examples do you find in this passage? How effective do you find them to be?

This question is an invitation for a scavenger hunt. Your students should turn up a dozen comparisons worth noting and discussing. Two that strike me as being particularly interesting are the house metaphor in paragraph 4 and the series of metaphors with which the passage opens.

The house metaphor, comparing a book in the making (tenor) to a house being renovated (vehicle), strikes me as being both unexpected and accurate. Even in shorter manuscripts, the serious reviser will sooner or later hit on a passage that *must* come out, even though it will bring some or all of the essay tumbling down when it is pulled. The house metaphor, by transforming the logical or emotional structure of a piece of writing into the physical structure of a building, captures precisely the sinking feeling I have when I face this situation. And Dillard captures the emotional flavor of the hard decision precisely: "There is only one solution, which appalls you, but there it is. Knock it out. Duck."

I'm less pleased with the line of words as "a miner's pick, a woodcarver's gouge, a surgeon's probe," largely because I find the comparisons so unclear.

Picks, gouges, and probes excavate, but in what sense is the writer excavating, burrowing into the world? It seems more precise to say that the writer is *constructing* a world. And even if we accept the burrowing metaphor, it's a bit difficult and unpleasant to imagine a surgeon's probe digging "a path you follow," particularly since the path leads to a "box canyon" and can be strewn with crumbs that are eaten by birds. Dillard's exuberance sometimes leaves me breathless and bewildered.

Discussing half a dozen of Dillard's comparisons will be time well spent. You may then want to ask your students how they feel about the collective effect of these comparisons. My own feeling is that, wonderful as many of Dillard's metaphors are, they are so numerous that they make her page too busy, finally distracting readers more than enlightening them. You may disagree. Discussing the question, however, allows you to remind students that overwriting is a real danger.

E. B. WHITE
Moon-Walk

Obviously, this is not a reading in the ordinary sense, but a combination of documentary proof and material for a research project. Merely *looking* at the drafts can make a strong impression on students, since the multiple versions show graphically the volume of rewriting that may go into a carefully constructed paragraph. The image of White's worked-over first draft alone should place in students' minds the idea that their own writing might be better if their drafts were so thoroughly reworked.

But a deeper examination of the progression of the drafts will be more fruitful still, since White's paragraph changes quite dramatically in tone and substance as it is revised. In fact, the paragraph illustrates nicely some of the observations Dillard makes in "Erase Your Tracks":

> Now the earlier writing looks soft and careless. Process is nothing; erase your tracks. The path is not the work. I hope your tracks have grown over; I hope birds ate the crumbs; I hope you will toss it all and not look back. . . It is the beginning of a work that the writer throws away.

Of the 305 words of White's original draft, only fifteen survive to the final draft, and a close look shows that his ideas change along with his words.

QUESTIONS

1. What became of the first third of White's initial draft? How do you account for the change?

Drafts 1–3 begin with a passage that changes very little, one that compares a trip to the moon to a trip to the beach, saying that both require "sometimes fateful decisions" about "what to take along, what to leave behind." This lighthearted comparison (featuring dill pickles and a rubber horse) leads up to White's challenging the appropriateness of planting an American flag on the moon. After the third draft, this comparison to the beach trip vanishes, leaving no tracks.

How can we account for the change? This question can provoke a good discussion if you draw ideas out of your students. An important clue can be found in White's telegram to Shawn, written to withdraw that third draft: "My comment no good as is. I have written a shorter one on the same theme but different in tone." The theme that stays the same is the call for internationalism, an important framework for much of White's writing after World War II. The shift in tone, it seems to me, is away from a false lightheartedness that doesn't really come off. To make the comparison to a beach expedition work, White had put himself in the awkward position of comparing NASA's successful engineers and scientists to picnickers incapable of making the right decision about a jar of dill pickles. Not only is the comparison silly, it belittles a great accomplishment. My feeling is that White dropped this beginning because he realized he was being a spoilsport. The brief new beginning starts the comment on a more positive note, and the clause "it was a moment not only of triumph but of gaiety" certainly gives the occasion more dignity.

2. How do the final sentences of the drafts vary, and how are they related to White's framework?

White's perspective is antinationalist, or (if you prefer) internationalist. His thesis could be stated as "this moon-walk should not have been marred by a display of nationalistic pride." But White was never a preacher, and part of the challenge he faced in this comment was to deliver his internationalist statement in a lighthearted way. In the first draft, he leads up to his closing sentence with comments on the international influence of the moon (on tides and lovers). The closing sentence as originally typed is fairly blunt:

> What a pity we couldn't have planted some emblem that precisely expressed this unique, this incredible occasion, even if it were nothing more than a white banner, with the legend: "At last!"

The internationalism comes through, but not with any particular wit, and the sentence seems to try to borrow punch from inflated adjectives: "unique" and "incredible." The second draft works up to the final sentence by a similar route and (in its first typing) reads this way:

> What a pity we couldn't have played the scene as it should have been played[:] planting, perhaps, a simple white handkerchief, symbol of the common cold, that[,] like the moon[,] belongs to mankind impartially and knows no borders.

The internationalism is preserved here, and the idea of using the handkerchief for a banner because the common cold belongs to mankind impartially is amusing. But the sentence is overlong and trips over its own feet at several points. The third version of the sentence has a sweeter cadence:

> What a pity we couldn't have forsworn our little Iwo Jima scene and planted instead a banner acceptable to all—a simple white handkerchief, perhaps, symbol of the common cold, which, like the moon, affects us all.

The fourth draft changes this sentence only slightly, by an addition: "What a pity *that, in our triumph,* we couldn't have forsworn . . ." In the fifth and sixth drafts, the sentences are virtually identical, and the ways that they differ from the fourth illustrate White's ability to make a very good sentence better still:

> What a pity that in our *moment of* triumph we *did not forswear the familiar* Iwo Jima scene and *plant* instead a *device* acceptable to all: a *limp* white handkerchief, perhaps, symbol of the common cold, which, like the moon, affects us all, *unites us all!*

You might ask your students what the difference is between "a triumph" and a "moment of triumph." Or what the difference is between saying "our little Iwo Jima scene" or "the familiar Iwo Jima scene." Or the difference between saying "a simple white handkerchief" and "a limp white handkerchief." But the master-stroke is the addition of "unites us all!" which perfectly completes the sentence's rhythm and blends the sentence's humor with White's higher purpose.

3.   How does White's attitude toward the men who decided to send an American flag to the moon seem to change from the first draft to the last?

If your students look closely, they will see that White begins by treating the decision to send a flag as a downright mistake: "We're not sure they planned well, when they included the little telescoped flagpole . . ." His first draft does not soften this negative judgment with any mitigating explanation. In the second draft, however, he inserts a new sentence: "It is traditional among explorers to plant the flag." This concession is presented in an even more accommodating way in the final draft: "It is traditional, *of course,* for explorers to plant the flag . . ."

Meanwhile, the idea that the planners had made any straightforward mistake has vanished from the fourth draft on. It appears that White began drafting the essay in a rather foul mood, ready to condemn. He ends it ready to regret a missed opportunity, but in the process of drafting, he seems to have realized that there was no reason to be a dog in the manger and that he was as capable as the next person of admiring and enjoying what the scientists and astronauts had accomplished.

CHAPTER 3

Writing Autobiographically

Purpose

Chapter 3 has three closely related purposes. The first is to make it possible for you to assign personal experience papers without seeming to invite bad imitations of belletristic writing. Most instructors like to assign some essays based on direct experience early in the semester, if only to avoid immediately adding the difficulties of research to the difficulties of writing. But personal essays can be a trap unless the student sees that even the memoir trades in ideas. The chapter therefore recommends three types of intellectual frameworks for the student's essay.

The second purpose is to connect personal experience writing to the writing students may do in other classes. To this end, we have chosen frameworks that correspond roughly to academic disciplines: history, sociology, and psychology.

The third purpose is simply to reinforce the central idea of Chapter 1: that an essay is an interpretation that requires a framework as well as a subject.

Overview

The *chapter proper* divides into five parts, the first four of which include internal readings:

1. A general discussion of memoir writing
2. A discussion of memoirs in historical frameworks
3. A discussion of memoirs in social frameworks
4. A discussion of memoirs in psychological frameworks
5. Advice on writing memoirs

The *assignments* following the chapter proper include an essay analyzing a memoir, an analysis of an initiation story, and—of course—a memoir.

The *readings* at the chapter's end are all by members of *The Riverside Guide*'s panel of featured authors:

George Orwell's "Shooting an Elephant," a memoir in which historical and social frameworks are important

Mark Twain's "The Mesmerizer," an account of Twain's introduction to the joys of deception when a hypnotist visited his hometown

Maya Angelou's "Powhitetrash," in which the author relates how she learned under her grandmother's tutelage the difference between proper behavior and the impudent behavior of poor whites living in her community

Mary McCarthy's "Names," a classic memoir with both personal and social dimensions

Orwell's memoir is from young adulthood; the rest are from childhood and adolescence. The reason for stressing memoirs about growing up is simply that good autobiographical writing requires perspective, and showing young undergraduates models of good writing about childhood may help them deal with topics far enough in the past that perspective is possible.

The Chapter Step-by-Step

General Discussion of Memoir Writing (pages 80–82)

After reminding students of the importance of having a framework as well as a subject, the text goes on to show that writers of autobiography necessarily play two parts. They are present as part of the subject ("the author as character"), but they also stand outside the action and impose a reflective framework on it ("the author as interpreter"). To drive this point home, I've included an amateur memoir by my great-aunt. Here both "authors" are clearly present, the six-year-old girl and the reflective seventy-three-year-old woman. After the examination of this memoir, there is a short homily on the need to present personal experiences in a framework that will generate reader interest.

The Historical Framework (pages 82–85)

A brief discussion of what is meant by a memoir in a historical framework precedes this section's example, a passage in which Theodore White recalls an earnest teacher's attempts to help him understand American history. The example merits discussion in class. In addition to having one hilarious moment, it shows the way the concerns of the "author as interpreter" frame the story of the "author as character." In this case, it may well be worth discussing each of the questions that appear in the margin of the excerpt. Here are some notes that may be useful:

How is the "meaning" of Thanksgiving different for this group of students than it might be for another group? The "author as interpreter," with his long interest in history and his consciousness of America as a nation of immigrants, must have enjoyed the ironies of this situation. For English-speaking students from Protestant families, Thanksgiving means one thing: they are clearly prepared to identify with the Puritans in the play about the first Thanksgiving. But for a boy like "Itchie" Rachlin, the meaning is not so clear: would he identify himself more strongly with the Puritans than with the Indians? If he did identify with the Puritans, he would probably think of Thanksgiving as a holiday meaningful to *immigrants* rather than as a religious holiday celebrating a bountiful harvest. The framework shapes the meaning.

Does White present the play as a success or a failure? Does White as interpreter see it as White the character does? From Miss Fuller's point of view, the play is a catastrophe, and young White (the character) tries his best to make it work on her terms. He fails, and from his sixth-grade perspective, so does the play. The older White clearly looks back on the play with glee, and to that extent, White as interpreter must view it as a success. He may also view the play as a success in another sense, because it *did* illustrate an important truth about American history: the waves of immigration, cultural conflict, and assimilation that began with the Puritans did not stop with them but have continued in the twentieth century. The play was successful in bringing home the point that "history connected to 'now,' to 'us.'"

What is the connection between Miss Fuller's interpretation of American history and her own situation? What is the connection between her version of history and White's situation or "Itchie" Rachlin's? We ask these questions to keep the issue of frameworks present in students' minds. Miss Fuller saw America as "being all about freedom" largely because she herself was benefiting from the freedom to move up in our society. Young White, the accomplished speaker of English and star pupil, was on his way to similar upward mobility and so may have had reason to share her view. It is at least worth thinking about the possibility that "Itchie" would be less likely to believe the freedom story until he had seen what it meant for his own life.

What is the connection between the "meaning" of Thanksgiving and the Immigration Act of 1924? White does not make the connection explicit, but can he have missed the fact that the Thanksgiving play is about Indians welcoming English settlers to America and the Immigration Act is about shutting the door in the face of another wave of immigrants? I assume that he sees the connection (or contradiction) and expects his reader to see it too.

What is the significance of this list? Why is the list in this order? I believe that White put this list together not just because it names a series of great men but because it names men whose careers are part of the story of American freedom and its difficulties: the signer of the Emancipation Proclamation, the Great Compromiser who delayed the crisis over slavery, two radicals of the Revolutionary War era, and the Puritan governor of a tiny colony dependent on the tolerance of surrounding Indian tribes. The list also matches the content of Miss Fuller's class—American history from the founding of Boston to the Civil War. By working backward in time, White knits the passage together: Bradford was White's part in the Thanksgiving play, and by ending with his name, White forces us to see the connection between the play and the more serious discussion of America's immigrant history.

Some students seem to be immune to the allure of history. Those who are not, however, will surely feel some of White's excitement about discovering the connection between his own life and so many lives that came before.

Exercises 1–4 (page 85). The way that we have used these exercises is to require students to write brief responses at home as preparation for class discussion, then have the students sit in groups of three or four to talk about what their thinking had uncovered that might be useful in a paper. The discussion, whether conducted in small groups or among the whole class, is important. Individually, students may be so little accustomed to recalling historical events that they are simply stumped by Exercise 1. When they begin to talk, they may remember a number of things—the shooting of President Reagan, the Ethiopian famine, the Iran hostage crisis, the trial of Oliver North, the disasters at Bhopal and Chernobyl, the Alaskan oil spill, the crumbling of the Berlin Wall, the crackdown on the democracy movement in China. None of these may have quite the same psychological force that Pearl Harbor, Sputnik, and the Kennedy and King assassinations had for previous generations, but as students discuss them, they begin to realize that they have lived through a good deal of history, and this awareness is the key to effective memoir writing in historical contexts.

The Social Framework (pages 85–90)

The brief definition of social frameworks is worth pausing over for clarity's sake: the social framework has to do with the discovery of distinctions between "them" and "us," distinctions that interest the anthropologist and sociologist almost as much as they do the child. The two examples need very little explanation. What might be emphasized in discussion is the tone of the passages and the distinction between the child experiencing events and the adult reporting on the experiences by putting them in a framework. The questions in the margin should help focus your students' attention on these matters.

If students think about the Angelou passage and the questions, they will realize that Angelou the adult and Angelou the child are both evident in the way the passage is written. The child might be skeptical about the humanity of white folks because their feet are too small and their skin is too "see-throughy." But the observation that the complete segregation in Stamps kept black children from knowing precisely what whites looked like is definitely an adult observation. And, despite Angelou's statement, I have some doubts that the association of "white" with "the powerful," "the rich," "the worked for," and "the well dressed" could have been articulated so neatly by a child. The political framework is adult.

The Johnson passage also mixes the observations of the adult and the child. The observation about the grandmother's coining new words by mispronouncing Biblical names is clearly adult and has a tone of gentle amusement that no child I have known is capable of. The impression that a mile is a very long walk clearly belongs to the child and helps us remember how young Johnson was when the event he describes occurred. The way that Johnson reports the incident has the adult tone of detached amusement.

Exercises 5–8 (pages 89–90).   As with Exercises 1–4, we had good luck with these exercises when we required students to write out short answers at home and then discuss their answers in small groups. One of the more interesting paper topics that evolved from these discussions was the first encounter between a white child, full of prejudices, and a black woman in his new neighborhood. Another was about the conflict of identity created by living in a home with a Chinese mother and an American father.

The Psychological Framework (pages 90–94)

This section begins by defining a psychological framework as one related to some "element in our character that can't be entirely accounted for by the times we live in or by the attempts of society to mold us." This definition may not hold up well under philosophical scrutiny, but it does produce a different focus from either of the other two types of frameworks.

The "author as interpreter" dominates the "author as character" more completely in the Twain passage than in any other in the chapter. You might ask your students to locate the sentences that make even the slightest attempt to re-create the world as viewed by the young Sam Clemens. If there are any, they are at the beginning of the second paragraph. In general, Mark Twain keeps young Clemens at arm's length. And the tone of the passage is clearly the rather world-weary tone we associate with the late Twain—still humorous, but not without bitterness. The humor deflates pretenses, undercuts the idealism of youth.

The McCarthy passage, in contrast, follows the thought of the "author as character" very closely in the first paragraph and brings forward the "author as interpreter" in the second paragraph. The extreme seriousness of the character's concern about damnation and the relative levity of the interpreter's concern may raise the eyebrows of some students and produce class discussion about McCarthy's attitude toward religion. If you feel that religion is a sensitive topic among your students, be prepared.

Exercises 9 and 10 (pages 92–94).   Pure fun was half our reason for inserting these exercises. Humorless memoirs, particularly those focusing on personality, can be unpleasant reading, and we've found that many students are inclined to write gravely about themselves. But these exercises (like many of the memoirs included in the chapter) are not any less serious for allowing humor. One student, after rating herself on the discord-harmony scale in Exercise 9, wrote an interesting paper about a situation in which she had to choose between endangering a friendship or becoming an accomplice in a cheating scheme (and she chose friendship!). We're likely some day to receive a humorous and perceptive paper with a title like "My Life as a Leo."

Advice on Writing Memoirs (pages 94–95)

This section encourages students to concentrate on two things as they draft their memoirs: the introduction of clear, fresh details and the placing of these details in the framework of a controlling idea. The questions for peer review continue this focus on the content of the memoir, its ability to produce and enclose vivid details. Such questions are particularly important if you are having students read early drafts of each other's essays. If they are reading later drafts, you should direct students' attention to the peer-review checklist on pages 65–66, which is appropriate for a more polished essay about to be submitted to the ultimate audience.

The Assignments

Assignment 1: Analysis of a Memoir.   Instructors seriously attempting to use their course to prepare students for the demands of other classes should consider this assignment, which is modeled on assignments used in several departments at University of Moisouri, including sociology, psychology, and history. In the early part of the semester, when you are requiring short papers, it is best to require analyses of short memoirs only. Later in the semester, however, you may want to offer your students an opportunity to write an analysis of a book-length memoir. Page 96 provides a list of some promising subjects.

Assignment 2: Analysis of an Initiation Story.   The chapter's emphasis on memoirs from childhood and youth should give students tools to work with in analyzing the initiation stories listed. Don't feel that you need to skip this assignment in order to save the short stories for the study of Chapter 10, "Writing About Literature," where the assignments ask for papers of a very different sort. It might even be beneficial for a student to write about the same story twice.

Assignment 3: A Memoir.   We mention no length limitation here, feeling that you must choose one appropriate to your syllabus and intentions. Our preference has always been for short memoirs, which force students to focus sharply and choose details carefully. As the examples in the chapter proper show, something significant can be accomplished in fewer than a thousand words.

Note: Sample papers and additional assignments are available in the package of supplemental material that accompanies the main text.

End-of-Chapter Readings

GEORGE ORWELL
Shooting an Elephant

Anthony Manzo, a fine teacher and researcher at the University of Missouri, Kansas City, has an interesting approach to teaching this essay, one that shows students the way that their background knowledge can help reveal the framework of an essay. *Before* students read, Manzo tells them (if my memory is correct) that he is going to teach them how to read telepathically. He then writes the name of the essay and the name of the author on the board. Next he asks, "Where do elephants live?" The students respond (eventually) with "Africa" and "India." "Good," says Manzo. "What country was once called the brightest jewel of the British Empire?" Someone answers, "India." "Good," says Manzo.

"What country would someone with a name like George Orwell come from?" Some students suggest "England," others "America." "Good," says Manzo. "Now, what do you think this essay will be about?"

Opinions vary, of course, but the class tends to think that the essay will have something to do with the role of the British in India. While the geography is a hair off, this is a good telepathic reading (aided somewhat by leading questions).

Thanks to Tony Manzo for that idea and to Melody Daily for the answers to Questions 3 and 4.

QUESTIONS

1. Of what larger story is Orwell's narrative a part?

A roomful of students should include some who will give odd answers to this question: man's exploitation of nature, perhaps, or the importance of finding a career for which one is suited. I think, though, that most students will soon decide that the story is primarily about the relationship between the British and the Burmese, or the relationship between the colonizer and the colonized, or the relationship between the oppressor and the oppressed. These are the frames that fit most naturally around the episode.

2. What distinction can be made between the thoughts and emotions of Orwell as character and those of Orwell as interpreter?

The first two paragraphs are the key here: Orwell (the interpreter) makes it clear that he is looking back on a much younger man, one who had only recently made up his mind "that imperialism was an evil thing." This "young and ill-educated" fellow "did not even know that the British Empire is dying." He "could get nothing into perspective." His confusion made him feel things that we can be fairly sure the older, wiser Orwell would not have felt (or not have felt in the same way):

> With one part of my mind I thought of the British Raj as an unbreakable tyranny, as something clamped down, in *saecula saeculorum*, upon the will of prostrate peoples; with another part I thought that the greatest joy in the world would be to drive a bayonet into a Buddhist priest's guts.

Once the first two paragraphs have done their work of establishing the older Orwell's perspective as the true framework of the story, the focus is on the consciousness of the younger Orwell, with little explicit commentary. Commentary is not needed, however, because the careful reader already knows that the feelings of Orwell the character are not endorsed by the management.

3. Who or what ruled Burma at the time of this incident?

Ostensibly, the British were the rulers of Burma. After winning three Anglo-Burmese wars fought between 1824 and 1885, the British annexed the whole kingdom of Burma, and in 1886 made it a province of India. That political decision added insult to injury because the Burmese differed from the Indians in race, language, culture, and religion, and the Burmese bitterly resented India for having fought on the side of Britain during the Anglo-Burmese wars. Nevertheless, the British government did not separate Burma from India until 1937, and Burma did not become a sovereign independent republic until 1948. When Orwell served in Burma, Britain dominated its colony economically, politically, and militarily.

But in this essay Orwell tells us that when he realized he would have to shoot the elephant because the Burmese onlookers expected it of him, he finally understood that, in a colonial system, the white man is nothing more than "an absurd puppet pushed to and fro by the will of those yellow faces" (paragraph 7). It is not, however, entirely accurate to say that the Burmese ruled the country. If that had been the case, they would have expelled the British.

If neither the British nor the Burmese rule, who or what is in charge? Orwell seems to be suggesting that the system itself, the colonial psychology, takes command. The white man does what he thinks the natives expect him to do, and the natives expect him to do the kind of thing they think white men do. The ruler's behavior is shaped by his perception of his subjects' expectations, which in turn are shaped by the subjects' perception of the ruler's behavior. Imperialism becomes a gigantic shell game.

4. If you judge this piece as a narrative, what are its strengths?

Orwell carefully structures the entire essay to build suspense. The title hints at the event that is to occur, but the death of the elephant is not a certainty until the penultimate paragraph. In the first two paragraphs Orwell gives us the necessary background information; he sets the stage for the drama that is to unfold. And indeed, this particular tragedy has the classical five-part structure: introduction, rising action, climax, falling action, and catastrophe.

The rising action is set in motion in paragraph 3 when the sub-inspector telephones Orwell to report that an elephant is "ravaging the bazaar" and requests that Orwell "do something about it." At that point neither Orwell nor the reader knows what he can do, especially with only an old .44 Winchester, but like him we are curious enough to go along to see what is happening.

From that point on, Orwell advances and retreats. Like the crowd, the reader continues to wonder what he will do next. In paragraph 3, we learn about the destruction the elephant has caused, and we know Orwell will have to act. But in paragraph 4, it seems that no one knows where the elephant has gone. We are ready to go home. Then the body of the coolie is discovered, and Orwell sends for an elephant rifle. We assume he plans to shoot the animal, but he surprises us by saying "I had no intention of shooting the elephant" (paragraph 5), and he spends the entire next paragraph explaining why he knew with "perfect certainty" that he ought not shoot the elephant.

Paragraph 7 is the turning point. Orwell looks at the crowd and realizes that he has to shoot the elephant because he cannot disappoint the two thousand people who have gathered to watch him. But the falling action prolongs the suspense. Orwell hesitates. In paragraphs 8 and 9, he weighs his alternatives. Finally he decides that although he is not afraid of death, he is afraid of being laughed at. He has to shoot the elephant.

Even the catastrophe is suspenseful. Once Orwell shoots, the question changes to whether he will succeed in killing the poor animal. In spite of Orwell's efforts to end the elephant's suffering, the animal and the reader agonize until paragraph 13.

MARK TWAIN

The Mesmerizer

Before your students read this memoir, you may want to make sure its time frame is clear. "The Mesmerizer" is part of Twain's autobiography, which was compiled rather haphazardly over a number of years; this segment was written in 1903. Twain would have been sixty-eight years old, looking back on an incident that happened more than fifty years earlier. You may also want to direct students' attention to the profile of Twain (page 163) for additional biographical information. Finally, a few of our students have been confused by the shift in time in paragraphs 13–15, which recall an earlier incident in order to set up the rest of the memoir. You may want to warn your class that the memoir contains a flashback to a still earlier time.

QUESTIONS

1. Through which of the three frameworks discussed in Chapter 3 is this memoir best understood?

Because the event took place in a time and society fairly remote to us, both the historical and social frameworks are significant. Twain shows us how, despite the widespread disbelief in mesmerism, a small community can be caught up in the sensation of it all and find a way to believe. At the same time, Twain is recounting this event from the perspective of 1903, when the study of human psychology had become scientific, adding an interesting dimension to the memoir if we read it in light of intellectual history. For the most part, however, the historical and social frameworks are most important for the way they add texture to the dominant framework, the psychological. With the focus of the entire memoir on the difficulty of sorting out truth from deceit, even in our own memories, the small-town setting and antics of the mesmerizer provide a perfect vehicle for analysis.

In showing us the psychology of his younger self, Twain is quick to step into the memoir and interpret for us. In paragraph 11, the boy proudly declares that though Hicks could not stand the pain of pins being stuck into him, "I didn't wince!" And then the older Twain responds, "The miseries that a conceited boy will endure to keep up his 'reputation'! And so will a conceited man; I know it in my own person and have seen it in a hundred thousand others." As in "Cadet of Temperance" (pages 90–91), Twain uses his personal experience to illustrate what he considers to be universal truths. Though we would never wish to limit the memoir to one interpretation, one way to read it is in light of this universal theme (the troubles the conceited bring on themselves). But the larger issue, the problem of distinguishing illusion from truth and appearance from reality, provides a more complete reading of the memoir.

2. What does Twain reveal about himself, both as a youth and as an older man? What does Twain accomplish through his method of presenting the two perspectives?

The joy of a well-written memoir is the sense of being in two places at once, completely caught up in the story of youth at the same time that we are joining the adult writer in observing and interpreting from a distance. Since the adult Twain can hardly stay out of the story for more than a sentence or two, our focus is generally with him; at the same time, however, he repeatedly allows us to plunge back into the story, obviously amused himself with the cleverness of his youth.

One way Twain keeps us involved in the story of his younger self is his method of characterization. He remembers well the youthful desire to show off and be the center of attention, as well as the unquenchable envy and longing to prove better than the "Hicks's" around us. Look at paragraph 5 for the most complete list of details; while Twain is speaking of himself as a boy, we cannot help but wonder, given his delight with his own writing, if he has changed at all in the following fifty years.

3. How does Twain characterize the role of memory and imagination in our personal lives and in writing?

In the first paragraph of the memoir, Twain demonstrates his interest in the process of memory and how it works. He states initially that memory is selective: he remembers the month but not the year of the event to be recounted. But he does not stop there; instead he characterizes memory as if it were a capricious child, with "no more sense than [a person's] conscience and no appreciation whatever of values and proportions."

Just as he has recalled an incident that happened over fifty years ago, so does he describe Dr. Peake's recounting of a fire witnessed nearly forty years before the mesmerizer's arrival. Yet it was not solely the memory at work re-creating the event but the imagination as well. Because the adults remembered vivid details, the young Twain was able to take part in the incident: hearing those details "made history real" for him, as it had never been before.

Though he does not say so directly, Twain implies that the memory is largely manipulated by the imagination. Without the imagination's power to give events and details life and significance, the memory has little means of retaining them. The problem, of course, is keeping the imagination in check so that it does not embellish the memory more than it should—and an imagination as strong-willed as Twain's gives us cause to wonder which faculty is in command.

4. What about the memoir reminds us that it is written by Twain the humorist?

Built into this memoir are layers and layers of irony. First, Twain is clearly re-creating an event from the distant past, relying on both his memory and imagination to do so. One point of his memoir is to emphasize how easily people can be fooled into believing that a lie is the truth; additionally, he lets us know up front that he is the best liar of all. And by re-creating the event, he demonstrates to us his craft, telling us specifically how he managed to make his vision of the Richmond fire believable by feeding his audience a little at a time, building momentum as he got them hooked, and then throwing "the valves wide open and [turning] on all the steam" (paragraph 18). Ironically, the story is about a marginally good fake, the mesmerizer, and about a more successful one, Twain himself. Without the ending, the careful description of a repentant man attempting to persuade his own mother of his falsehood and to make us see the horrible burden of being a great liar, we might think the entire memoir was fabricated. And yet, perhaps the ending is Twain's "throwing the valves wide open"—duping us just as he has Dr. Peake.

Twain's mother's argument is by itself wonderfully humorous and ironic; it may be fun to try to sort out her reasoning and look at its logic and illogic. But it may also be interesting to pull apart the complete memoir and have your class decide how much memory and how much imagination went into Twain's account of the mesmerizer coming to town.

MAYA ANGELOU

Powhitetrash

"Powhitetrash" is the name we gave to Chapter 5 of Angelou's *I Know Why the Caged Bird Sings*; along with the other early chapters of the book, it focuses on defining the various communities within the small town of Stamps, Arkansas. Like "My Sojourn in the Lands of My Ancestors," much of this memoir focuses on what separates (and what unites) people in communities. But as much as Angelou desired to break down barriers between people in her account of traveling in Africa, here she seems determined to create barriers in order to distinguish herself and her family from the ill-mannered and dirty "powhitetrash." If you haven't yet, you may wish to direct your students to the profile of Angelou (page 132) for additional background information.

QUESTIONS

1. To what extent does Angelou's memoir sound like a re-creation of the experiences and thoughts of a child, and to what extent does it sound like the reflections of a mature woman? What does she gain by her mixture of the child's perspective and the adult's?

This question should prevent your students' overlooking the dual perspective Angelou creates in this passage. With a keen eye to detail, she captures a child's view of life: from the nuisance of bathing, to the fear of the dark and of snakes, to her unique point of view when she hides behind the screen door or looks up to see Momma hovering over her. Small details also reveal a black child's confusion over differences among people; Angelou can't resist pinching a white child to see if it is real, and she violently resists Momma's acknowledging the white girls as "Miz."

But what makes the memoir complete is the voice of the adult Angelou looking back on the experience. When she pauses to assert that her "lifelong paranoia was born in those cold, molasses-slow minutes" or to realize that she was "as clearly imprisoned behind the scene as the actors outside were confined to their roles," we know that Angelou the adult is making sense of what had happened. She recognizes the event as an introduction to the injustice of racial conflict and to the complexity of it: in spite of her intense anger, she knows that the white girls are simply acting out learned behavior.

Yet Angelou devotes very little of her memoir to direct interpretation, allowing us instead to view the incident primarily through the eyes of the child (a good contrast in terms of the mix of adult and child observation is Twain's "The Mesmerizer"). Instead of identifying a framework through which to view her memoir, she relies on technique to direct our attention to the contrasting subjects and to focus our understanding. But the dual perspective is clear; in order to get a better sense of the interaction between the adult and youthful voices, you might have your students compare the style of this memoir—and of "Whitefolks" (pages 86–87)—with Angelou's "My Sojourn in the Lands of My Ancestors" (pages 33–37), which deals with a later portion of her life and is a very different kind of memoir.

2. How do the historical, social, and psychological frameworks contribute to our understanding of "Powhitetrash"?

The historical aspect of Angelou's writings will always be important because she is so directly tied to one of the most crucial aspects of American history; the long and painful process of establishing equality for African-Americans is certainly at the heart of this memoir. At the same time, Angelou's depiction of herself as a child forced to deal with racial tension reveals much about human nature and specifically about the psychology of an African-American youth. But because Angelou clearly moves beyond self-discovery in this memoir and because she carefully constructs three types of people within a particular society, she seems to emphasize most the social framework.

Notice how, throughout the memoir, Angelou plays the adult world off that of children while contrasting the character of the black community with that of the poor white community. The memoir seems to be divided into four sections, the first of which (paragraphs 1–6) contrasts Angelou the child with her grandmother and then sets forth the "customary laws" that both reveal Momma's character and establish a means of comparing "correct" behavior with that of the powhitetrash. The next section (paragraphs 7–13) completes the contrast by describing the girls who tormented Angelou by shopping in Momma's store. Angelou suggests their inferiority by subtly comparing them to animals (they were a smelly "gaggle" that "crawled" over everything in the store). By also focusing on Momma and Uncle Willie's response to them, Angelou emphasizes the irony of the social scene: though the white people rented land from Momma, they still had the power to treat her as an inferior.

Finally, the event itself divides into two parts. The first part (paragraphs 14–32) contrasts Momma's reaction to the insulting behavior of the girls with Angelou's own response; the second part (paragraphs 33–37) is the resolution that elaborates on Momma's quiet but certain victory. Though we learn much about individuals throughout the memoir, what stands out most is what the various responses to racial tension teach us about the social situation in Stamps in the late 1930s.

3.   What exactly did Momma win?

Angelou's memoir draws its strength largely from what it does not tell us directly. It is as if Angelou knows that we will understand Momma's victory better emotionally than we would intellectually, so she focuses her attention on helping us to *feel* what was going on. Notice the details Angelou has selected to keep our attention focused on the "battle" and Momma's fight. First, Angelou points out that Momma could have avoided the confrontation by coming into the house, and in the middle of the incident, we find ourselves wishing she had. As the girls grow more and more insulting, Momma continues to hum softly and steadily to herself; only the occasional trembling of her apron strings indicate her struggle to maintain control. The battle culminates, of course, in Momma's determination to give the girls respect by addressing each as "Miz" despite their despicable behavior. We *know* at this point, without being told, that Momma has proven that personal dignity can be maintained in the face of racial injustice. Her goal was not to prove anything to the white girls, who may or may not have understood the impact of the incident, but to teach Angelou what her response should be—and given the resulting memoir, we know she succeeded.

4.   What is the purpose of the patterns Angelou creates in the dirt yard?

Without elaborating on her grandmother's character, Angelou shows us the impact Momma had on shaping Angelou's own. Although Momma seems rather stern in the opening section of the memoir (sending the children out into the freezing weather to ensure cleanliness at all times), she teaches as much through her example of goodness as through her commandments. As a child, Angelou obviously worked hard to please her, imitating her fastidious desire for perfection by creating patterns in the dust, turning the bare yard into a work of art. Because this action frames the encounter with the white girls, it works as another image with more emotional than intellectual impact. Like the sound of the familiar hymns that Momma hums, the patterns in the dust suggest a hope we cannot quite describe. Angelou and Momma have shown us they can create something meaningful and "right pretty" out of the dirt that surrounds their lives.

MARY MCCARTHY

Names

Of the memoirs included in this group of readings, "Names" is arguably the most profound in its ability to present a simple incident from childhood in frameworks that extend through psychological and social constructs to universal and timeless questions. "Names" tells the bittersweet story of growing up, with humor (McCarthy describes her encounter with the mother superior as being "rather like a round" in which they were singing two very different songs) but also with solemnity (McCarthy sees herself ultimately, and reluctantly, as an outsider)—all because of the power of names to make people and situations what we perceive them to be. Before your students read the memoir, you might start them thinking about their own experiences with being labeled by other people or by themselves; to reinforce the concept of frameworks, you might remind them of Chapter 1 and the effect of naming as "symbolic speech" or "antisocial behavior" an incident in which a flag was burned. You might also direct their attention to the profile of McCarthy (page 329) for additional biographical information.

QUESTIONS

1. What does the lengthy discussion about names that introduces McCarthy's story (paragraphs 1–5) add to the memoir?

As if teaching young children to read by saturating them with the rich sounds of words, McCarthy lays before us name after name, engaging us in the delight of their sound before asking us to consider what they mean. But if we had to state a theme for the first five paragraphs of "Names," it would have something to do with the power of context to give names meaning. In the context of the convent, the sound of foreign names "bloomed like prize roses among a collection of spuds"; similarly, the larger context of the "still-pioneer" Pacific Northwest rendered foreignness in a name a quality to be valued, though in a slightly different context, such as the Midwest, the same name meant ridicule or shame. McCarthy then narrows the discussion to the power of Catholicism to endow a name with even greater meaning, linking it to the past, to specific saints, and to some mystical association; at the same time, through Catholicism McCarthy first named herself, and this act at the time of her confirmation suggests a degree of control that we may have over our identity. Beginning her memoir with this introduction, McCarthy invites us to consider the complexity inherent in all names and to examine the role of naming in our discovery of who we are.

2. What framework predominates in "Names"?

Certainly the psychological framework is the most obvious, for "Names" largely recounts the process of growing up as McCarthy experienced it. What she chooses to portray about her life in the convent is both typical of childhood and wonderfully surprising, set in a framework of self-discovery that moves beyond the particular to the universal in a refreshing way. That is, McCarthy takes two common life-altering events (the onset of puberty and the loss of faith) and focuses not on what each meant to her but on the confusion caused by each occurring within the peculiar context of the convent.

Within the stiff, reserved convent setting, McCarthy learned that not only does honesty not pay, but sometimes it isn't even an option. She felt forced to hide her denial of Catholicism in order to keep peace, and so "gave up" her loss of faith for a feigned religiosity. But even more absurd, she believed, was having to pretend to "be a woman," not to avoid ridicule, but because she had no choice: the nuns heard only embarrassed protesting when McCarthy told them the truth. In effect, the convent forced names on her that she could not claim for herself, that made her feel guilty and ashamed, and that made her see herself, reluctantly, as an individual who didn't quite fit in. McCarthy's self-discoveries are surprising in their honesty, for at this point she does not feel the liberation or excitemn of finding her identity, but only confusion and isolation.

In light of its psychological framework, "Names" is an excellent parallel to "First Communion" (pages 91–92), which is also about McCarthy discovering what she is not and what she is. Read together, the two encapsulate the difficulty of being known—by oneself as well as by others.

3. What does McCarthy's dual perspective add to the memoir?

Above all, humor. Because she tells it with the sense of humor of one looking back on the awkwardness of a preadolescent girl, the memoir on the surface seems hilariously absurd. McCarthy's innocent cut on her leg and her inability to get anyone to believe in it, coupled with her lively encounter with the mother superior, give the memoir the tone of one finding the humor in the traumatic experiences of childhood.

At the same time, however, McCarthy's mature voice takes the memoir beyond the childhood framework to pose larger questions about identity. The very nature of naming, McCarthy suggests, binds it to deception, for with a name comes an odd assortment of associations and expectations over which we have little or no control. In accepting the names of "Catholic," "woman," and "Cye," McCarthy saw herself as "a walking mass of lies" (paragraph 15). The memoir should make us somewhat uneasy, then, for ultimately McCarthy focuses on the mystery of establishing our identity as something that we often cannot understand. McCarthy never knew if Elinor and Mary told the school about her solemn (though faked) regaining of the faith; she never found out what C.Y.E. meant; and most importantly, she could never understand why she did not fit into the convent ("the nuns, evidently, saw something about me that was invisible to me," she explains in paragraph 14). But beyond the particulars of McCarthy's convent experience (and prevalent in the complete *Memories of a Catholic Girlhood*) is the larger problem of an orphan attempting to discover the truth about her family and her own identity.

4. What role do Elinor Heffernan and Mary Harty play in McCarthy's exploration of the meaning of names?

Elinor and Mary add an ironic dimension to the memoir, for they were defined by their very act of naming others. They were a "clownish pair" who "entertained the high-school department by calling attention to the oddities of the younger girls" (paragraph 6). They gained surprising power over the other girls simply by their act of assigning nicknames: since the nicknames were as likely to be flattering as insulting, the others did what Elinor and Mary commanded, and McCarthy never learned what her nickname (C.Y.E.) meant since even her best friend was afraid to tell. But in taking on the role of "clown," each girl also became known for her laziness, nonconformity, and low standing in the school—in essence, as an amusement not to be taken seriously except in the role they defined for themselves.

CHAPTER 4

Writing Reports and Observations

Purpose

Chapter 4 is similar in structure and purpose to Chapter 3. Once again the aim is to make it possible to assign a common type of paper (the observation or description paper) without having students fall into a common trap (naively producing a barrage of detail without discriminating between the important and the unimportant). Once again there is an attempt to show that the type of paper students write has its analogue outside the classroom (in this case, in the worlds of journalism and business). And once again there is reinforcement for the central idea of Chapter 1, the need for an essay to be an interpretation with a framework as well as a subject.

The principal difference between the two chapters lies in the nature of the subject students will be writing about and the sources of information they will use. In Chapter 3, the students look inward and backward, writing from memory. In Chapter 4, they look outward at the world and usually write from direct observation rather than from memory.

If you are teaching from a crowded syllabus and are eager to move on to the argument chapters, you may want to choose between Chapters 3 and 4. If you have time for both, I think you'll find the parallelism of the two chapters a virtue.

Overview

The *chapter proper* divides into five parts, the middle three of which include internal readings:

1. A general discussion of report writing.
2. A discussion of reports on places. This discussion has subparts: the first half concentrates on the physical environment, the second on the character of the inhabitants.

3. A discussion of reports on occasions. This discussion also divides into sub-parts: the first half focuses on single occasions, the second on a series of occasions that must be telescoped by the writer.
4. A discussion of reports on personalities. This section divides into two sub-parts: the first half deals with the portrayal of a type, the second with the portrayal of individuals.
5. Advice on writing reports based on observation.

The *assignments* include reports on places, occasions, and personalities, plus a Theophrastan character and a report on a character from literature.

The *readings* are, once again, all by members of *The Riverside Guide*'s panel of featured authors:

Charles Darwin's "Copper Mining in Northern Chile," a traveler's report on a place, excerpted from *The Voyage of the Beagle*

E. B. White's "Education," which contrasts a private New York City school with a public school in rural Maine

James Weldon Johnson's "Salt Lake City," a traveler's report on a place and on events that transpired there

George Orwell's "Reflections on Gandhi," an essay that evaluates the man in two frameworks—as a saint and as a politician

Theodore White's "Jimmy Carter," a report that places the former president in several frameworks

Joan Didion's "Amado Vazquez," a report on an interesting noncelebrity

These readings, along with the passages by Orwell, Darwin, Maya Angelou, Theodore White, Theophrastus, and Ellen Goodman in the chapter proper, give students a wide range of models to consider when they undertake their own reports.

The Chapter Step-by-Step

General Discussion of Reports (pages 118–119)

This discussion continues *The Riverside Guide*'s emphasis on framework and introduces another term by way of reinforcement—*drift*. The passage by John Henry Newman that uses the term is not an easy read, but I hope you can persuade your students to consider it carefully. Other words and phrases Newman uses—"idea beyond itself" and "relation"—have a good deal of heft to them. Once students have read Newman, you might find such terms useful in praising or criticizing student papers.

Reports on Places: The Physical Environment (pages 119–120)

This section begins with a passage intended to remind students that unselective (truly objective) reporting is impossible and that reporting that sets out to be unselective is boring and pointless. This preliminary discussion leads up to the selection from Orwell's "Marrakech Ghetto," in which he describes the city's Jewish quarters.

The Orwell passage is illuminating here because it seems to be both selective ("subjective," as people often say, disapprovingly) and honest. The ethics of reporting are probably as ambiguous as any other ethical code, but Orwell is as good an example as any of a writer who could present his perspective on a subject without violently rearranging the thing on which he was reporting.

The first two questions in the margin draw attention to some of Orwell's techniques for getting the reader to recognize and share the writer's view of what he sees. By saying "you go," Orwell puts the reader directly in his own shoes and so removes an element of psychological distance: it is one thing to have the experience of reading a report by a man who has seen a river of urine; it is another to seem to see it with our own eyes. Orwell's similes go beyond what the eyes can see, however. They allow him to introduce emotionally charged images: children clustering like flies, booths that are like caves, and so on. The third marginal question is discussed in the final paragraph of the selection.

Exercise 1: Objective and Subjective Language (page 120).   Since this exercise is a general hunting license, there should be some variety in what your students collect. Here are a half-dozen rather arbitrary examples:

"sore-eyed children"—an accurate observation made more pathetic because Orwell focuses on children rather than adults

"like clouds of flies"—not the most objective bit of description, this expression seems to convey Orwell's emotional reaction rather than what he sees

"a little river of urine"—accurate enough, and Orwell manages to yoke two words ordinarily sweet and innocent with one not so sweet

"fly-infested booths"—accurate as well as powerful because "infest" carries connotations of disease

"dark holes"—not the sort of description one likes to have associated with buildings inhabited by humans; here Orwell chooses an expression that is more emotional than objectively descriptive

"crawling out, groping the air with his hand"—at times Orwell's emphasis on pathetic details approaches the surrealistic

Listing such expressions on the board and discussing them will give your students a lesson in both style and epistemology.

Reports on Places: The Character of the Inhabitants (pages 120–122)

The Charles Darwin passage given as an example of a "place characterized by the behavior of its inhabitants" raises similar questions of emphasis and reliability. The first of the marginal questions merely points to Darwin's selection of details—he has surely picked the most extreme example he could to show how fascinating he was to the people of the region. The other two questions raise a more interesting issue: it could be argued that Darwin's amusement at the ignorance of the Uruguayans is actually provincialism on *his* part. The Englishman who is so amused because people in Uruguay don't know what London is might consider how few of his countrymen could identify the geographical feature that separates Montevideo from Buenos Aires.

Exercise 2: Action as an Element of Description (page 122).   The intent here is simply to draw attention to writerly technique. Here is a possible list of actions:

1. The people ask Darwin to demonstrate the compass.
2. Darwin points the way to various locations.
3. The young woman sends for Darwin.
4. The people ask Darwin whether the earth or sun moves, etc.
5. Darwin ignites matches with his teeth.
6. People collect their families to watch.
7. Someone offers Darwin a dollar for a match.
8. A man "cross-questions" Darwin about why he washes his face.
9. Travelers ask for lodgings at the first convenient house.
10. The guides tell the people about Darwin's behavior.

Like one of those medieval paintings filled with figures busy with one thing or another, Darwin's passage achieves interest by recording activity. Your students' papers may be more interesting if you pause to drive this point home.

Reports on a Single Occasion (pages 123–124)

After a brief explanation of the distinction between reports on places and reports on occasions (occasions are fleeting), we plunge into a passage in which Maya Angelou describes a society soiree in the 1960s. Readers gain a strong sense of the party because the passage is an interpretation: the details line up like iron filings in the grip of a strong magnet.

The marginal questions are aimed at helping students see the ways that Angelou implies a framework. The comparison to a minuet is pertinent to the framing idea—that the party goers have a sort of preening sophistication. The emphasis on colors suggests the artificiality of the scene: the young men have dyed hair (I wish she had said what color), the "predatory" women have red lips and crimson fingernails. The older women have pale pink lips and heavy mascara. But the most significant references to color are not to a single shade but to iridescence. The party's pretty people are explicitly compared to "iridescent dragonflies," the young men "rustled like old cellophane," the older men are ready to go "where the conversation was more scintillating," and the young women have "the exotic sheen of recently fed forest animals." Even when the particular image is not visual, Angelou keeps in front of us the idea of iridescence: everything shines like carnival glass.

Exercise 3: Figurative Language in Descriptive Writing (page 124).   Though every passage in this chapter contains some interesting metaphors, Angelou's may provide the best opportunity for study because hers are so insistent and so frequent. Some of the more striking are

1. The guests' movements in "minuet patterns." I doubt that the movements resembled a minuet, and I doubt that many readers would know what minuet movements look like, but the connotations of the word are apt.

2. the young men "who rustled like old cellophane." I confess I don't get the meaning here, though I get an emotional impression. Is Angelou actually talking about the noise that the men's clothes make, and if so, what can the clothes be made of?

3. the young women "who had the exotic sheen of recently fed forest animals." Again, I don't see the meaning here exactly. Is the sheen from fur coats? From the women's hair?

4. the crimson fingernails, "as pointed as surgical instruments." Here the meaning is perfectly clear and the image is striking.

5. the chains and bead necklaces that unsuccessfully "shielded" the unattractiveness of the older women. Your students may have to look twice to see the comparison to armor.

6. the comparison of the unattractive older women among the pretty people to "frogs buzzed by iridescent dragonflies." This is the masterstroke of the passage, I think, an image with an unpleasant edge to it but one that points clearly to the framework.

Though Angelou's metaphors and similes do some descriptive work, it seems to me that their main function is to clarify the passage's perspective or framework. They pull their weight emotionally.

Reports on a Series of Occasions (pages 124–126)

The Theodore White passage is no more neutral than the Angelou passage. It gives one man's compressed impression of a series of events that lasted for many hours and must have been vastly more complicated than his report suggests. In class discussion, one of our students made a sensational observation about this passage: it reads like a religious convert's description of his savior's appearance on earth or a description of a soul-shaking sexual experience. Had Freud read the passage, he would surely have seconded this comment: White's description is permeated with the "oceanic feeling" Freud believed to be the essence of religious experience.

The marginal questions are aimed primarily at helping students see how highly colored the passage is. White's syntax in the first sentence is mimetic: the sentence that describes the surge seems to surge itself. The adjectives encourage stereotyping: the "frowzy woman," the "harsh-faced woman," "the grizzled workingmen and union men." White is laying on Kennedy's appeal to the working class with a trowel. The "one remembers" refrain of the last paragraph is organizationally no more than a way of building a list, but it gives a rhythm to the passage that suggests exactly the "oceanic feeling" our student detected.

Except that they are carefully selected, the details present in the passage probably depart little from the literal truth, but the combination of selection and syntax creates a version that is strictly White's—and nearly purple. If you find this passage is overwritten, you might want to point out to your students that it occurs as an emotional crescendo amid many calmer passages and that a description of an occasion need not be so highly wrought.

Exercise 4: Verbs in Descriptive Writing (pages 125–126). You should decide before plunging into this exercise how finicky you are going to be about distinctions among various forms of verbs. My own feeling is that no damage is done at this point by calling main verbs, participles, gerunds, and infinitives all "verbs" or "verb forms." By this broad definition, some verbs to look at might be as follows:

Line	White's Verb Form	Dull Substitute
3	surging	coming
4	squeeze	press
5	splinter	give way
8	muttering	saying
12	crayoned	made
13	chalked	written
17	pouring	coming
25	bursting	coming
26	grasped	took
27	squeezed	pressed

White's choices are sometimes predictably "colorful," but sometimes they show remarkable craftsmanship. "Splinter," "crayoned," and "chalked" are particularly effective—verb forms convey a good deal of meaning very compactly. In a single word, the verbal creates the wooden barricade and the danger of its breaking, or conjures the classroom with children coloring at their desks, or evokes the construction site with future walls and conduits drawn in chalk. The less graphic alternatives bleed the life from the passage.

Exercise 5: A Brainstorming Session on Reportable Events (page 126). This assignment is important as a preliminary to Assignment 2. It will work well with a class capable of productive group work. If you don't want to parcel your class into groups, you might consider making a list on the board and suggesting that students seriously consider the potential of each subject proposed.

Reports on Character Type (pages 126–128)

The discussion of reports on personalities is built on the assumption that good reporting on people usually involves an interaction between an abstract "type" and a concrete individual. The type is connected with what we have been calling framework, and the individual is the subject. To make this "type" and "individual" distinction clear, the text first presents an example of a pure type—the Theophrastan character—and then gives an example of an individual (C. Everett Koop) portrayed as belonging to a type (the man of duty).

Theophrastus's "The Faultfinder" is a very clear and amusing example of type writing and may produce some witty imitations (Assignment 3). At the same time, as the text points out, the essay is not merely an exercise in humor. The character serves a serious purpose.

Exercise 6: A List of Character Types (page 128). This exercise should lead to an amusing few minutes at the chalkboard if you decide to collect lists of types. It may also lead to a modest philosophical insight, since students—even though they may want to dismiss stereotypes as false—tend to agree that some types are more "true" or "real" than others. The highlight of our first experience with this exercise was a discussion of "people who wear black," a type the class immediately recognized as tied in with a certain type of music and certain cultural attitudes. When a student in the back row said that he thought of himself as a person who wears black, we all had something to think about.

Exercise 7: A Rewrite of "The Faultfinder" (page 128). If your students get hold of this exercise properly, they can have productive fun with it. The key is to find details that give a dual shock of recognition: yes, that is just like a faultfinder; and yes, that is a representative bit of our everyday culture. "If his parents give him a compact disc player, he points out that it only has four-times overdubbing." "If she goes to Cancun for a vacation, she comes back complaining about how small the hotel room was." The possible responses are endless.

Reports on an Individual (pages 128–131)

The Goodman profile of Koop works so well in this type-and-character scheme that it requires little comment. The questions in the margin draw attention to some of Goodman's better strokes. She chooses quotations very carefully to contrast two views of Koop—the stereotypical religious conservative and the dutiful physician. She arranges her surprises in order of their surprisingness: that a religious conservative should oppose smoking is less surprising than that he should produce a scrupulously fair report on the effects of abortion. She also carefully distinguishes (as Koop did) between the public man and the private, leaving us with the impression that Koop's triumph was that the man in uniform rose above the prejudices of the private man.

Exercise 8: A Counter-Characterization (page 131). Whether you ask students to write this exercise or merely to discuss it, you probably shouldn't pass it by. Goodman's portrayal of Koop confidently assumes that the reader shares a value system that puts the public welfare before private morality. But you can be fairly confident that some students in your class will at least be uneasy with this value system. Shouldn't there be some absolute moral values, regardless of benefits to the public? they might think. A counter-characterization of Koop might present him as a man of once-firm moral principles who, when he rose to high public office, lost his way (if not his soul). It might even say that Koop became enamored of his image as a crusading Surgeon General and betrayed his principles in order to court the good opinion of liberals and opinion makers like Goodman.

Advice on Writing Reports (pages 131–134)

Experience tells me that students writing from observation tend to become (or try to become) recorders rather than reporters. They can more easily be persuaded to pile on details in quantity than to take an active stance that will create a principle for selecting details. The emphasis in this section is therefore on boldness, on getting what reporters call an angle. The peer-review questions stress angle and detail and are particularly appropriate for evaluating early drafts. Later drafts would benefit from a review using the checklist on pages 65–66.

The Assignments

Assignment 1: A Report on a Place. Some students have written reports on places so often in their primary and secondary school English classes that this assignment may produce intellectually dull and stylistically unsound prose *unless you insist that students take the journalistic role seriously.* If the rule of the road is that the paper will be evaluated as if it had appeared in a newspaper or magazine, you may be able to avoid essays that start something like this: "My grandparents' house has always meant so much to me. Its leafy trees wave in every passing breeze." Remind students, if you must, that newspapers are read by bankers, auto mechanics, lawyers, and insurance salespeople as well as high school English teachers.

Assignment 2: A Report on an Occasion. Once again, it is important to emphasize the breadth of the audience for which students should write and the need to find a subject of more than personal interest.

Assignment 3: A Theophrastan Character. The obvious thing to do with this assignment is to use it as a warm-up for the longer and more difficult papers in Assignments 4–6. Because Theophrastan character essays are quite short and follow a fixed formula, they can produce wonderful class discussions. We like to duplicate two unmarked examples (ideally one we would give a B+ and one we would give a strong C) and have students assign and justify the grades they would give the two.

Assignment 4: A Report on an Acquaintance. Here the assignment specifies classmates as the ultimate audience. The advantage of such a specification is that classmates are real and present. The disadvantage in some classes might be that students don't have a particularly elevated opinion of what might interest other students. You could broaden the audience specification and ask students to imagine that their work will be published in a newspaper or local-interest magazine.

Assignment 5: An Interview-Based Report on a "Public Figure." This is the most time consuming of the assignments because of the difficulty of arranging and conducting interviews, but it may be the most rewarding for both the student and the teacher. Figure that students may need a week to get their research together and another week to take their essays through drafts. Students who undertake this assignment should probably read Jessica Mitford's advice on interviews (pages 421–422 of Chapter 11).

Assignment 6: A Report on a Character in a Short Story or Poem. Character studies are a very common assignment in literature classes, and this chapter should lay a foundation for students to produce better-than-average ones. The predictable error students make in character studies is falling into plot summary: telling what happened to a character rather than showing what type of person the character is. If you can convince students to build their character studies on the pattern presented in this chapter, you may be able to forestall the plot-summary error.

Sample papers and additional assignments are available in the package of supplementary material that accompanies the main text.

End-of-Chapter Readings

CHARLES DARWIN
Copper Mining in Northern Chile

Not a tightly organized essay but a traveler's observation, this passage from *The Voyage of the Beagle* nonetheless shows the difference between the observations of a thinker and writer and the observations Newman attributes to sailors who "gaze on Pompey's pillar, or on the Andes; and nothing which meets them carries them forward or backward, to any idea beyond itself."

QUESTIONS

1. List the hypotheses you can find in this passage.

If your students look at you uncomprehendingly when you ask them to do this task, explain that you simply mean for them to list the instances in which Darwin develops a theoretical or speculative explanation for what he sees. For example:

a. In paragraph 1, he hypothesizes that men who are not "obliged to act and think for themselves" will "acquire no habits of carefulness." This theory is offered to explain the extravagant and apparently foolish behavior of the Chilean miners.
b. In paragraph 3, he hypothesizes that the failure of the British mining associations in Chile was caused by incompetence.
c. In paragraph 5, he hypothesizes that habit alone (without significant help from diet or physique) will enable a person to endure great labor.

I may be stretching the meaning of hypothesis in listing these three, but it is in a good cause. Darwin is a splendid example of an observer who collects details of a subject and constantly tries out theoretical frameworks on them. His own journals bear out his dictum that no one can be an accurate observer who is not also an active theorizer.

2. What sort of support does Darwin muster for these hypotheses? How convincing is the support?

For the assertion that carelessness and extravagance can be created by a way of life that includes no responsibilities, Darwin uses comparison. Sailors, like Chilean miners, live under the domination and protection of their masters, and they are equally extravagant. The miners of Cornwall, who (if I understand correctly) own and manage a part of the vein, are not extravagant and irresponsible. By choosing the comparisons he does, Darwin seems to eliminate variables. It isn't mining that makes people extravagant, since Cornish miners are not extravagant. Nor does irresponsibility appear to be linked to race or nation, since sailors everywhere are irresponsible. The form of the argument seems good, though Darwin hasn't much evidence and generalizes from few cases.

For the assertion that the failure of the British mining associations was caused by incompetence, Darwin gives a good deal of evidence. He eliminates the possibility that there wasn't enough potential profit margin by showing what a remarkable bargain the mines were, and he enumerates a series of obviously foolish actions.

For the assertion that habit alone can enable a man to endure very heavy labor, he also has evidence to offer. That the Chilean "Apires" do almost incredibly heavy labor he documents meticulously, and he also documents their poor diet and describes their slight physique. If neither physique nor diet accounts for their endurance, habit (or, as we would now say, conditioning) seems the only plausible explanation.

Two important tendencies of Darwin's mind are apparent in these half-developed arguments. First, when he sees something unexpected, he looks for explanations. The miners of Cornwall are sober and responsible, but the miners of Chile are extravagant: why the difference? British mining companies bought Chilean mines at a fraction of their value but failed to turn a profit: why the failure? Chilean miners carry burdens that would stagger a beefy Englishman: how do we account for this?

Second, when Darwin searches for an explanation, he works largely by elimination. He eliminates the possibility that occupation or race accounts for the miners' irresponsibility and is left with conditions of employment. He eliminates a slender profit margin as an explanation of the mines' failure and is left with mismanagement. He eliminates diet and physique as explanations of the miners' strength and is left with habituation.

Curiosity about the unexpected is a quality that every reporter must cultivate, and learning to sort through alternative explanations is a key to clear thinking.

3. Travelers' tales are notoriously unreliable. What (besides his now-famous name) makes Darwin's report credible?

This question should point your students to the fourth paragraph, where Darwin, skeptical about the reports of Captain Head, decides to see for himself how heavy the load is that the miners carry up the deep shafts. Not only does he pick out a load and feel its weight for himself, but he has it weighed to the nearest pound. The combination of skepticism about reports of wonders and scrupulousness in investigation tends to make the reader trust Darwin's observations and judgments.

E. B. WHITE

Education

Though "Education" and Johnson's "Salt Lake City" seem like very different reports, largely because of their contrast in tone, the two resemble each other in many respects because they both contain the elements we expect to find in reports on place. Both Johnson and White clearly define place in light of their own experiences, both use contrasting scenes to make the point of their descriptions clearer, and both leave us thinking about the course of progress (though two very different aspects of it) in this country. You might have your students read the two selections together, along with the profiles of each author (pages 59 and 88), in order to emphasize the power of a person's background to shape his or her perception of place.

QUESTIONS

1. How effective is "Education" as a report on place, and how effective is it in persuading us that a public country school is better than a private urban one?

In this brief, six-paragraph sketch, we get a description not only of each school but of the clothes the boy wears to class, the methods of transportation used to get him there, the various teachers, and the methods of teaching, of eating, and of recreating. The completeness and brevity with which White describes each school, besides offering us a sharp image of each place, should draw attention to his economical use of words.

The tone of the essay is an important element, in part because it shapes our interpretation. A first reading may give students the impression that White is easygoing and not terribly concerned about which school his son attends but is focused instead on simply presenting a portrait of each school. The content, after all, has little to say about quality of education, and after a year the only difference White can see between the two locations is that in the country the boy sleeps better (and that's probably due to the air, not the school). Yet if we look closely at White's technique, we may decide that his intent is to make an argument *for* the public school. And if he is not, his careful word choice and organization at least prove the pointedness of his report.

Notice first how White begins the essay with a portrait of the public school teacher, able to discharge a host of responsibilities and be regarded by the boy as "his great friend" as well. White also tells us his own bias, admitting that he himself is the product of public education, and then presents his portrait of each school. Though he maintains a "no-complaints" attitude toward the private school, which was modern, electric, and colorful, his choice of verbs makes it quite clear that this is the private-school-as-machine: White does not introduce us to any individual teacher in this description, though we can assume the presence of one as the boy is "worked on" until he has to be "revived" with his mid-morning juice; through supervised play and supervised work, the boy "learned fast, kept well," and the machine operated smoothly enough to keep his parents satisfied. But the only living organism in the private school system, according to White's description, is the school bus, the growling, ferocious being that gets the boy to school on time (being, in fact, "punctual as death").

On the other hand, the alternate portrait is the public-school-as-human, and White stresses his preference for the natural vitality (and even the limitations) of this school. That the teachers "teach what they know themselves, just as fast and as hard as they can manage," and that the children are forced to find their own amusements, being deprived of supervised play, come across as perfectly acceptable to White. Your students may notice the lack of vivid verbs and adjectives in the description of the public school and may argue that the passage's flatness is a sign of White's lack of interest in it; if White is saying anything by his selective use of strong and weak words, perhaps it is that there is a place for the electric and a place for the natural, and his "third-grade scholar" (who just might not need to be a scholar so soon) benefits much more from the health, peace, and opportunity to develop his own imagination than from the hothouse atmosphere of the private school.

2. Where do you find White's style of writing surprising, and what is its effect?

Your students will most likely see first White's occasionally odd choices of words, such as in the first paragraph. Not only are we surprised by the incongruity of "third-grade scholar," but we also pause to wonder how the teacher can be a guardian of "[the pupils'] mothers" as well as of the children's health and habits. And that the teacher "can cool their passions or warm their soup" may come across as little more than clever wording. Any examples like these that catch students' attention should allow you to discuss the value of language that calls attention to itself. In the case of the "third-grade scholar," students may agree that it reflects White's bias against highly regimented learning for young children; however, students may feel that the other phrases do less to clarify White's meaning than to make us pause, possibly for no valid reason. White is not Orwell; he does not write prose clear as a windowpane.

The second paragraph contains at least two fine examples of White's economical use of an image to give us a strong and complete picture of what he is thinking. White admits that his bias against the private school may be "an involuntary defense against getting kicked in the shins by a young ceramist on his way to the kiln." With this one sentence, we get the sense that White is not only defending himself but also vaguely attacking the type of activities encouraged in a public school and the type of children such an environment produces. Similarly, when White claims that his wife, "never having been exposed (in her early life) to anything more public than the washroom of Miss Winsor's," knew little about public schools, he indirectly emphasizes the atmosphere of the private school (as prim and aristocratic as "Miss Winsor" herself) while humorously discrediting his wife's bias against the public system. Economizing on words as White does is not simply a matter of conciseness, for throughout the essay he proves the power of suggestion as he makes us see the two schools, and perhaps see them as *he* does, without his being compelled to present us with a thorough argument.

3. How precisely does White match his description of one school with his description of the other?

Although his structure is not as strict an organizational pattern as you may ask for from your students, White's report loosely follows the divided method (see Chapter 13, page 483). His essay is typical of the type of comparison/ contrast structure students will find most often in their reading of professional essays; while the structure does not break into neatly paired paragraphs, you will want to point out how careful White is to cover the same elements in each half of the report: clothing, transportation, learning, eating, teachers, and recreation.

JAMES WELDON JOHNSON
Salt Lake City

In order to prepare students for reading "Salt Lake City," you will want to direct them first to the Johnson profile (page 88); an awareness of Johnson's life, particularly of the prominence he had obtained by the time he traveled to the West, should put into perspective the difficulties he encountered in Salt Lake City. You might also remind students of one of the major premises of Chapter 4: "Good reporting on places comes from an interaction between the place itself and an idea of the place, constructed in the writer's mind and conveyed to the reader largely by a judicious selection of details." Once again we are confronted with frameworks—this time the writer's sense of insulted dignity shapes his view of a whole city. To reinforce students' awareness of how a perception (framework) shapes reporting, you might read them Mark Twain's description of Salt Lake City in the 1860s:

> Next day we strolled about everywhere through the broad, straight, level streets, and enjoyed the pleasant strangeness of a city of fifteen thousand inhabitants with no loafers perceptible in it, and no visible drunkards or noisy people; a limpid stream rippling and dancing through every street in place of a filthy gutter; block after block of trim dwellings, built of "frame" and sun-burned brick—a great thriving orchard and garden behind every one of them, apparently—branches from the street stream winding and sparkling among the garden beds and fruit trees—and a grand general air of neatness, repair, thrift and comfort, around and about and over the whole. And everywhere were workshops, factories, and all manner of industries; and intent faces and busy hands were to be seen wherever one looked; and in one's ears were the ceaseless clink of hammers, the buzz of trade and the contented hum of drums and fly-wheels.

The armorial crest of the state, he adds, was "simple, unostentatious, and fitted like a glove": "a Golden Beehive, with the bees all at work!" It is hard to believe that Twain and Johnson are writing about the same place. Reading Johnson's description in light of Twain's, then, should make clear the difference between a place and the idea of it.

QUESTIONS

1. How do Johnson's own history and personality affect his view of Salt Lake City?

The best place to begin answering this question is with the biographical information in the profile of Johnson (page 88). Clearly, Johnson lived in a time when most whites would not expect an African-American to be a person with dignity, education, and experience of the world. And one assumes that in Utah, then an essentially all-white state, stereotyping would have been particularly severe. Yet here was Johnson, highly and widely educated, having been a high school principal, a lawyer, a singer-songwriter, and a student of theater—all before he traveled in the West.

Johnson creates an impression of his personality in the essay itself, primarily by his tone. He maintains reasonableness throughout, as well as a sense of dignity and of fairness to himself and others (see Question 3). Above all, he keeps a sense of larger-than-personal perspective. His anger at the way he was treated must have been to some degree personal at the time, but his essay subsumes the personal in the political. He is angry for all African-Americans who must endure these sorts of affronts. The incident was important not only in itself but as a representation of the injustice throughout the "hell of a 'my country,'" and Johnson devotes a large portion of the passage to his analysis of the segregation issue.

2.   Since a report on place is shaped by its judicious selection of details, what details in "Salt Lake City" are most crucial to our seeing the place as Johnson did?

As if alluding to the perfection of Twain's Salt Lake City, Johnson carefully places details that ironically emphasize what the city proves *not* to be. Since this is the city of the Mormon Tabernacle—the "city of the Latter-Day Saints"—we are right to wonder why the only "compassionate soul" is the Irish cabman. Similarly, though they asked only for a good hotel, Johnson and his party are taken to "the best"—and again, the behavior we would expect in such a place is completely absent. By encouraging us to set our expectations high, Johnson emphasizes the despicable behavior produced by racism.

Johnson also uses details to focus on racial tension at a more personal level. As a contrast to the strained and embarrassed behavior of the hotel clerk, Johnson depicts the "stare of a crowd" he and his companions faced when refused service at a restaurant. These details force us to feel the awkwardness as well as the anger that have too often plagued African-Americans. Even more personal, then, is Johnson's note that after a long and difficult day, the travelers cannot bring themselves "to bear the touch of the soiled bedclothes"; this brief scene brings Johnson's sense of his own dignity into sharp contrast with the indignity of his surroundings.

The effect of Johnson's details, then, is to help us see the situation as he does, as a reasonable man with his dignity under considerable strain. Johnson's manner of presenting the incident impresses this framework on us, so that he does not need to elaborate on his feelings. Certainly the string of emotions he felt ("humiliation, chagrin, indignation, resentment, anger") coupled with the list of difficulties African-Americans face ("unfairness, injustice, wrong, cruelty, contempt, and hate") leaves no doubt in our minds of what Johnson expects us to see in the incident. It may be worthwhile to return with your students to the "Jim Crow" passage in Chapter 1, pages 12–13, to reinforce how carefully Johnson selects his words.

3.   Although "Salt Lake City" is primarily a report on a place, Johnson includes several brief portraits of people encountered there. What do these characterizations add to the report?

You will probably wish to begin by having your students characterize each of the personalities Johnson depicts. Our first impression is of the hotel clerk, busy at the key-rack, who delays, gets flustered, and finally tells Johnson and his companions a lie. Johnson reveals much of himself in this incident, for his response is that he "could detect a sense of pity for the man who had to [tell the lie], for he was, to all appearances, an honest, decent person." The clerk demonstrates the complexity of racial injustice as Johnson focuses on the perspective of one caught in the middle.

Next we encounter the Irishman; jovial, desiring to please and to console, he is "the only compassionate soul . . . in the whole city" and is so frustrated by the travelers' plight that he "gave vent to his feelings in explosive oaths," making it his mission to find them a place to eat and sleep for the night. The cabman is something of an outsider himself, but he nevertheless shows that empathy is possible in the city; at the same time, his characterization demonstrates Johnson's freedom from racial bias. His problem is not with whites but with bigots.

Although she kept the house for laborers and did little to keep it clean, the lodging-house keeper hesitated before letting Johnson and his companions stay there, and then only if they "got out before her regular lodgers got up." While the hotel clerk and the cabman are primarily revealed by their actions, this woman is characterized by the filth she lives in, particularly as it reveals her racial attitude: bad as her hotel is, it is too good for African-Americans. Johnson's portrait of this woman is not kind. He strips her of dignity almost as ruthlessly as she had stripped him of his. Compassion has its limits.

Johnson's means of identifying these people points to how characterization of people is similar to description of places. We still see the actual person, revealed in what the person said and did, but at the same time, we see Johnson's idea of him or her. And as we see the fairness that Johnson generally maintained, acknowledging the embarrassment of the clerk and the compassion of the cabman, we are reminded of Johnson's character as well.

GEORGE ORWELL

Reflections on Gandhi

Before sending your class off to read Orwell's essay, you may wish to introduce it by allowing students to discuss what the name Gandhi means to them, to construct their own framework through which they tend to view the man Gandhi. A reputation that has scarcely been tarnished over the years, coupled with the recent release of the movie of Gandhi's life (which several of our students claim their mothers made them watch), will probably result in a positive, if not reverent, response from your class. Reviewing the profile of Orwell (page 275) may be helpful, particularly if you want to emphasize the weight Orwell's own life and experiences add to his argument.

QUESTIONS

1. Explain the two frameworks (in this case, types of people) in which Orwell places Gandhi. What is the effect Orwell achieves by using two frameworks instead of limiting himself to one?

We can break the essay into two means of viewing Gandhi: as a man (and/or saint) and as a political theorist and activist. While each framework itself is somewhat complex, that Orwell separates the two is significant, for positive views of Gandhi often seem unable to distinguish one from the other. When we look at each framework individually, however, what is most remarkable is how carefully Orwell constructs the stereotype, defines what it means to fit that stereotype, and then characterizes Gandhi according to how he fits the stereotype in some respects and doesn't in others.

In viewing Gandhi the man, Orwell devotes two extended paragraphs to extolling Gandhi's personal virtues, most notably his physical courage, his fairness to all people, and his inability to act out of envy or a sense of inferiority. In fact, Orwell even finds favor with Gandhi's means of taking up his extremist positions—he was neither a rash person moving from a position of extreme sin and worldliness to extreme piety, nor a saint from birth, but rather a cultured man who, with careful deliberations, gave up the benefits of his position for what he believed he had to do to serve the world. Thus, Orwell praises him as a man of character, a type that Gandhi fits well. But at the same time, Gandhi fits even more snugly in the saint category, which by definition—in Orwell's opinion—puts him in an extremely negative light. What Orwell most obviously opposes is the "other-worldly, anti-humanist tendency" of Gandhi's teaching. He felt Gandhi made a huge mistake by excluding personal friendship and love from his life and, at the least, cannot "feel much liking" for him. The problem here is not Gandhi's inability to fit the stereotype but rather his fitting too well into one to which Orwell feels no man should aspire.

Turning to Gandhi as a political leader, Orwell carefully characterizes Gandhi's own definition of pacifism, then demonstrates once again how Gandhi fits the type too well. The example will undoubtedly stay with your students: Gandhi believed it was better for the Jews to commit mass suicide during World War II than to be killed, so they could at least die significantly. Yet in his fairness, Orwell also offers a more positive example: how Gandhi's pacifism worked in getting the British out of India without war. While it is again the type that gives Orwell doubts (he finds fault with much of Gandhi's theory), this type is at least workable for Orwell, perhaps the solution to preventing a third world war.

By presenting the two most prevalent aspects of Gandhi, Orwell proves the complexity of character, the limitations and problems of strict stereotypes, and his own ability to serve as a model for fair judgment.

2. How does Orwell's presentation of himself compare to his presentation of Gandhi?

Though Orwell talks (in "Why I Write") about his struggle to efface his personality in his writing, the personality is always present, and in this essay the reader gets a virtual double portrait—of Gandhi and Orwell. In important and obvious respects, the portraits contrast. Orwell's treatment of Gandhi's saintliness certainly reveals as much about the English writer as about the mahatma. Orwell is resolutely (to some, shockingly) antiascetic: "sainthood is also a thing that human beings must avoid" (paragraph 6). And unlike Gandhi, he is inclined to think that totalitarianism creates situations in which pacifism means appeasement and therefore acquiescence in evil (paragraph 8). Students need to see that

Orwell often uses Gandhi as a foil for himself and himself as a foil for Gandhi: the contrast shows each man's profile more clearly.

On the other hand, all is not contrast. If Orwell is hostile to asceticism and saintliness, he is attracted to honesty, and he repeatedly praises Gandhi for avoiding the hypocrisy of other pacifists. The honesty he praises is mirrored in the manner of his argument, which bends itself into a pretzel to be scrupulously fair. First of all, though we know beyond doubt that Orwell finds Gandhi's personality disagreeable, he devotes a large part of the essay to praising Gandhi's strengths. Even in his opening paragraph, he emphasizes that the questions about Gandhi do not place him strictly in a box but allow us to judge "to what extent" he fits in one characterization or another. Further, Orwell chooses as a means of judging Gandhi's character Gandhi's own words—his autobiography—so that there can be no question of unfair play. Thus, even as Orwell presents his portrait of a man whose honesty and fair-mindedness he respects, the writer shows himself to be honest and fair-minded.

3. Orwell is known for his frank (and sometimes offensive) statements of opinion. Where do you find such statements, and what effect do they have in the essay?

The way students answer this question will depend largely on what they think of Gandhi and partly on what they think of Orwell. The following examples may come up:

- "Saints should always be judged guilty until they are proved innocent" (paragraph 1).
- ". . . to what extent was Gandhi moved by vanity—by the consciousness of himself as a humble, naked old man, sitting on a praying mat and shaking empires by sheer spiritual power" (paragraph 1).
- ". . . sainthood is also a thing that human beings must avoid" (paragraph 6).
- "One must choose between God and Man, and all 'radicals' and 'progressives,' from the mildest liberal to the most extreme anarchist, have in effect chosen Man" (paragraph 6).
- "I have never been able to feel much liking for Gandhi" (paragraph 9).

Very likely, you will have as many students unruffled by these statements as students offended by them. In part, students often are reacting from their own level of ability to see their past thinking challenged. But students are more likely to respond to Orwell's method of presentation; by embedding his harshest criticism of Gandhi in passages that praise (or at least seriously consider) his characteristics or ideas, Orwell emphasizes the balanced nature of his critique.

As a variation, you might have students look for surprising statements coupled with reasonable language. Examples may include:

- "Whether he was also a lovable man, and whether his teachings can have much value for those who do not accept the religious beliefs on which they are founded, I have never felt fully certain" (paragraph 4).

- "This attitude [that one should die rather than commit the sin of eating meat] is perhaps a noble one, but, in the sense which—I think—most people would give to the word, it is inhuman" (paragraph 6).

- "One may feel, as I do, a sort of aesthetic distaste for Gandhi, one may reject the claims of sainthood made on his behalf (he never made any such claim himself, by the way), one may also reject sainthood as an ideal and therefore feel that Gandhi's basic aims were anti-human and reactionary: but regarded simply as a politician . . . how clean a smell he has managed to leave behind!" (paragraph 9).

The extreme care with which Orwell presents his opinions, as well as the honesty with which he reveals his feelings about Gandhi, encourages us to see the merit of the writer's position, if not to agree with him altogether. "Reflections on Gandhi" serves as a fine example of reasonable argumentation; teaching it as an example of persuasive reporting prepares students well for the chapters ahead.

THEODORE WHITE

Jimmy Carter

The emphasis in Chapter 4 has been on reports that leave a single strong impression of the subject. But a conscientious writer will sometimes find that his or her subject cannot be honestly treated by the single-framework formula. A professor who is a model of refinement in the lecture hall may turn out to be a loud, bawdy, bumptious character off campus. A city neighborhood may be one place to the rich and another to the poor, or one place by day and another by night. A concert may be a technical and even artistic fiasco and yet be redeemed by the personality of the performer. In such cases the writer may feel that complexity and even contradiction are at the heart of the matter.

White's portrait of Carter falls into this category and can serve as a model for students who want to undertake a paper that views the same subject in a number of frameworks.

QUESTIONS

1. How did White gather the information used in this report?

White, who is primarily a storyteller rather than a scholar, does not identify all of his sources explicitly. The effort of attempting to identify them should give students both some insight into the nature of journalistic research and some understanding of why more explicit documentation of sources is valuable.

It appears that White's report is put together from roughly five sources:

a. The most conspicuous source is White's interview with Carter in Plains (paragraph 3). Every student should name it. If you intend to use Assignment 5, you might pause to note the brilliance of his "single-track" question about the beginning of modern American history; the question is non-threatening and since there is no standard answer, every response is bound to reveal something about the interviewee.

b. Carter's open letter on creationism (paragraph 4) is apparently another source, one that White probably read in its entirety or in excerpts reprinted in other sources.

c. The account of Carter's praying at breakfast with Ed Koch (paragraph 4) and the account of Carter's behavior at the opera in Vienna (paragraph 9) obviously were not based on direct observation. White was a voracious reader of newspapers, and one suspects that these tidbits were picked up from such reading.

d. The story of the "prominent New York Democrat" who finds Carter knee-deep in the Air Force budget (paragraph 9) *might* have come from the Democrat himself, but it may have been obtained secondhand.

e. The conversation with the pilot named Peterson (paragraph 8) turns out to be the most serendipitous source, providing not only a picture of Carter the engineer learning to operate the plane's instruments, but also a more revealing picture of Carter the believer pausing in mid-campaign to try to coax Mrs. Peterson into attending church.

This is not particularly deep research. It is certainly unimpressive by comparison to the legwork White did for his books on the 1960 and 1964 campaigns. But it will remind your students that a reporter benefits from consulting several sources that can confirm or contradict each other and add new depth of detail.

2. How many layers does White find in Carter's personality?

I count five: the true believer, the engineer, the yeoman (paragraph 10), the mechanic of politics (paragraph 10), and the wary small-town outsider (paragraphs 10–11). Obviously, not all are equally developed, and this uneven development should probably be brought to the attention of students who have been trained in producing papers that have a mechanical symmetry about them. White has decided that two facets of Carter's personality are most important, and he concentrates his attention on them, merely noting the rest.

These facets White develops with several examples of Theophrastan clarity, and he makes it clear that he is dealing in abstract types. Note, for example, that he says that "one could invent a Jimmy Carter on the model of Sir Isaac Newton." White was very conscious that the presentation of a personality is always a matter of interpretation, of invention.

3. What is White's judgment on Carter as a man and as a politician?

Just as Orwell, writing on Gandhi, separated the man-saint from the politician, White seems to some degree to separate the man Carter from the president. Although he may be somewhat uneasy with Carter's "archaic" fundamentalism, he seems finally to admire its sincerity and the "motivation of love and mercy" (paragraph 5) that it created. He is particularly positive about the way Carter's religion shaped his attitude toward civil rights (paragraph 3).

But in politics good intentions are not enough, and White seems finally to conclude that the combination of "engineer" Carter and "small-town" Carter hampered his political effectiveness as president. You might ask your students whether the report moves generally from negative to positive or from positive to negative. Clearly, it does the latter, and so leaves us with the impression that White's overall judgment is negative.

JOAN DIDION

Amado Vazquez

When Didion reprinted this essay (originally titled "The Man in a Greenhouse of Orchids") in *The White Album*, she made it the middle section of "Quiet Days in Malibu," an essay in which she uses a few portraits of the people living there as a basis for characterizing the place. Vazquez comes onto the scene after Didion's portrait of the everyday life of a lifeguard; as with the greenhouses, Didion notices in this setting its moments of quiet, but the sense of action on the beach contrasts well with the quiet greenhouse full of growing plants. You might also wish to compare "Amado Vazquez" to "Marrying Absurd" (in Chapter 1, pages 27–28) in order to emphasize aspects of Didion's technique that stand out when she characterizes place. In addition, the profile of Didion (page 15) and the summaries of "Marrying Absurd" in Chapter 1 might present students with the interesting task of fitting this characterization to Didion's life and other writings—or explaining the ways it doesn't fit.

QUESTIONS

1. How is "Amado Vazquez" a report of a place?

Though the title focuses our attention on the person of Amado Vazquez, we may read it equally as a report on place—greenhouses in general, and the Freed greenhouses in particular. At the same time, the essay characterizes Vazquez because he cannot be extracted from the greenhouses he tends. The prevalent characteristics of the greenhouses—their benevolent peace and quiet vitality—belong equally to the man who keeps them.

Didion reports on the Freed greenhouses as representative of one of her favorite places, featured because it contains "the most aqueous filtered light, the softest tropical air, the most silent clouds of flowers." While Didion is primarily attracted to the Freed greenhouses for the beauty and solitude they provide her, her description of what she experiences there suggests an ideal world, as if the setting were a place of escape not only from the activity and noise of California life but from the entire world as well. Among the priceless Freed orchids, Didion finds herself in a sort of Eden; the benign presence of Amado Vazquez watches over all, keeping the air, light, and even humidity in perfect order.

To emphasize the natural beauty of the greenhouse itself, Didion sets up a contrast of the business side of the growing of orchids with the beauty of the flowers themselves. We first see this side when the men in the business suits, from far and exotic places, invade the greenhouses. And Didion's description of the office fleshes out this side: the "dulled silver awards," the "genealogical charts," and Marvin Saltzman's *Sander's List*. Most unusual is Saltzman's telling of the "old story," the explanation of the evolution of orchids, seemingly scientific yet magical at the same time, particularly to Didion. The two sides of the greenhouse production cannot be entirely separated, though the two worlds seem to have very little in common. Yet in Didion's mind, the office is nothing but unnatural in contrast to "the primeval silence of the greenhouse beyond the office window."

Similarly, Didion stresses the ideal nature of the greenhouses by contrasting their orderly and perfectly controlled environment with the natural habitat of the orchids: the jungles of Malaysia. In the wild, the orchids have little chance to survive, suffering from bouts of wind, boas, and monkeys; in Vazquez's greenhouse, orchids seem to live forever, pollinated meticulously by Vazquez himself (though at full moon and high tide), destined to at least outlive those who grow them. Didion very carefully mingles the natural and artificial until we begin to believe that the greenhouse is the most perfect of places.

2. How is this essay a report of a person?

While Amado Vazquez is most readily identified with the greenhouses he tends, he is by no means limited to the Edenic garden he has created there. Didion begins and ends the essay with a look at his life outside of the greenhouse, though the effect is undoubtedly to reinforce the portrait of him among his orchids. The first and last paragraphs discuss Vazquez's background, emphasizing his affinity with Mexico; although he has lived most of his life in California, he maintains the look, the "personal conservatism," of one from Mexico, and after all those years, he is unable to give up his devotion to his native country. A resident alien, Vazquez stands apart from the Freed family, which represents the business and profit aspect of the greenhouses.

The devotion with which Vazquez regards his homeland is surpassed, however, by his devotion to his orchids. "It seemed to me that day that I had never talked to anyone so direct and unembarrassed about the things he loved," Didion explains. The orchids are like his children; he expects much out of them, he loves them, he gets up at night to care for them. "My whole life is orchids," he says. In addition, Vazquez's entire family is connected to the greenhouse business in some way, and his vacations are all trips to look for more orchids. Didion has been introduced to Vazquez as one of twenty great orchid growers in the world, and therefore as a legend. Didion's characterization approaches adoration: in his delicate care of his orchids, in his ability to grow and care for flowers as few can, and in his power to produce a breed that will live for possibly two hundred years, he seems almost godlike.

Your students might be interested to know that Vazquez eventually bought the Freed greenhouses and moved them to his own location. But the final image that Didion leaves us with is Vazquez as a lover of orchids: the essay ends with his own words, "I will die in orchids."

3. How is the essay also a report on Didion?

Didion initially recalls herself as a child, longing for the solitude and beauty of greenhouses. By revealing her lifelong love of greenhouses, Didion reveals that part of her personality that is drawn to the peace and beauty she found there. This aspect of Didion may surprise some readers who think of her as the "first lady of angst," someone who seeks out disorder and battens on grim irony. What we seem to find revealed in "Amado Vazquez" is a picture of the world Didion would like to inhabit, the ideal against which the various fallen worlds she has reported on must be measured and found wanting. While being introduced to the business of the Freed greenhouses, Didion could not "take [her] eyes from the window"; she could not stop gazing at the greenhouse itself beyond the confining walls of the office. The peace and serenity are magnetic to her. The closing image of Didion is as fitting as the characterization of Vazquez: she is standing in a "sea of orchids," endowed with a huge bouquet with "more blossoms maybe than in all of Madrid."

PART II

Writing and Argument

CHAPTER 5
Preparing to Argue

Purpose

Argument is a word with several definitions and strong and varying connotations. Some students are alarmed by the combative overtones of the word, and one of my colleagues argues (combatively) that it should be purged from the vocabulary of composition because it suggests that the meek can't inherit the earth until they learn to comport themselves like prosecuting attorneys. Some students, of course, love combat and see argument as a free-for-all in which they can join without being restrained by either good manners or good sense. Others, particularly those who have been exposed to the "if *P*, then not *Q*" formulas of logicians, expect arguments to have an unearthly precision in terminology and reasoning.

This chapter defines argument in a way that distinguishes it from combat without denying that it is grounded in disagreement. The emphasis is on the arguer's purpose and tone, and the chapter builds a picture of the ideal arguer as someone comfortable with the idea that on many questions there is both room for reasonable disagreement and an opportunity to change people's views without twisting their arms.

This emphasis on courting the opinion of others shuts off the idea that an argument can be won either by bullying or by a crushing deployment of logical force. Argument becomes indistinguishable from persuasion—all to the good, in my opinion, since the distinction has done much damage.

But I want to put one type of persuasion outside the pale—the attempt of an arguer to sell an unexamined idea or an idea that he or she finds utterly without merit. Therefore, the process of preparing to argue is presented as a process of scrupulously examining one's own opinion before attempting to persuade others to accept it. I encourage students to argue with themselves before they argue with anyone else.

Overview

The *chapter proper* divides into three parts:

1. Observations about the nature of argument
2. A discussion of the psychology of clichéd thinking
3. A description of a five-part heuristic to dechannel thought, illustrated by a student example

I want to draw your attention especially to the student example because it so perfectly exemplifies the open-minded, flexible attitude students need to cultivate for Chapters 6–9. Some students tend to skim over student examples, feeling that they are beneath their notice, but this one deserves close reading as a true model.

The sole *reading* for the chapter is Mark Twain's "Corn-Pone Opinions," a bitterly amusing essay on the tendency of individuals to follow "public opinion" or "swarm with their party" rather than think independently. If your students read both the dechanneling heuristic and Twain's essay, they will find that each sheds light on the significance of the other.

Although there is no formal writing *assignment* for Chapter 5, the exercise on page 164—the five-part heuristic—requires a significant amount of writing and thinking and could certainly weigh as heavily (both for emphasis and for grading) as some of the short assignments in the book.

The Chapter Step-by-Step

The Nature of Argument (pages 156–158)

It may seem odd to start this chapter with two pages on what argument is *not*, but the tendencies to be quarrelsome and to speak in absolutes are so strong that I thought it best to campaign against them early and often. If you want to reinforce the point on page 156, you might ask your students what Baker's mother and grandmother were actually quarreling about. In one way or another, students will probably say that the dispute was about dominance or control far more than it was about the consequences of eating between meals. At that point you can explain that the type of argument you hope students will write will have less to do with the assertion of ego than with the pursuit of truth.

The discussion of syllogisms is deliberately minimal. Our own experience is that class time spent working on the mechanics of categorical reasoning does little or nothing to improve the logic of students' arguments; indeed, it may do damage by encouraging sweeping generalizations. Instead I have tried in the text to focus on the most valuable insight students can gain from the syllogism: arguments require a connection between the particulars of the subject and some generalizations about principles or probabilities. If you want to reinforce this point, ask your class to find some general statements in the student example illustrating the heuristic and to link these general statements to particulars, syllogism-fashion, to lead to a conclusion. For example, item 2(c) on page 161 might generate something that looks like this:

> Generally, the college shouldn't adopt policies that will lead to conflict between new and old employees.

> The proposed hiring policy could lead to such conflict.

> Therefore, the college should think twice about adopting this policy.

Or, item 3(b) on page 162 might produce the following:

> The college wants more women to become professors.

> Women will become professors only if they know there is work available to them.

> Therefore, the college should make work available to female professors.

Such arguments would make a pure logician cringe, but students who can identify them are clearly aware of how argument actually proceeds.

The Psychology of Clichéd Thinking (pages 158–160)

This discussion is linked to the discussion of foggy thinking in Chapter 2 and anticipates much that is to come in Chapters 6 and 7, where students are asked to think twice about facts and about rules. One of the rarely acknowledged goals of higher education is to train the mind to slow itself down a bit on the way to a conclusion.

If you feel that your class needs to slow down a bit on pages 158–159, you might ask them to join you in assembling a list of common-sense truths from the past that we now think are erroneous. Here are some examples:

1. Most women are incapable of profound or prolonged thought.
2. The sun, moon, and stars rotate around the earth.
3. The Japanese are capable of manufacturing only cheap imitations of American goods.

After making your list, you could ask students to discuss what made the old pattern of thought attractive and what disrupted it. If your students read "Corn-Pone Opinions," they'll have the benefit of Mark Twain's thinking on the subject.

The Five-Part Dechanneling Heuristic and Exercise (pages 160–164)

Reading the example will give students some sense of what the heuristic does, but what really counts here is getting students to work through the heuristic themselves. You will probably want students to write on a question that might be used for their next paper, but if you have not yet settled on the assignment, you could consider having them choose among the factual controversies given in Assignment 1 of Chapter 6, pages 191–192.

End-of-Chapter Reading

MARK TWAIN

Corn-Pone Opinions

Writing long before Edward de Bono, Twain knew well the problem of being "blocked by openness." Twain's general attitude is like de Bono's, but the position he takes is more extreme, claiming that not only do our minds tend to follow the most accessible channels but they do so because they are nearly incapable of digging out their own. In making this claim, Twain has presented us with a fact we may wish to dispute, and his essay serves not only as an illustration but as a basis for argument as well.

QUESTIONS

1. Which of Twain's examples best illustrates the "blocked by openness" problem? What current examples can you add to Twain's?

Students will recognize the truth in Twain's observations about our literary tastes and table manners, but because students are often more interested in clothes than in literature or etiquette, the example of the hoop skirt may be the one that strikes home. What is most familiar is the way Twain describes our reaction to changing fashion: we are often shocked or amused but soon find ourselves accepting, and sometimes adopting, the very fashion we laughed at only months before (paragraph 10). Equally on target is Twain's explanation of how our response comes about, for it is true that we often give changes little intellectual consideration but merely observe and conform (in our opinions if not in practice).

When you ask students for examples of their own, you will certainly get a broad range of answers worth pursuing. The movement up and down in the length of skirts and in women's heels, the recent insistence on Guess jeans instead of Levis or on Nike Air Jordans instead of Converse shoes, the steady increase in co-ed colleges and co-ed dorms, the conservative swing in student politics (or the liberal swing that preceded it), the preference of young readers for Stephen King instead of Jack Kerouac, and even the recent supplanting of Walt Disney characters by Teenage Mutant Ninja Turtles—all these examples suggest that we desire to conform more than we desire to think.

2. Outline Twain's essay. What makes his organizational strategy effective?

I.   Preface (paragraphs 1–8)
     A. Twain introduces his topic through an anecdote (paragraphs 1–5).
     B. He offers two modifications.
          1. People do not conform by calculation and intention.
          2. Firsthand opinions rarely exist.

II. Summary and discussion of thesis (paragraphs 9–17), which encompasses both of Twain's modifications: "I am persuaded that a coldly-thought-out and independent verdict upon a fashion [of any kind] that is projected into the field of our notice and interest, is a most rare thing—if it has indeed ever existed" (paragraph 9).

   A. First three examples stress our habit of observing and conforming rather than forming firsthand opinions for ourselves (paragraphs 10–13).
      1. Example from fashion (paragraphs 10–11)
      2. Example from manners (paragraph 12)
      3. Example from literature (paragraph 13)
   B. Final examples—of morals, politics, and religion—stress *how* we conform, not by calculation but by habit and by our natural desire for approval (paragraphs 14–17).
      1. Corn-pone opinions come from our desire for self-approval, which is grounded in the approval of others and results in conformity (paragraph 14).
      2. While financial gain is sometimes a motivator, our primary motivation is our desire for approval (paragraph 15).
      3. People may think upon political questions, but they think with their own party (paragraph 16).
      4. We all act almost exclusively out of feeling, which we merely mistake for thought (paragraph 17).

By outlining Twain's argument, we are more conscious of its clever organization. The essay divides into two parts: a preface that introduces and leads into the topic gradually (see Question 3), and the body of the essay that develops Twain's thesis. Twain divides his examples into two types, first using trivial and commonplace ones to make his point clear and then emphasizing the gravity of his argument by citing serious examples. This strategy—to progress gradually and to use repetition to drive home a point—makes what begins as a humorous essay a serious indictment of human nature.

3. What does the opening scene add to Twain's argument?

To get a sense of the importance of the prefatory scene, ask your students to erase it from their minds the best they can, and then begin reading to them starting with paragraph 9. After a few sentences, students will probably sense the difference even if they can't articulate it: without the preface, we hear Twain matter-of-factly telling us how *we* are, describing a problem with *our* minds. This is the sort of message that can give offense, particularly if the writer shows any trace of arrogance. By telling us that he got his ideas from a slave when he was fifteen and that he was drubbed by his mother for listening, Twain avoids starting out on his high horse. We are more inclined to listen to him because he doesn't *start out* by judging us as if from on high.

4. Apply the five-part dechanneling procedure (page 160) to Twain's thesis.

Since it would be foolish to try to anticipate a student response, I will respond to the questions myself, providing you with a sample work-through for your students to comment on. First, of course, you will want to define Twain's thesis: people's opinions do not come from rational and independent thinking but from their natural inclination to conform to the opinions of others. My response would be that Twain's position is not completely valid, and I would propose that people's opinions come from a balance between their inclination to conform and their conscious effort to make independent judgments.

1. *Explain what it is in your past thinking or experience that makes one answer "naturally" appealing to you.*
    As an educated person, I want to believe that I think for myself. As an educator on a college campus, I want to believe that it is possible to teach people to think for themselves.

2. *List reasons to doubt this answer.*
    a. People tend to change their opinions when they change their groups of friends; many of my friends, for example, changed to the political party of their spouse when they got married, and even more gave up their own religious denomination for that of their spouse.
    b. Even I find myself liking a fashion trend once it is around long enough, and I fight fashion trends more than almost anyone I know.
    c. Ninety percent of my freshmen students, when asked about their favorite authors, mention Stephen King, and 100 percent went to see *E.T.*.
    d. Bandwagon arguments, while obviously fallacious, work: people often persuade others that a certain movie is "good" simply by appealing to public opinion—"Everybody's seeing it."
    e. Last week a friend of mine defended her choice of a piece of silver for a wedding gift merely by stating "That's what we do."

3. *List reasons to accept this answer.*
    a. If people cannot form independent opinions, then why are there so many different opinions?
    b. Some of the most popular news and opinion shows on television feature debates on current events in which the disputants seem to agree on *nothing*.
    c. People have, on occasion, changed their lives radically because they felt compelled to follow their own very unpopular beliefs: Gandhi is a prime example.
    d. If you ask people why they hold a certain opinion, few will admit that they do so primarily because of the influence of someone else.

4. *Explain why this is not an open-and-shut question.*
    Twain's argument is a sweeping generalization; mine is only slightly less sweeping. Unfortunately, many people almost always get their opinions from others, while a few form theirs almost entirely from independent thinking. It is an important argument in that it gets us thinking about how we think, but it is also a difficult one to get control of since we can only deal in generalizations.

5. *Explain the consequences, long-term and short-term, of persuading an audience to accept one answer or another.*

In the long run, if we persuade people that they are capable of forming independent judgments—but also that they conform as often as they think for themselves—it will raise their awareness of their thinking process and make them more responsible decision makers. In the short run, we may diminish their self-confidence by making them doubt their first impulses, but in most cases, this may not be a bad thing.

Twain's hypothesis is more an argument of fact than of policy making, so it produces a heuristic somewhat different from the example in the chapter. Having students experiment with it can be good preparation for Chapter 6.

CHAPTER 6

Arguing When Facts Are Disputed

Purpose

The principal purpose of this chapter is to help students overcome an obstacle to any serious attempt at argument. This obstacle is what psychologist William G. Perry, Jr., has called *dualism*: the tendency to treat every statement as simply right or wrong. Many students are committed to the view that "facts are facts," and that since somewhere there is an Authority who can tell us the Truth, there is not much point in arguing about facts. This theory of knowledge creates a severe hierarchy, with "those who know" at the top and the rest of us ignoramuses at the bottom. Students who understand the world in these terms tend to see an assignment that asks them to argue about facts as utterly senseless: facts aren't something you argue about; they are something you look up.

You may remember your own eye-opening discovery that facts are not the steel-jacketed nuggets you had taken them to be, that experts often disagree about what appear to be fairly elementary facts. The experience can be disorienting, but it is also liberating: it *makes argument possible*. The first aim of the chapter, then, is to give students a strong nudge toward a more sophisticated view of facts. For that reason, it concentrates on a "fact" that most students would treat as unchallengeable—that Shakespeare wrote the Shakespearean plays. If students can be brought to see that even *this* assertion rises and falls in likelihood according to the arguments made about it, they should have a sense that there are many "facts" that they can argue about rationally and articulately.

The chapter's second purpose is closely related to the first: to show students that they argue better when their view of persuasion is less than absolute. If the only successful argument is a "win" that absolutely crushes the resistance of skeptics, who can argue well? If the aim is to nudge the audiences *toward* the arguer's position, then arguing well is a more achievable goal.

The third objective is, naturally, to help students see what sort of arguments and evidence will be effective in moving an audience toward their position.

Overview

The *chapter proper* divides roughly into five parts:

1. An examination of the Shakespeare controversy, including two major exercises in which students practice evaluating the significance of pieces of evidence
2. A discussion of some key issues in arguments about facts: purpose and tone, level of certainty, and burden of proof
3. A discussion of logical fallacies
4. A discussion of the ways that we evaluate flawed arguments and the weight of evidence
5. Points to consider and questions for peer review regarding the persuasive essay about disputed facts

The *assignments* include a "temperate" position paper, a strong advocacy of an unpopular position, a balanced treatment of a local dispute, and an analysis of a persuasive essay.

The *readings* include arguments on a wide variety of subjects—personal, scientific, and political:

"The Truth About Roy McCarthy," Mary McCarthy's carefully reasoned argument against the accusation that her father was a "periodical drunkard"

"What Was the Acheulean Hand Ax?"—a bit of detective work by a fledgling anthropologist

"White Lies," Sissela Bok's argument that the consequences of innocent deception render it something other than harmless

"Lotteries Cheat, Corrupt the People," George Will's argument that the actual effects of state-run lotteries are not ones that the government should sanction

"Unconscious Selection and Natural Selection," Charles Darwin's argument that natural selection is a strong enough force to account for major changes in species

The Chapter Step-by-Step

A Walk Through the Shakespeare Controversy (pages 168–173)

There are two keys to teaching this section of the chapter. The first is to be sure that students understand the significance of the discussion of probabilistic reasoning (surmising) on page 171. The second is to get them actively involved in the exercises.

The discussion of probabilistic reasoning is so simple that in itself it probably won't generate much class discussion, but you may find that you need to call attention to it in order to reinforce the point that *an estimate of probability is an essential logical step* in arguing about disputed facts. The arguer who says that Shakespeare's father was illiterate and therefore Shakespeare couldn't have written the plays is either talking nonsense or implying an argument like the following: "Shakespeare's father couldn't write, and in sixteenth-century England it was highly unlikely that the son of an illiterate father could acquire the sort of learning that the plays reveal. Therefore, it is highly unlikely that Shakespeare wrote them."

Exercise 1: Weighing Facts (pages 172–173).   Here is a key exercise in seeing how facts introduced as evidence can affect the reader's judgment on a disputed fact. To get the maximum effect, students should follow the instructions fairly literally, preferably as homework. After they have done the exercise individually, they should be in a position to enjoy and benefit from class discussion. The discussion is crucial because it gives students practice in articulating arguments that lead from "established facts" toward the acceptance or rejection of a disputed fact.

For discussion's sake, imagine a student who identifies her position on the Shakespeare question as 95, giving as her principal reason for this ranking that it is unlikely that the whole academic world could be wrong on such a simple question; she is not, however, at the 100 position because she recognizes a discrepancy between Shakespeare's background and the greatness of the works. Her mind might move as follows:

> Fact 1 would likely move her down the scale, to 93, let's say. Her reasoning might be that, as she knows from previous reading, Shakespeare never formally studied law. The Chief Justice's statement that the plays show a deep knowledge of the law therefore makes it less probable that Shakespeare wrote them. That the Chief Justice seems qualified to make the judgment gives it more weight.

> Fact 2 could move her up the scale, perhaps to 94, if she believes it unlikely that Shakespeare's contemporaries could have been fooled about the identity of the playwright. Actually, this bit of evidence is less impressive than it first appears, since it is not clear which contemporaries are speaking and how well (if at all) they knew Shakespeare and his background.

> Fact 3 could move her further up the scale since it weakens the argument based on John Shakespeare's "farmer-class background" and presumed illiteracy. Here is a fact that, if accepted, suggests that John Shakespeare could quite possibly have signed with a cross and yet been a man of means and influence, a man who could send his son to the best school available. Perhaps our student is now at 95.

> Fact 4 could be a powerful persuader. It might move our student up to 98. The argument would be that Jonson could hardly have been fooled, and there is nothing in evidence to suggest that he had a motive to lie.

> Fact 5 could also be a powerful persuader. The argument would be that Shakespeare's fellow parishioners, people who saw him every day, would be hard to fool. If they believed him to be a writer, likely he was. On the other

hand, might they have a motive to accept his great reputation and promote it? On balance, the argument from this fact would probably not shake our student from the 98 position.

Fact 6 obviously, but very slightly, weakens Fact 5's effect.

Fact 7 may sway some students, but it shouldn't. This fact can only be used in an argument based on the bandwagon fallacy.

Fact 8 is a harder call. Are English professors all experts on this topic? Probably not, since few have examined the evidence closely. Because the faculty's opinion is essentially indistinguishable from the voice of the people, the student should be unmoved.

A Temperate Treatment of the Shakespeare Question (pages 173–177)

Students who have discussed Twain's anti-Stratfordian arguments and the facts in Exercise 1 are in a position to read the excerpt by Brown and Spencer with some insight. The marginal questions on this passage have no particular hidden agenda, though the question about the treatment of the Bacon controversy should give students pause. Bacon's candidacy receives the lion's share of attention, even though it has been more thoroughly discredited than the candidacy of Oxford, Derby, and Marlowe. There may be some slanting here: Brown and Spencer give in detail arguments they know they can discredit.

Exercise 2: Weighing Additional Facts (pages 175–177).   The facts in Exercise 2 are somewhat more complex than those in Exercise 1. Students working in groups or as a whole class are more likely to see all the implications than are students working in isolation. The exercise prepares students for the discussion of logical fallacies on pages 181–185.

Fact 1 would seem to discredit the argument for Marlowe and so indirectly strengthen the argument for Shakespeare. But the weight of the fact is worth discussing. On the one hand, it challenges Hoffman's status as an expert, and this seems legitimate. On the other hand, the line between challenging credentials and arguing *ad hominem* is often hard to draw (see item 4, pages 182–183).

Fact 2 may cause quite a sensation, particularly among students for whom the reference to *Scientific American* is itself a powerful persuader. However, even if Barrell's reading of the X-rays is correct, their relationship to the authorship question isn't obvious. Perhaps the best anti-Stratfordian argument to be gleaned from these facts is that a close relationship of some sort existed between Shakespeare and de Vere. But how do we get from the close relationship to the authorship hoax?

Fact 3 returns to the question of Shakespeare's supposedly illiterate family. It seems that great damage is done to the illiteracy argument by showing that men who (like John Shakespeare) chose to sign with a cross may well have been quite capable of signing their names.

Fact 4 combines two problems in evaluating the significance of evidence. If Burgess is right, how significant is the fact that de Vere owned these books (and Shakespeare apparently did not)? Let your students argue about that one a bit. Then let them consider whether the source affects the way they evaluate the evidence.

Fact 5 damages Twain's argument that if Shakespeare had written the plays he would certainly have been a great celebrity. Both the weight of Harbage's expertise and his citation of a strong example help the Stratfordian cause.

Fact 6 is another one to puzzle over. Obviously, it could be used by anti-Stratfordians to show that intelligent people who know something about literature have their doubts about Shakespeare's authorship. How likely is it that this distinguished group could be taken in by anti-Stratfordian arguments unless there is some merit in such arguments? On the other hand, only Furness has a real claim to expertise on Shakespeare, and we don't know how strongly these people doubted or why.

Some Key Issues in Arguments About Facts (pages 177–181)

Much of the chapter's work in establishing a productive attitude toward argumentation is done in these few pages on levels of conviction, the arguer's purpose and tone, the appropriate level of certainty, and the burden of proof. In effect, these pages compose a little lecture on the psychology, logistics, and ethics of argument. The section is so short that we won't summarize it here.

Logical Fallacies (pages 181–187)

This treatment of the "informal fallacies" of argumentation is fairly traditional. It is perhaps a bit clearer and more practical than such presentations, because the fallacies are illustrated using the Shakespeare material students have been studying throughout the chapter.

Exercise 3: Evaluating Arguments (pages 185–187). Textbook examples of flawed arguments are sometimes unrealistically simple, and so they reinforce students' tendency to think about arguments as things that are either simply right or simply wrong. The five examples given here are far more representative of the way that arguments tend to be fallacious by degrees.

In the first example, for instance, Rockefeller cites various pieces of evidence to show that legalized abortion is "in the mainstream of world opinion." If, as he pretends, he were doing this only to show why liberals may have a false sense of security, there would be no fallacy. But he is writing for *Newsweek* and knows he is not preaching entirely to the converted. Surely he hopes that some readers will be swayed by the implication that what so many people *believe* to be true or just *must be* true or just—the *bandwagon* fallacy.

The second example appears to be an example of the *either/or* fallacy. Surely many laws (perhaps most laws) are a mixture of justice and injustice. In the context of King's essay (reprinted in the text; see especially pages 304–305), the distinction between just and unjust laws is clarified by some "tests" that King provides. But even in that context, the logician and the legal scholar would surely find the division of all laws into two kinds: stark and oversimple.

To understand the third example, students will need to think a bit about what Winn's purpose is. The title of her book and the drift of this passage should tell them: she is attempting to demonstrate that television is decreasing the ability of parents and children to communicate. But even if we assume that the one nurse she has talked to has given her a correct impression of the behavior of children and parents in most hospital emergency rooms, we can question the representativeness of her sample. Is the conversation in the hospital emergency room really typical of the normal conversation between parents and children? Is it possible that the stress of the accident that brings them there and the alienness of the environment stop the tongues of both parents and children? There seem to be at least two hints of *hasty generalization* here.

In the fourth example, Jill Knight at least flirts with an oversimplification of cause related to the *post hoc* fallacy and to *tenuous chain of causation*. She asserts that the two reasons many women opt for abortion during what is "the 'best' time" medically speaking are (1) the depression that comes in early pregnancy and (2) "the knowledge that the highest authority in the land has sanctioned" abortion. This picture of what is happening implies, of course, that these women are incapable of a rational decision, are slaves to their pregnancy-induced emotions, and are profoundly affected by the government's attitudes toward morality. But surely many pregnant women are capable of making rational decisions and have their own opinions on moral issues regardless of what the government says. By creating a stereotype of women who seek abortions, Knight allows herself to oversimplify the causes of their behavior.

The fifth example may raise the most difficult question of judgment. Patricia Taylor comes perilously close to an *ad hominem* fallacy here. Her argument amounts to saying that nothing the alcohol companies do or say can be motivated by anything but greed. When they claim that they endorse moderate drinking, even when they produce advertisements discouraging excess, they *must* be lying, because moderate drinking would decrease their profits. But isn't it possible that some high-placed executives in alcohol companies have a conscience? On the other hand, the officers of corporations are legally obliged to maximize profits for shareholders, so it isn't clear that the *ad hominem* attack is unjustified.

Evaluating Flawed Arguments and Weighing the Evidence (pages 187–189)

The two paragraphs on evaluating arguments containing logical fallacies are particularly important in helping to break down the dualism in students' thinking. An argument can be flawed and "right"; there can be some dispute about whether a flaw is really a fault. Students need to know these things, *especially if they are going to critique each other's essays*. Since virtually all arguments are to some degree flawed, a student who searches mercilessly for flaws in another student's essays will certainly find them. We need to give both the writer and the reviewer some sense of proportion on the matter.

To those who have given much thought to the way that we evaluate the factuality of things, the discussion on weighing evidence may seem to belabor the obvious. But students who are "dualists" or who see knowledge as something to be received passively have great difficulty evaluating evidence critically. The same is true of the somewhat more sophisticated students who believe that "everyone has a right to their own opinion" and so blind themselves to distinctions between stronger and weaker evidence.

Points to Consider and Questions for Peer Review (pages 189–190)

This little advice section speaks for itself. You'll notice that it contains a reprise of the chapter's emphasis on the uncertainty of the "facts" a paper may be trying to establish, the need to think critically, the need to think in terms of changing the reader's estimate of probabilities rather than beating him or her into submission, and the need to be aware of one's own judgments and logical flaws.

The Assignments

Assignment 1: A Temperate Statement of Your Position on a Publicly Disputed Fact. This is probably the most ambitious assignment in the chapter, requiring students to react critically to questions they may have thought closed (like the moon landing) or to questions that have roused strong emotions (like the invasion of Grenada). Students are required to do justice to the other side and then to answer the other side's argument in a cool, reasoned way. This is hard work, emotionally and intellectually. The key to making the assignment work is to make it clear that *being temperate is part of the job.* Some students tend to write diatribes or resort to easy ironies on assignments of this sort, thereby eliminating work as well as a chance to grow intellectually.

Assignment 2: A Strong Advocacy of an Unpopular Opinion. This assignment will be good fun for some of your students and next to impossible for others, so we do not recommend making it the only option for a whole class. You might require students to tell you in advance what opinion they intend to advocate so that you can be sure it is genuinely unpopular—a minority report from a fresh perspective. We have had students argue that sports build character, apparently assuming that most people disagreed, but the absence of real disagreement enervated the essays. The emotional impetus for this assignment ought to be a desire to set the world right on something it is wrong about.

Assignment 3: A Balanced Treatment of a Factual Dispute Closer to Home. Recently on our own campus, a huge, out-of-control party resulted in a black teen-ager being beaten by some white fraternity members who had mistaken him for another black teen-ager. The police say that the incident was "not racially motivated"; some witnesses and commentators disagree. The dispute over the cause of this incident might serve as a good subject for this assignment. Every campus is the setting for controversial incidents that produce disputes about the "real facts."

Assignment 4: An Analysis of a Persuasive Essay.   This assignment reviews everything that has been said in the chapter and is a fine exercise in critical reading. Any of the essays at the end of the chapter lend themselves to such analysis, but the effect might be better if you sent students to the library to find their own examples of essays in which authors dispute facts, causes, or effects.

Sample papers and additional assignments are available in the package of supplementary material that accompanies the main text.

End-of-Chapter Readings

MARY MCCARTHY

The Truth About Roy McCarthy

Few of us will ever air a family dispute to so large a public as McCarthy does here, but the manner in which she airs it can serve a model for argument in an area of uncertainty. At no point do we feel that McCarthy is taking a merely partisan view: she seems to be earnestly attempting to discover the truth, and this earnestness wins our trust and respect. Knowing that no one will ever know with certainty the truth of this matter, we may be more inclined to trust McCarthy's version than Uncle Harry's, even though Uncle Harry presents himself as an eyewitness and McCarthy must get most of her information at second hand. As Aristotle pointed out 2,500 years ago, when the truth cannot be established with mathematical certainty, the audience must decide whom to trust, and most readers will find that McCarthy sounds trustworthy.

McCarthy's assessment of conflicting evidence is a fine example for students to follow, for if they have spent much time listening to their parents, grandparents, aunts, or uncles discussing particular family members, they should be well aware of conflicting characterizations at least, and possibly of not-so-well-kept family secrets. You may wish to encourage students to conduct similar investigations of their own as they practice writing arguments based on disputed facts.

QUESTIONS

1. Is McCarthy's reasoning about the evidence plausible? Sketch out the logic of each of McCarthy's main points and comment on the effectiveness of her method.

McCarthy's goal is to prove that Uncle Harry's claim about her father's drunkenness is not a fact at all. Her first step is to prove that her father was not an alcoholic when she was a child:

> Because children's sense of smell is sharper than that of adults, because children do not like the smell of alcohol, and because she has no recollection of her father drinking when she was a child, McCarthy concludes that her father was probably not a drunkard when she was a child.

She amasses other evidence as well:

> Because "Roy's wine" brought laughter rather than trouble to the family, because children are quick to notice anything wrong in a household, and because she does not remember any trouble, McCarthy concludes that her father was probably not a drunkard when she was a child.

Students may wish to question some of McCarthy's statements; some of my students, for example, believed that alcohol was a rather pleasant smell to them when they were very young, and they did not want to let McCarthy off so easily. The important issue is the extent to which McCarthy's statements push us either to believe or doubt her argument. Once you have established where your students register on this question, ask them to consider McCarthy's shift to a different line of attack:

> Because McCarthy's mother's brother did not know this story, because her mother's family apparently did not know of the problem before the marriage, and because her mother's family would have known of her father's problem if he had not reformed, McCarthy concludes that her father was probably not a drunkard when she was a child.

With this point, McCarthy shifts to an attack that depends not on her own memory but on the evidence of adults present at the time; she also opens up a new possible explanation—that her father may have reformed before marrying her mother—and will now have to discount it:

> Because periodic drunkards almost never reform, because if periodic drunkards do reform they cannot touch alcohol, and because her father did drink occasionally, McCarthy concludes that he was probably never a drunkard.

Again, you will want to have your students register their response at this point. McCarthy moves beyond personal experience to the testimony of eye-witnesses and then presents logic based on external evidence of drunkards in general to apply to this specific case. Her method is surprisingly thorough for such a brief argument, and though students may want more proof of her assumptions, they should be somewhat persuaded by her means of deriving them. Finally, McCarthy shifts to an investigation of motives to complete her argument:

> Because her father's marriage was the "last straw" in his family's eyes, because Uncle Harry wanted McCarthy (after her parents' death) to side with his family, and because Uncle Harry was fond of McCarthy's "lovely mother," McCarthy concludes that Uncle Harry may have fabricated, or at least exaggerated, the story.

Laying out each step in McCarthy's argument should demonstrate to students what a model argument it is. McCarthy gathers and deploys evidence in a way that, on balance, makes us doubt Uncle Harry's version of the truth and believe her version; at the same time, she keeps us from feeling that she has concealed facts that would help the other side. In fact, her description of her father's appearance with the red roses ("a drunkard's appeasing gesture") adds evidence that Uncle Harry never mentioned.

2.   Imagine a scale numbered from 0 to 100, with each point on the scale representing a level of conviction. For the purpose of this exercise, the zero point will represent the conviction that there is no chance that Mary McCarthy's father was a periodical drunkard; 100 will represent certainty that he was a periodical drunkard; and 50 will represent a precisely balanced lack of inclination to believe one way or another. Begin this exercise by reviewing McCarthy's discussion of the question and placing yourself on the scale to show your current level of conviction as precisely as possible. Explain in a few sentences how the evidence and McCarthy's treatment of the evidence affect where you place yourself.

After you read each of the following "facts" (some of which are invented), reassess your position on the scale and explain briefly why you have or have not changed your level of conviction. The facts should be treated cumulatively: that is, when you move on to each new fact, you should assume that the preceding facts are still true.

   a. McCarthy tells us that Uncle Harry was an old man, and rather far gone in his cups himself when he made these charges
   b. Medical research indicates that children, especially the children of alcoholics, are not offended by the smell of alcohol. Most find it mildly pleasant, and few can identify it for what it is.
   c. A newspaper clipping from a Seattle newspaper indicates that a man named Roy McCarthy was arrested for driving while intoxicated in 1917.
   d. McCarthy's mother's brother says that his sister joined the Women's Christian Temperance Union a few weeks before meeting McCarthy's father.
   e. W.C.T.U. documents show that McCarthy's mother joined the organization a few weeks after marrying McCarthy's father.
   f. A survey of forty-four students who have read McCarthy's argument reveals that thirty-one of them believe that McCarthy's father was "more likely than not" a periodical drunkard. Five students have no opinion, and eight think it more likely than not that her father was not a problem drinker.

As you work through this exercise, ask students to explain what it is about each fact that gives it weight. Then have them try ranking the relative persuasiveness of five forms of evidence: (1) eyewitness accounts, (2) written documents, (3) medical research, (4) McCarthy's reasoning, and (5) the judgment of a general audience. Students may be surprised to find that while written documents and eyewitness accounts can be very persuasive, they also can be doubted, and often it is the personality of the arguer that ultimately persuades us one way or another.

EILEEN O'BRIEN

What Was the Acheulean Hand Ax?

Students sometimes resist O'Brien's article on the grounds that it lacks relevance, so you will want to introduce the essay before you send your students off to read it. Even though they may not believe that knowledge of the Acheulean hand ax is crucial to their personal lives, you may be able to convince them that a close study of O'Brien's technique could improve their writing and arguing skills considerably. Or you may tell them that (as one of my students said) the paper reads like a detective story, full of clues and reasoning.

In many respects, the essay is organized like a typical scientific paper: O'Brien first gives the necessary background information and reviews previous work on the topic; she then explains her method of research and what she found; and she concludes with a discussion of her findings. As important as her organization, however, is O'Brien's tone. Revising her original article for a general audience, she goes to great lengths to keep her reader engaged and her argument clear. You may wish to draw your students' attention to both of these elements; you may also wish to have them review the original article in *Current Anthropology* (February 1981) to see for themselves how accommodating O'Brien is when revising for a general audience.

QUESTIONS

1. Where do you find O'Brien using factual, logical, and psychological appeal? (See page 168 to review the definition of each.)

The factual appeal consists of O'Brien's deployment of her own knowledge of the hand ax, the people that used it, previous studies, and of her own experiment. If your students look closely at the facts O'Brien chooses to report and the manner in which she reports them, they will see that she is not merely giving a catalog of what is known but is building an argument as well. The description of the dimensions and shape of the hand ax (paragraph 2), for example, prepares the reader for the description of its flight pattern and its tendency to land with its edge "slicing deeply into the thawing earth" (paragraph 12). To make a tight "fit" between the object and its behavior, she is extremely thorough in her description of the nature of the ax itself and in her description of her experiment.

The logical appeal may be said to include O'Brien's appeals to authority, first to back up her own beliefs, such as when she cites "most anthropologists" (paragraph 3) and specific scholars of various sorts (paragraph 6), and then to add credibility to her experiment, such as when she cites the "head of the museum's casting department" (paragraph 9). Most often, however, we find O'Brien appealing to common sense: she asks us to believe with her, for example, that since the hand ax was "a source of raw material," *Homo erectus* would have reused it and then transformed it into a smaller tool (paragraph 5). She is probably correct, though she did claim in the first paragraph that *Homo erectus* was "small-brained."

Finally, O'Brien uses psychological appeal throughout the essay in many subtle ways. By progressing through her ideas meticulously, O'Brien establishes herself as a writer who cares about her readers and about the evidence. We are likely, then, to be psychologically willing to trust her.

2. Which appeal is most convincing, and why?

Students may be most persuaded by the factual evidence—about the hand ax, about the people who used it, and about O'Brien's experiment—or by the psychological appeal—through which O'Brien presents herself as a person we would have no trouble trusting and believing; we will focus here, however, on the logical appeal.

A good place to begin is the opening section in which O'Brien, while providing background information, carefully begins to refute other theories of the hand ax. You might lead your students through paragraphs 3 and 4 as an example of using the logical appeal to discredit other theories. O'Brien raises other possibilities for the hand ax and then refutes them in paragraph 3, by first raising one issue, then refuting it with an authority ("most anthropologists"); raising another, then refuting it by citing the lack of evidence; and raising a third, then refuting it with the "common and traditional interpretation." After admitting that any of the competing theories *could* be accurate (in a brief concession in paragraph 4), she then gives a logical defense of her own theory: other tools were present alongside the hand ax that were more suitable for the purposes other theorists propose; assuming that *Homo erectus* would probably use the most suitable tool, O'Brien concludes that the hand ax was probably not used for these purposes. Her pattern of reviewing past notions, conceding their strengths, and then offering a better hypothesis is both fair and logical.

O'Brien's use of analogy is another example of her careful argument: if we can understand how other prehistoric weapons worked by comparing them to modern forms, then we can also understand the hand ax by so comparing it. Given the size and shape of the ax, she decides that the discus is the closest form, and she proceeds to her experiment accordingly.

A final example of her logic is her method of answering her initial question of why hand axes are found so often in watery areas and so rarely in dry ones. If thrown at a herd of game gathered at a watering hole, the axes would be unretrievable and would "accumulate like golf balls in a water trap" (paragraph 19). But when used on land they would have been easy to retrieve and so would rarely be abandoned for the benefit of future anthropologists. The facts fit the hypothesis neatly.

3. How does O'Brien present herself through the essay (what is her tone), and what effect does it have on her argument?

O'Brien's argument succeeds largely because of the tone she takes. She is both cautious and personal, presenting herself as a serious and sensitive person. Paragraph 5, for example, demonstrates her open-mindedness: the phrase "whatever its function" implies that she is willing to listen to other arguments for the use of the ax. In addition, rather than stating directly what she believes to be true, she leads us through her process of discovery. She also stands out of the way at times and allows a greater authority to speak: the phrase "if we let the evidence speak for itself" begins paragraph 6, where she proposes that the evidence logically leads to the question of the hand ax's use. And when we finally get the word on O'Brien's own theory, she introduces it with the modest phrase "the possibility that occurred to me" rather than with a bold statement of fact. Nevertheless, as the article develops, we tend to agree with O'Brien, perhaps because her position is presented in such a moderate, reasoned fashion. By the end, she is offering "a simple explanation" of what very well "could" have happened, and she is very likely entirely correct.

A comparison of this essay with the original *Current Anthropology* version reveals the personality O'Brien puts into the revision. In the more scholarly original, she refrains from using the first person and relies instead on the passive voice ("experiments were performed") to convey a detached and "objective" tone; in the revised version, she uses the active voice and first-person narration and reminds us that her experiments were part of a personal discovery. She also makes us part of the discovery by giving the evidence before she gives the conclusion, thereby allowing us to reason along with her. Even the language invites us to get caught up with her in the actual experiment, as in paragraph 11 when she describes Karl Nyholm's throw: "With a great exhalation of breath, he hurled himself out straight and let go. Silently, gracefully spinning, the hand ax soared." We may feel an unscientific urge to marvel (or cheer) at the sheer beauty of the thing.

4. On a scale of 1 to 100, where would you rank your level of conviction? If you do not register 100 (full conviction that the hand ax was a projectile weapon), what keeps you from fully accepting O'Brien's argument?

This question is an important one for considering the barriers that keep us from complete belief. I would place my conviction level at 80 or so, for a variety of reasons. First, O'Brien's method of arguing suggests that she is not without doubt, since she admits to other possibilities for the hand ax and to the need for further research; unless we are archaeologists with greater knowledge of the Acheulean hand ax than O'Brien herself has, we probably will not be more certain than she is about her conclusions. In fact, our own ignorance is a large part of the problem. We are forced to trust O'Brien to give us the "facts" about the hand ax, about *Homo erectus*, and about the supposed waterways and habits of the animals congregating there. Although she presents herself as a trustworthy scholar, when dealing with facts largely constructed from hypotheses over the centuries, we have good reason to doubt. At the same time, O'Brien's logical argument is so strong that if we *do* accept the facts, we are very likely to believe her theory as well.

5. Can you find any logical fallacies in O'Brien's argument?

This question may prove helpful in solidifying students' familiarity with the fallacies, although it will be difficult to locate any in O'Brien's argument, primarily because she is so careful in her manner of presenting her ideas. For example, students may question her use of analogy: is the link between the hand ax and the discus valid, and if not, does the analogy hurt her argument? While the analogy is not a perfect one, it does no damage because O'Brien's argument does not depend on her asserting their similarity; instead, she uses a discus thrower to *test* the possibilities for throwing a hand ax. If we believe that the fiberglass replica is suitable for testing, then the analogy should give us little trouble.

In addition, students might accuse O'Brien of committing the either/or fallacy, since her article suggests that the hand ax was not a hand-held tool but a projectile weapon. O'Brien does use the lack of hand axes in campsites to prove the projectile theory, but she does not make the claim that they could not have been used there as well. In fact, she explains why they might not have been recovered there: older axes could have beeen salvaged to produce other, smaller tools. And the strongest statement she makes is that "hand axes were in general used as projectiles" (paragraph 6). By concentrating not on trying to disprove the use of the hand ax as a tool but on proving that it was primarily a weapon, O'Brien saves herself from committing a fallacy.

6. How are the introduction and conclusion fitting to the type of essay O'Brien is writing?

Students should notice how carefully O'Brien sets up the problem, giving minimal background information that captures our attention while stressing the importance of the question she raises. In this relatively brief introduction, she acts as a reporter, introducing us to the *what* (the hand ax), *when* (1 to 1.5 million years ago), *where* (Africa, Europe, and Asia), and *why* (made because tools/ weapons were needed) while setting up the *how* (how the hand ax was used) as the question that must be answered. By the end of this first paragraph, she has clarified her purpose for writing the article and given us specific expectations for what will follow.

The conclusion is a fine blend of summary, reasoning, and speculation. She shows how, given a set of "facts" about the weapon and another set about *Homo erectus*, she can fit the two together to add weight to her argument. But after constructing her argument carefully throughout the article, O'Brien ends in speculation. First she suggests that the hand ax may fit with the general defenselessness of early humans in a world of large, dangerous animals and with the corresponding strategy of killing from a distance. Then she raises the *possibility* that the Greeks got the idea of throwing the discus from the ancient tradition of hand-ax use. The suggestion strengthens her argument and again gets our attention, but O'Brien does not get herself in trouble by asserting as "fact" what is clearly only speculation.

SISSELA BOK

White Lies

In order to introduce this section, consider reading the opening quotations to your students before sending them off to read the essay proper; a brainstorming session at this point could produce a long list of "white lies" that students are familiar with and even accustomed to committing. You might then have the students rank these untruths from most offensive to least offensive and have them explain their rationale. It's a safe guess that most students worry little about white lies, being much more inclined to good manners than to absolute honesty: most could probably recall at least one white lie told in the past day or so. Introducing the essay in this way should get the students more personally involved, and with their own reputations on the line, they should be better able to rate their level of conviction after reading the essay.

QUESTIONS

1. Write a brief summary of "White Lies."

Because this essay is so long and because students may have trouble defining Bok's argument precisely, writing a summary may be the best way for them to grapple with her argument and the troubles they have understanding it. The exercise also gives students practice sorting through a large amount of material and fitting it into a concise and useful form. The following summary may serve as a sample; it is roughly 250 words in length.

> Bok begins her essay by noting that though white lies are trivial and common, they are a form of deception. Examining some common white lies, such as those used in social situations to avoid insult or bad manners, Bok admits that they are often harmless and completely well-intentioned. But she also believes they are too closely related to more harmful deceptions for us to draw a clear line between the two. While acknowledging that some white lies do more good than harm, Bok argues that their cumulative effect is inevitably a loss of trust.
>
> Bok's main examples of damaging white lies are placebos and inflated letters of recommendation. Placebos are harmful, she argues, because of their costs: financial loss to patients who pay for them, health risks to those who trust them and so don't seek further medical attention, a loss of trust in the medical profession, and potentially harmful side effects. Likewise, inflated letters of recommendation are dangerous because they help the applicants who receive them but unwittingly harm other applicants whose letters are honest and therefore somewhat less than topnotch evaluations. The only solution to this problem is for people to begin promoting honesty in evaluations.
>
> Bok concludes that we "cannot dismiss lies merely by claiming that they don't matter," and we must aim to eliminate as many white lies as we possibly can. Their cumulative effect on truth telling in general and their inevitable potential for harm outweigh the benefits of a few individual cases.

2.   Chart your level of conviction (from 1 to 100) throughout your reading of the essay. At what points did you feel your attitude changing, moving either closer to Bok's position or further away, and why?

Most students will probably approach Bok's essay feeling pretty unconcerned about white lies. They are probably used to greeting people with half-truths about how good they look, getting out of awkward social invitations by inventing prior engagements, and concocting excuses for their tardiness—to use on their teachers if not on their parents. Frankly, as I lean toward this position myself, I was taken by surprise by the first paragraph: Bok's use of "deception" and "duplicity" to define white lies made me pause to reconsider the validity of my attitude. Also, students may agree that as Bok demonstrates a degree of moderation (paragraphs 2–5), allowing that some white lies can be excused, she encourages us to see things a little more her way. Bok's refutation of the utilitarian argument, coupled with her description of how white lies get out of hand and lead to such things as false advertising and lying to children (paragraphs 9–11), brought me still another step closer to agreeing with her.

Of the two extended examples, the placebo case may more strongly persuade students toward Bok's position because of the manner in which she presents it. While I began reading the section assuming that she was going to outlaw something I believed beneficial, after considering the costs, the seriousness of the case study she included, and then her amassing of negative effects, I felt compelled to agree that in most cases placebos have the potential for more harm than good. The letters of recommendation will probably strike your students as more relevant yet also more frightening since they might be the innocent victims of an honest evaluation. At this point, you may get a more mixed response.

Bok's final section might also turn students' opinions as she appeals to our sense of integrity. In her conclusion she calls us to change our own lives so people don't feel compelled to lie to us (paragraph 50) and urges us to take responsibility for how we handle the truth (paragraph 51). If students are still not buying her argument, I'd push them to explain why. It may be that the thoroughness with which Bok argues tires students before they reach the end, or perhaps they are simply unwilling to take the risks involved in eliminating white lies.

3. What kinds of evidence and support does Bok offer for her argument, and what parts of the argument do you find most persuasive?

This question gives you the opportunity to examine Bok's technique and scholarship and consider their effect on her credibility. Most readers would agree that logical and factual appeals are Bok's strengths. She proves her case primarily by quoting from a variety of notable authorities (such as major medical journals) and by laying out facts extensively (such as her use of an authentic case study); both sources speak for themselves while also presenting Bok as a knowledgeable person we can trust.

You may use this question to build on Question 2, now encouraging the students to explain *why* certain parts of the essay were effective in shaping their opinions. The following examples may come up:

a. Bok's presentation of her argument in the first paragraph. While appealing to us psychologically in the first few sentences—to our sense of right and wrong—she also proves her own reasonableness by admitting that the triviality of white lies makes her argument seem unnecessary.

b. Bok's refutation of the utilitarian argument. Here Bok mixes her psychological appeal with a logical one. She first presents the utilitarian case with fairness (paragraph 8), then concedes that the triviality of a lie should be taken into consideration (paragraph 9). Her logical argument is actually based on her concession, then, for she will agree that in *isolated cases* the utilitarian argument holds true, but the broader consequences are so detrimental that they outweigh the occasional positive effects. Bok then returns to a psychological appeal in claiming that the "Kantian analysis"—the extreme of her own position—is equally wrong and in effect establishes her own position as the most reasonable one.

c. Bok's argument against placebos in particular. What is most interesting about this section of the essay is how Bok uses authorities as both psychological and logical appeals. When she cites health professionals rationalizing and even joking about their use of placebos (paragraphs 15–18), we might be somewhat alarmed by what *they* may be doing to *us*. Later, to prove the credibility and consistency of her argument, Bok cites studies done by professionals who wish to protect us from those who do not take placebos seriously.

In general, Bok's article should prove helpful to students as an example of a solidly researched argument; she is able to use the force of authorities as well as her own reasoning to prove her case.

GEORGE WILL

Lotteries Cheat, Corrupt the People

Although Will is known for his conservatism, he cannot be pigeonholed as a typical Republican and is not entirely predictable in his opinions; you may want to introduce this essay by introducing Will via the profile on page 229. Will's political views, in particular his apprehensions about laissez-faire capitalism, reflect the belief that one function of government is to encourage and uphold traditional values—an underlying message in "Lotteries" that should evoke a variety of responses from students. In addition, the essay demonstrates a method of constructing an argument that differs from O'Brien's in "What Was the Acheulean Hand Ax?" for example: Will primarily attacks the rationalizations of his opposition rather than devoting his efforts to making his own case. Teaching both essays will give your students two very different patterns for organizing arguments.

QUESTIONS

1. What sort of appeals does Will rely on to prove his argument in "Lotteries," and to what end?

As we might expect, the essay is built on factual, logical, and psychological appeals; its strength lies in how Will weaves the three together to make a persuasive argument. Despite a few holes in his research, Will fills the essay with facts, generally in the form of statistics; for example, he plays the $15 billion dollars Americans spent on gambling in one year off the fact that 99.9 percent of all those who play are losers. Will is equally strong in his display of logic, which we rarely find reason to question. His first argument, for instance, is hard to argue with because of the way he presents it: how can we disagree that "there is evidence" that legalizing gambling makes it more respectable, that respectability draws in new gamblers, "some of whom," because of the better odds, move into illegal gambling? By tempering his argument with reasonable language and creating a cause-and-effect pattern that is very likely to hold water, Will presents logic we cannot easily dispute.

Oddly enough, despite the relatively objective tone Will maintains throughout the essay, the psychological appeal is perhaps the strongest. On the surface, it seems that Will is staying out of the essay, allowing the facts—and the words of others—to speak for themselves. Notice, however, the emotional appeal inherent in the apparently emotionless statement that "grocery money is risked" during gambling seasons: Will's careful selection of facts makes a harangue unnecessary.

2. Notice that rather than arguing for his own case, Will argues against the opposition. What does he gain—and lose—by this method of argumentation?

You may wish to remind your students of the opening quote from the Will profile about people who read op-ed articles such as "Lotteries": they are "people who have an interest in public affairs and hold settled opinions about them." Here, in Will's view, lies his audience, and his strategy should match his assumptions about it. Why, then, would he initially opt to discount opposing views instead of concentrating on his own?

First, Will is probably correct in assuming that most of his readers know what state-run lotteries are and have formulated some opinion of them. He also may assume that his readers know something about Will himself and perhaps have come to expect the "conservative line." By focusing on the opposition, Will gains his readers' attention, particularly because he is telling those who favor the lottery what they think, and once he has that attention, he then can safely close the article with his own views.

Will's argument also gains force by shifting the burden of proof. After delineating the key rationalizations of those who support gambling (which, by the way, may not be the strongest ones but rather those that best suit his argument), all he has to do is prove their weaknesses in order to "win." Also, once he has thrown the opposition into a negative light, he is free to present his own ideas while under less pressure to prove his own absolutely. Once he makes us see that gambling hurts some of the people who engage in it and that it does involve some innocent victims, we should agree that it *is* a moral issue—and we should be prepared to listen to his own argument (paragraphs 12–16) concerning the moral responsibility of state governments.

3. Although Will focuses his essay on the ideas of others, he is presenting his own at the same time. What weaknesses can you find in his argument?

One of Will's primary arguments is that gambling "blurs the distinction between well-earned and 'ill-gotten' gains." The assumption behind this statement is that "well-earned" gains are easily identified, and he extols those who earn money "by the sweat of their brows" or "by wrinkling their brows for socially useful purposes." These ideas lead to questions students need to think over: How often are monetary gains the result of socially useful work and thrift? How do people who get ahead typically do so? Students may see little distinction between the lottery and being lucky in guessing when to buy or sell stocks, or being lucky enough to be born into a wealthy family, or happening to know the right person at the right time. Will concedes that there are "windfalls." But some of your students may argue that they are not as exceptional as he implies: in this society it could be true that at least as much money is gained by chance as is "well-earned" by elbow-grease.

Will covers himself fairly well in his final paragraphs, however, when he places the blame on the states that sanction gambling rather than on those individuals who participate in it. In essence, his argument is that the state must be held to a higher standard of conduct than the individual: the state has a responsibility to educate and train. It abrogates that responsibility when it encourages speculation as a way of getting what we want from life.

4. What do the quotations by Jefferson, Jackson, and Van Buren contribute to the essay?

Most students will have a high regard for the three presidents quoted: they may not be all our traditional history lessons have them cracked up to be, but they were wise, or cunning, enough to be elected president. But what their words add to the essay may be a matter of dispute. First, students may question the relevance of Jefferson's extolling "virtue-instilling" agricultural labor to our post-agrarian society, as well as of Jackson's argument against the nineteenth-century Bank of the United States. Will accomplishes little more than identifying himself with the past, with former leaders, and with traditional American values; the quotations reinforce Will's criticism of contemporary capitalism and clarify his conservatism in a way that will please those who agree with him—and will scarcely persuade those who don't. In addition, in an argument about gambling, students may justly see the quotations as a bit tangential.

That Will relies on these quotations should lead to a discussion of how and why to quote. Where in the essay would a quotation from an authoritative source be of greater value? What sources, comparable to the presidents, may have been more appropriate and relevant to our present situation? Do students have any qualms about Will taking quotations out of context?

Students may find the words of the presidents perfectly acceptable; after all, Will is only using them to reinforce key points he has made, or will make, himself. At times an argument is substantially strengthened by the illusion of community agreement, even if the community consists of people and ideas far removed from our present situation.

5. Will is one of the most prolific journalists in this country today, regularly producing biweekly and bimonthly columns in addition to writing books. He obviously has little time for extensive research and revision. Where can you find problems with the essay that could have been remedied by either of these?

While I would not dwell on the essay's faults, pointing to a few may stress the value of both research and revision to argumentation. At times Will is ambiguous or unclear. "Lotteries took in 24 percent more" (paragraph 4) leaves us wondering "More than what?" More than $15 billion, or more than they did in 1976? And when Will talks about "the injury done to society's sense of elemental equities," we have some trouble making meaning out of the tangle of syllables. Such lapses in clarity are not critically damaging to his overall argument, but they may cause serious readers to pause and perhaps become irritated; when attempting to persuade, we can rarely afford to lose our audience over such minor problems.

Similarly, Will too often assumes his audience will believe what he says without proof. We have a right to know, for example, in what respect "gambling is severely regressive" (paragraph 8), and we may need proof in order to believe it. In the same way, how do we know that "gamblers are drawn disproportionately from minority and poor populations" (paragraph 9)? Surely Will could find sources that would add credibility to these statements. You may find that using this essay as a springboard, pointing out its weaknesses as well as its strengths, may help students criticize their own writing in similar ways.

CHARLES DARWIN

Unconscious Selection and Natural Selection

Most people today find Darwin's ideas either so completely logical or so fundamentally unacceptable that they have trouble understanding the controversy that surrounds them. You might therefore preface your discussion of this essay by placing Darwin's theories of selection into the context of his own time. In the middle of the nineteenth century, Darwin's ideas could have been interpreted as blasphemous and seditious; it was dogma in most Christian churches that God personally created each new species. The typical religious outrage evoked by Darwin's ideas may be represented by Charles Hodge who, writing in 1874, protested that the human eye was obviously "planned by the Creator, like the design of a watch evinces a watchmaker," and that to deny this design was to deny the existence of God himself. Darwin tried to prepare himself for the hostility with which his ideas were received. Writing in his notebook while first drafting *The Origin of Species*, Darwin reminded himself to "mention persecution of early astronomers" and stress society's acknowledgment of the valuable work of other recent scientists. Still, such a radical change in the course of human thinking was upsetting to Darwin as well as to the whole of Victorian society; in fact, distress and anxiety over his own findings may have been the cause of Darwin's forty-year illness (see the sample research paper in Chapter 12).

QUESTIONS

1. Explain in your own words what Darwin means by *unconscious selection* and what he means by *natural selection*.

Having students define and distinguish these terms is a good way of being sure they have sorted out the essence of the essay. Their definition of unconscious selection should acknowledge that it is selective *breeding* of animals or plants by *humans*, and that it is unconscious in the sense that the breeders have no intention of altering the species. The person who likes to keep lots of small dachshunds will tend to give the larger puppies away and keep the runts. Eventually the person will be surrounded by runty dachshunds, who will mate with each other and produce more runty dachshunds. The owner will give the larger ones away and keep the smaller ones around. These will mate with each other, and after several generations, the aged owner will have produced a strain of smaller dachshunds *without ever having set out to do so*. This is the essence of unconscious selection.

By natural selection, Darwin means the process by which species of plants and animals in *nature* undergo gradual modifications in the process of adapting to their environment. Darwin uses the examples of wolves from the Catskill Mountains adapting to the type of available prey and of insects and flowers adapting themselves to each other to illustrate how plants and animals in nature are modified over long periods of time. No human breeder is selecting here: the environment is selecting those fittest to survive.

2. How does Darwin's discussion of methodical selection and unconscious selection prepare the reader to understand the process of natural selection?

Darwin introduces unconscious selection by comparing it to the methodical selection used by breeders to create a new and superior strain—a common enough notion that Darwin's readers would probably understand and accept without question. Once his readers have been reminded that conscious selection can alter a breed dramatically (making it virtually a different species), then they are prepared for Darwin's well-documented argument that unconscious selection can accomplish much the same thing.

Once readers accept the idea that unconscious selection by humans can alter species dramatically, they are prepared for Darwin's argument that the environment may also select. A mind, after all, is not essential to the selection process. To many readers, Darwin's logical progression has seemed inexorable. The important thing for your students to note is that it is *gradual*. Darwin is a good rhetorician. He knows that if he is going to lead his readers into new and frightening territory, he must begin with the familiar and nonthreatening and move forward by small steps that build one upon the other.

3. What strategy does Darwin use to make his arguments persuasive?

The essay consists largely of assertions backed up by specific and thorough examples. It provides an excellent exercise in evaluating the weight of proof from direct observation, from secondary observation and the works of authorities, from demonstrating logical relationships in cause and effect, and from the reasonable presentation of the argument by the writer. Your students may agree that the sheer weight of Darwin's evidence leaves us so exhausted that by the time we finish the essay, we scarcely have the energy to resist his conclusions.

A good example of Darwin's use of direct observation in persuasive argument is his "hypothetical" explanation of the pollination of plants, in which a detailed description convinces the reader that the plant with the most nectar and with the most prominent reproductive organs would be crossed with other plants most often and, by natural selection, would contribute to the creation of "vigorous seedlings which consequently would have the best chance of flourishing and surviving" (paragraph 12).

Darwin's argument is also strengthened by his use of secondary observation and appeal to authority. In proving the possibility of unconscious selection, Darwin relies on the studies of experts on cattle and sheep (see notes on Robert Bakewell and William Youatt), as well as those authorities who have had firsthand experience with the breeding of dogs. Likewise, in describing changes in the pear, Darwin again relies on a trustworthy source (Pliny) to which he compares his own observations.

A characteristic strength of Darwin's arguments is his ability to show the plausibility of cause-and-effect relations that other observers had not recognized. For example, Darwin notes that domestic breeds that are very similar in their internal anatomy often vary greatly in their external appearance. What causes this effect? Unconscious selection by breeders who value visible oddities, Darwin argues: "it is in human nature to value any novelty" (paragraph 9). If your students are skeptical about this cause-and-effect relationship, let them propose another cause.

4. How does Darwin's language reflect apparent variations in his level of conviction, and why?

Remind students before they begin to examine Darwin's language of his awareness of the hostility his ideas would encounter. *The Origin of Species* is a book written for a largely hostile audience.

In general, Darwin does not force his ideas on his readers but instead invites them to see things his way. He often backs up his ideas with a degree of reservation, using phrases like "there is reason to believe" or "some highly competent authorities are convinced." At other times, possibly to give his words more weight, he uses a more forceful claim, such as "there is not a suspicion existing in the mind of any one at all acquainted with the subject" that the method used by Buckley and Burgess to breed sheep is not completely valid (paragraph 3).

But look at paragraph 8: once Darwin has spelled out his argument, he breaks from his careful qualifying and states his views forcefully. "On the view here given of the important part which selection by man has played, it becomes at once obvious, how it is that our domestic races show adaptation in their structure or in their habits to man's wants or fancies," he begins, and follows up with still more forceful language, stating "man can hardly select," "he rarely cares," "he can never act by selection," "no man would ever try," and finally "I have no doubt." Darwin's argument may move forward on facts and logic, but he is aware of the emotional dimension of argument and knows how to move gradually from the low end of his level of conviction toward the high end.

CHAPTER 7

Arguing When the Rules Are Disputed

Purpose

Though I believe that for many students this may be the most difficult chapter in the book, its purpose is at least easily stated: to help students understand the principles of argumentation when the issue is not what *is* but what *ought to be*. Arguments about what *is* are treated in Chapter 6.

My conception of what needs to be accomplished in this chapter has been shaped by the work of psychologists who have studied the ethical and intellectual development of college students, particularly that of William G. Perry, Jr., (*Intellectual and Ethical Development in the College Years: A Scheme*) and that of Mary Field Belenky, Blythe McVicker Clinchy, Nancy Rule Goldberger, and Jill Mattuck Tarule (the authors of *Women's Ways of Knowing: The Development of Self, Voice, and Mind*, which reflects and modifies Perry's scheme). The research conducted by these psychologists suggests that many students are inhibited in their ability to argue well because they have either a world view in which all rules and all knowledge belong to unchallengeable authorities (in which case no argument is possible) or a world view in which all rules are equally arbitrary (in which case argument, even if amusing, is merely a game).

If students are to be successful arguers, we need to find a way to move them toward what Perry calls "committed relativism," a state of academic grace in which students acknowledge that a case can often be made for any of several rules, but there are good intellectual and ethical reasons to advocate one rule among the many. Their intellectual stance in argument then becomes "wholehearted but tentative," to use one of Perry's key phrases.

Of course, students will not have their world views changed by reading a single textbook chapter. Nor will they often change dramatically because of a single academic course. But the purpose here is to lead them from the states that Belenky et al. associate with "received knowledge" (uncritical acceptance of opinions delivered from the outside) or "personal knowledge" (surrender to an isolating subjectivity) toward "constructed knowledge." Once they are comfortable with the idea that knowledge (of the facts and the rules) is constructed, they can begin to play a role in that construction.

The principles of argument that students learn in the chapter are those that we all seem to discover inevitably as we move toward committed relativism or constructed knowledge. Once we are aware that not all the rules championed by parents, teachers, religious leaders, and scoutmasters are accepted everywhere, we begin to inquire why we should prefer some rules to others. At this point we begin to understand the nature of the appeals to authority, consistency, and consequences—the three persuaders the chapter encourages students to recognize, evaluate critically, and use.

Overview

The *chapter proper* divides into four parts and features two key exercises:

1. A discussion of the nature of arguments about rules, illustrated by a passage from Robert Bolt's *A Man for All Seasons* in which Sir Thomas More and Thomas Cromwell dispute the legal meaning of More's silence on the subject of the King's marriage
2. A discussion of the ways in which rules are justified, or argued into place, featuring an example written by a judge
3. A short discussion of the role that undisputed facts play in an argument about rules
4. General advice on writing arguments about disputed rules

The exercises at the end of the first and second parts (page 220 and page 228) may be the most important part of the chapter, and you will want to examine them carefully and give some thought to how they can best be used in your class. There is certainly adequate material in this chapter to keep a class productively occupied for three sessions: the first session going through Exercise 1, the second through Exercise 2, and the third discussing whatever writing assignments are given.

The *assignments* include paragraph-length arguments for a warm-up, six assignments based on a case study, and an assignment in which students are encouraged to write on a subject of their choosing following a disciplined form of argumentation.

The *readings* are among the most challenging in the book:

"*Miller* v. *California*," excerpts from a U.S. Supreme Court decision featuring the clash between Chief Justice Burger's rule that a state government has the right to regulate the distribution of obscene material that may offend "the sensibilities of unwilling recipients" and Justice Douglas's rule that the sensibilities of recipients cannot be allowed to restrict freedom of the press

"Let's Put Pornography Back in the Closet," Susan Brownmiller's argument in favor of Douglas's position

"Just Like Us?"—a panel discussion on the issue of animal rights, in which disputants offer arguments about what rules should regulate the relationship of human beings to other beasts

"Vivisection," in which C. S. Lewis makes his case for the rights of animals to be protected from exploitation in the laboratory

The Chapter Step-by-Step

General Discussion of Arguments About Rules (pages 216–221)

Textbook treatments of argumentation are often so burdened with special terms that they seem to be introducing students to a foreign language. I've attempted to avoid superfluous jargon in *The Riverside Guide*, but you'll notice that in this section words are sometimes used with a special emphasis or meaning. You need chiefly to alert your students to the use of the following:

Dispute is used to mean the whole context of disagreement within which arguments exist. In effect, I am using *dispute* to mean what students often mean by *argument* in such a sentence as "Fred and Mary were having an argument."

Argument is ordinarily used to mean a line of reasoning inside a dispute, one that (in this chapter) leads through a rule.

Rule is used to mean pretty much what it means colloquially—when, for instance, a teacher says that her rule is that late papers will be docked one letter grade. *Policy* or *principle* might be suggested as synonyms. Students need to realize that rules can be made up on the spot—not all of them come from rule books.

Court is used to refer to any party set up as a judge of arguments, though in some instances it may mean a court of law.

These very simple terms can be quite useful to you in clarifying what students are expected to do when they write essays arguing about rules. You will sometimes find students arguing what needs no arguing, in which case you may ask them to define the *dispute* they are trying to resolve. You may find others giving facts and drawing conclusions without creating a true *argument*, in which case you may point out that their argument should pass through a *rule*. If they write without consciousness of an audience that needs persuasion (if they preach to the converted), you may ask them to define their *court*.

Exercise 1: **Practice in Inventing and Stating Rules** (pages 220–221). Failure to identify the conflicting rules that shape a dispute is a common failing among students. For some students I have known, rules seem almost as ineffable as angels. They simply cannot state in the form of a general principle the rule that lies at the center of their argument, nor, of course, can they articulate the rule that lies at the center of their opponent's argument. This first exercise is aimed at improving that basic skill.

The exercise is not easy or trivial and could productively occupy a good portion of a class period. It is a very effective exercise for small group work, bound to create some productive disagreements within the individual groups and likely to produce disagreements among the various groups when you bring the class together again at the period's end.

Students will almost inevitably end up arguing about what justice demands in the case rather than merely state appropriate rules. That is, they will begin to offer justifications for the rules they favor and criticisms of the rules they oppose. You will, of course, want to *encourage this expansion of the exercise*, since practice in arguing about rules is precisely what students need.

The three legal cases used in the exercise are subtle reworkings of actual court cases. The first is based on *Vosburg* v. *Putney* (50 N.W. 403 [Wisconsin, 1891]), a case that has irritated several generations of law students. In the original case the family of Vosburg (our Verberg) prevailed because the court accepted the rule that when Party *X* intentionally strikes or touches Party *Y* without obtaining consent, Party *X* becomes responsible for any injury Party *Y* sustains as a result, no matter how unforeseeable. Another rule that would favor the Vosburgs is that when *someone* must pay for the consequences of an action (as someone must pay for John Verberg's medical treatments), the party most in the wrong should pay. Clearly Tom Piltney's behavior, forgivable as it may be, was *more* wrong than John Verberg's. Making the Piltneys pay may be irksome, but making the Verbergs pay is more irksome.

On the other hand, there are good rules to be offered on the Piltneys' behalf. A rule that says Party *X* is responsible only for the harm he or she could reasonably foresee would favor the Piltneys. A rule that says people are responsible only for the harm they intend to cause would also get the Piltneys off the hook. So would a rule that says however reprehensible the actions of a child may be, the family as a whole (the parents) cannot be held responsible—in which case the Verbergs could recover only as much as Tom Piltney had in his piggy bank.

The second case is based on the notorious *Katko* v. *Briney* (183 N.W. 659 [Iowa, 1971]), which was reported in newspapers across the nation because (according to the somewhat sensationalized reports) it awarded a "burglar" damages when he was shot entering someone's house. The court decided that Katko (our Karko) deserved compensation on the basis of much the same rule that governed *Vosburg* v. *Putney*: when Party *X* intentionally strikes or touches Party *Y* without obtaining consent, Party *X* owes Party *Y* compensation for any injuries sustained. That the striking was done with a shotgun trap rather than with a fist certainly did not keep it from being a striking. Your students may not see the shooting in the Karko case as analogous to the kicking in the Verberg case and may come up with some rule like "When one person deliberately harms another person, the person who did the harm owes compensation to the one harmed" or even "When one person shoots another . . . ." These are fine rules for our purpose, though you may want to ask (by way of sharpening some minds) if a single rule could serve both the Verbergs and Bill Karko.

What rules might have made the case go the other way? The obvious one would be that a person whose property is threatened has a right to defend it without incurring liability even if defending it means striking or shooting another person. Your students might end up in a lively discussion of whether this is a rule they would like to have applied in their own societies and neighborhoods. Would they want people to have the right to shoot a homeless person who breaks into a detached garage looking for a place to sleep in the winter? to shoot a child who is throwing rocks at the window? Where, as law professors are continually asking, do you draw the line?

The third case is based on *Mohr* v. *Williams* (104 N.W. 12 [Minnesota, 1905]), and in it the court decided in favor of Mohr (our Mayer). The rule was once again the same, or nearly so: a person who intentionally strikes or touches another person without obtaining consent owes that person compensation for injuries sustained even if the injury is only to the victim's dignity or psychological well-being. Except in cases of emergencies, the law doesn't recognize a distinction between a doctor's unauthorized touching for medical reasons and touching by anyone else. Mohr was offended by her physician's touch, and this, in the eyes of the court, was injury enough to merit compensation. Your students may make up a rule that says "When a doctor performs an operation that the patient has not consented to, the doctor owes the patient compensation." This is not bad, but you might ask whether they want this rule to apply to doctors only. Would they want *you* to perform an operation on them without consent? And you might ask them if they want to limit the rule to operations. What about unauthorized spinal adjustments? breast examinations?

One rule that might be introduced on behalf of the doctor is that a person should only have to pay compensation for behavior that physically *harms* another person: the "touch" that the doctor bestowed did no harm and actually conferred a benefit, and so by this rule, he could not be sued successfully. A second rule that would favor the doctor would be that when physicians in the process of doing their duty touch or strike someone, the touch is always allowed. A third would be that once a person has consented to be operated on by a physician, that person consents to whatever touching the physician thinks best for medical purposes.

Discussion of the Way Rules Are Justified (pages 222–230)

The debate that Exercise 1 is almost certain to generate should help students see the pertinence of what comes in this section. In situations where one rule or another *will* be applied, how do we persuade a "court" to prefer ours? Our answer here is by appealing to authority, consistency, consequences, or some combination of these. Argument by analogy is treated on pages 224–225 as a special instance of the appeal to consistency. All these appeals are used in the clearly argued opinion Judge Ward Hunt wrote in the Ryan case (pages 226–228).

Exercise 2: Practice in Justifying a Rule (pages 228–230). Here again we have a major exercise, one that cannot be done quickly but one from which students have much to gain. We recommend that you use it in one of two ways. First, you might simply require students to write the exercise outside of class, treating it essentially as you do a short essay (good answers will run in excess of 250 words). If you do this, I suggest that you give students an opportunity to rewrite after getting comments from you, since many will have difficulty with the assignment. Second, you might devote part or all of a class period to having students discuss the exercise, trying out and getting reactions to the arguments they might use. Probably the best way to do this is to have them work in groups, developing an argument collaboratively.

If you use groups, your best bet for avoiding confusion at the start would probably be to assign the same case to all the groups. You might leave the groups the choice of arguing for either side in the given case, or you might assign half the groups one side and half the groups another. Discussion among the whole class will probably be more fruitful if the groups haven't all argued the same side. A class period of collaboration is not likely to produce a complete draft. Instead, students will leave with ideas and notes for their own short essays.

Here is an example of a short argument for the second case (Karko versus Brawney):

> In the case of Karko versus Brawney, Karko might argue for the rule that a person who deliberately strikes (directly or indirectly) another person without that person's consent must compensate the victim for his or her injuries. Brawney might argue that people have a right to use force to defend their property against trespassers and thieves.
>
> Karko's rule seems the better of the two. The court established in the case of Scar versus Striker that a blow delivered by a trap requires compensation just as a direct blow does. The bucket propped over the door in that case is analogous to the shotgun trap in this case. Brawney's rule that a person need not pay compensation for such a blow if the person struck is a trespasser or a thief would have negative consequences if it were frequently applied. Property owners would become more inclined to arm themselves, set traps, and shoot intruders, believing that the courts will never hold them liable. The result would be an increase not only in the number of professional burglars injured but in the number of teen-age pranksters shot or killed, the number of neighborhood children injured, and even in the number of people injured by their *own* firearms and booby traps. In the case of Devlin versus Anglen, the court said that its "highest goal was to shape the character of the citizenry by rewarding behavior that is socially productive and punishing behavior that is socially destructive." Violence against people—even against those suspected of wrongdoing—is socially destructive, and the court should not encourage it by announcing its approval of a man's shooting another man in order to protect some old bottles and fruit jars.

An argument for the other side might begin with the same first paragraph but then proceed as follows:

> Brawney's rule seems the better of the two. It is true that in the case of Scar versus Striker, the court decided that a person struck by a trap deserves compensation just as much as a person struck directly, but in that case, there is no indication that the person trapped himself by engaging in a criminal action. Brawney's trap, on the other hand, was set off by a man who was illegally entering another person's house with the admitted intention of stealing goods. People who break into other

people's houses in order to steal must surely know that they run the risk of being battered or shot by a frightened or angry property owner. The threat of criminal activity sends property owners a clear signal to defend themselves and their possessions as well as they can, and the injuries intruders sustain fall under the rule the court used in the case of Guard versus Center: "If the person touched gives . . . reason to believe that the touch is acceptable, the toucher cannot be held liable for the consequences."

In addition, the consequences of forcing the owner to pay the intruder compensation for the injuries received are unacceptable. If criminals learn that the risk of being injured in the course of carrying out a crime is balanced by the possibility of being compensated for the injury, they will be more likely to break in and steal. And if property owners learn that they may be successfully sued by an intruder they resist, then they will be less likely to defend their own property. The police cannot be everywhere, and if owners dare not guard their own houses, then burglary will become a safer, more lucrative profession and presumably a more popular one. But the court said in the case of Devlin versus Anglen that its aim is to "shape the character of the citizenry by rewarding behavior that is socially productive and punishing behavior that is socially destructive." Breaking and entering is surely destructive and should not be encouraged by compensating thieves like Bill Karko for their injuries.

If you think your students are going to have trouble with this assignment, you could reproduce these answers as examples, discuss them, and then have students work on either the first or the third case (Verberg versus Piltney or Mayer versus Wilson).

Discussion of the Role of Undisputed Facts (pages 230–232)

The model of argument we are using in this chapter always begins with undisputed facts, moves to a disputable rule, and ends in a conclusion. But students may well wonder where these undisputed facts come from. The purpose of this section is to answer that question: facts *become* undisputed when (1) all sides agree from the outset to accept them; (2) when the arguer convinces the court (by methods discussed in Chapter 6) that the fact is probable enough to stand on: and (3) when the prior application of a rule has created a new fact.

Some students may be uneasy with this picture of how "fact" is established, preferring the simpler view that things that are true are facts and things that aren't, aren't. But my purpose in Chapters 5 and 6 has been precisely to help students see that this simple duality has to be overcome if they are going to understand the nature of reasoned arguments.

Advice on Writing Arguments About Disputed Rules (pages 232–233)

Once again the advice section serves as a reminder of the chapter's major points. The emphasis is on the key constituents of an argument: establishing a foundation in undisputed facts, identifying a rule that clearly applies, and making a persuasive case for that rule.

Peer review of arguments about rules is particularly important because student writers often have trouble viewing their work objectively. They tend to become partisans and to accept their side's version of the facts as indisputably true. Or they fail to see an obviously attractive rule that the other side could put forward and that needs to be either criticized or accepted. The questions for peer review are aimed at encouraging the reviewer to play devil's advocate to some degree. You may want to remind your students that in helping a fellow student hone an argument, being "nice" is not necessarily being useful.

The Assignments

Assignment 1: Paragraph-length Arguments.   Each of these brief scenarios could obviously produce a number of effective arguments. Because the resulting essays are quite short, you should be able to discuss the strengths and weaknesses of some examples in class. Or you could prepare students to write by having them work through the problems in groups, as suggested for Exercise 2 above.

Brief sample arguments for the first two cases follow, with some commentary on possible variations.

> *Case 1.*   Gina Davis was repaying a favor to Sally Seymore. She had benefited from Sally's generosity and promised to care for the fish as repayment of a debt. When a friend promises to care for another friend's property as part of such a tit-for-tat arrangement, then the friend must keep his or her promise or else pay compensation for the damage that results from failing to do so. The death of the fish was caused by Gina's not feeding them and checking on their condition. She owes Sally $20.

On the other hand, it could be argued that (to borrow language from Judge Ward Hunt, page 226) Gina can be held responsible only for the "proximate" or "natural and necessary" consequences of her failure to care for the fish as she had promised. Assuming that the fish died from lack of oxygen rather than lack of food, their death was not a "natural and necessary" result of her neglecting them; she could not have foreseen the failure of the aerator and so may reasonably have assumed that the worst consequence of a few days' neglect would be that the fish would have been hungry. This line of argument would suggest that no compensation is due. If you have some ichthyologists in the class, they may know that the Balinese fighting fish is a surface breather whose death cannot be attributed to the failure of an aerator, and they may come up with an argument that Gina owes Sally only $5.

In Case 2, some students may argue that Jim owes Alan the whole bundle ($1,515) on the principle that when someone borrows a friend's possession, he or she assumes an absolute obligation to compensate the friend for any loss or damage. Some may argue that Jim owes Alan nothing because Jim was himself negligent in letting the bike go to the mall with valuables in the carry-all. A more interesting and perhaps a sounder argument might go like this:

> *Case 2.*   Jim Curry must have seen the carry-all bag attached to the bike's seat, but there is no indication that he looked inside it, nor did

Alan Norton tell him what the bag contained. Under these circumstances, someone in Jim's position would naturally assume that the bag
contained nothing of extraordinary value, but there would be no reason
for him to think that it was completely empty. He might have expected
it to contain some small, practical, inexpensive items like a tool kit or
gloves, but not a gold watch. A good rule to apply in this case is that the
borrower is responsible only for what he or she could reasonably understand to have borrowed. Thus, Jim was responsible for the bike itself
(which he carefully locked) and for what a reasonable person might expect to be in the bag. He owes Alan $15 for the tool kit but nothing for
the watch because there was no reason for him to believe that he was bor-
rowing such an expensive item.

Case 3 will raise somewhat different questions from those raised by the first
two cases because students will have to decide what sort of compensation (if any)
Dawson owes Seymore for the lost labor and lost knowledge represented by the
notes themselves. Case 4 will raise the new question of what standard of care can
be expected of those who do not *borrow* goods or offer to care for them as return
for a favor but who have the goods *thrust* on them.

A number of overall rules might be offered. One possibility is that when
people knowingly take charge of a friend's property as part of an arrangement
from which they benefit, then they must care for the property as people ordinarily
care for things they own. If they fail to do so, they must pay their friend compensation for the "ordinary and natural" consequences of their negligence.

Assignments 2–7: Arguments About School Policy.   Some instructors (and
some students) may have knowledge about the way courts of law have handled
some of the matters raised in these assignments. If you have such special knowledge, please note that we are *not* dealing with the principles that would apply
in a state or federal court but with the principles that an individual school board
decides to apply. Everything is up for grabs.

There are two predictable pitfalls these assignments create for students inex-
perienced in writing on "case studies" or "hypotheticals." One is to try the ploy
that has sometimes worked for written examinations: devote a good deal of the
answer to repeating information that is in the question. You can help students
avoid this trap by reminding them that the audiences specified for the various
assignments all have considerable knowledge of the situation and that merely
repeating the information they already have will do no good. The second pitfall
is to fail to take into account all the information that is given. Very few students
in the classes on which we tested these assignments realized that John Dewey's
educational philosophy (as summarized in the plaque near the front door) could
be used to add authority to their arguments. Only about half the students considered the general constraints under which the school was operating.

Student answers will vary widely, and a good deal of the fun in this assignment
comes from comparing their arguments and approaches. Here are some notes on
what to look for:

Assignment 2 will provoke some arguments that Foster has made his bed and
must lie in it. The key to examining such arguments is to see precisely what

rule is being insisted on (or what *rules*, since more than one may appear). A good paper must articulate the rule clearly enough that we can examine it. "When the damage done to a person is largely caused by his or her own behavior, that person can't reasonably demand that other people undo the damage" is a good possible rule. "When the community's resources are limited, no one can demand more than his or her fair share" might be another.

Assignment 3 might produce such rules as "When a school hides the educational problems of students, it does damage that must be repaired"; "A school's obligation to give its community's children at least a minimal degree of education is absolute and doesn't end when the child receives a diploma."; or "A school that declares a student educated is obliged to make that claim a true one."

Assignment 4 will tend to produce such rules as "A teacher is obliged to serve students as a role model, both inside and outside of class" or "A teacher who undermines the community's attempt to raise children who will live within its moral code is neglecting his or her duty."

Assignment 5 will almost certainly produce some statement of the rule that employees should be judged only for their performance in the workplace. It may also produce a pragmatic rule that, given the difficulty in finding good teachers, the community should be generous in overlooking the after-hours behavior of teachers whose excellence in the classroom is well established.

Assignment 6 will produce arguments based on the rule that a student's grade for a course should reflect his or her success in studying the academic content of that course (regardless of the student's brilliance or dullness). Quince might make some ingenious use of Dewey's creed by arguing that learning to work within the classroom community is learning to enter into "proper relations with others."

Assignment 7 will produce arguments based on the rule that grades should be given to reflect ability and accomplishment (rather than good behavior). It may also produce some allusions to Dewey's creed, since Jenny's accomplishments may reflect a greater mastery of the "process of living" than would doing the standard assignments.

Assignment 8: An Argument of Your Choice.   This assignment needs little comment. You may want to insist that students follow the very general outline it recommends. Not all effective arguments follow such an outline, of course, but the discipline it imposes on students unfamiliar with the conventions of argument may benefit from them and produce more coherent papers.

Sample papers and additional assignments are available in the package of supplementary material that accompanies the main text.

End-of-Chapter Readings

CHIEF JUSTICE BURGER AND JUSTICE DOUGLAS

Miller v. *California*

Taking on a Supreme Court case is a fairly difficult task for the average under-graduate, though reviewers of the text were surprised at how easy this one is to follow. Students should have little trouble understanding the facts of the case and the goals of each side; analyzing each argument, however, will undoubtedly prove to be a challenging assignment. The following questions are designed to lead students through that process. The task is a valuable one for clarifying and rein-forcing the ideas in Chapter 7 as well as for preparing the students to write their own arguments.

In the years since the *Miller* case, vital Supreme Court decisions regulating ob-scenity include *Young* v. *American Mini-Theatres* (1976), which placed limits on the location of adult bookstores and theaters; *FCC* v. *Pacifica* (1977), which determined that "patently offensive" words were unprotected in broadcast media; and *New York* v. *Ferber* (1982), which denied child pornography First Amendment protection and was extended in an April 1990 decision to include the *possession* of child pornography. And the issue has been kept alive through the fall of 1990 as 2 Live Crew, a rap group performing in Miami, Florida, faced charges of obscenity because of the content of some of the songs they perform, and were acquitted. In addition, the battle to regulate artists receiving NEA fund-ing goes on. The main issues in question—First Amendment rights and the vague-ness of existing law—have not been completely settled.

One of the most interesting changes in the obscenity issue is its shift in focus: since the *Miller* case, the crusade against obscenity has been led by feminists who wish to define pornography by its violence and degradation of women and who have been joined all over the country by fundamentalist religious groups. You might therefore be just as interested in your students' *reasons* for defending or attacking obscenity as in which side they choose.

QUESTIONS

1. What are some facts no one disputes in *Miller* v. *California*?

Certainly both sides agree that Marvin Miller made available sexually explicit materials by means of a mass mailing of brochures that included photographs and drawings. In fact, although Douglas defends Miller, he admits that the mate-rials may well be "garbage" and agrees with Burger that people should not be forced to view them (paragraphs 16–17).

Both sides agree that the result of earlier Supreme Court decisions is to prohib-it "dissemination or exhibition of obscene material when the mode of dissemina-tion carries with it a significant danger of offending the sensibilities of unwilling recipients or of exposure to juveniles" (paragraph 1); Burger's citing of twelve cases to support the law proves not that the law is just but that it has not been overturned or substantially modified over the years. Douglas could not and does not dispute this fact.

Both justices concede that the Fourteenth Amendment applies in this case and that California may not make a law inconsistent with other parts of the U.S. Constitution (particularly the First Amendment).

Finally, both justices concede that the Constitution (particularly the First Amendment) gives no clear statement of how the publication of obscenity should be treated. Both sides agree that some further action must be taken by the Supreme Court or by the Congress if the publication of obscenity is to be regulated.

Possibly the most vital factual point that is *not* agreed on by the two justices is whether there is a general, shared sense of what "obscenity" is. Burger's arguments throughout depend on an assumption that although it is difficult to define obscenity in words, it is easy enough to predict what will offend community standards of decency. Part of Douglas's argument depends on the unpredictability of where an individual judge or jury will draw the line between the obscene and the acceptable.

2. What does the First Amendment have to do with obscenity, and what are the opinions of the two justices on the First Amendment issue?

Before attempting to map out the arguments of Burger and Douglas, students may benefit from talking out some of the key issues on their own. The First Amendment states that "Congress shall make no law . . . abridging the freedom of speech, or of the press. . . ." You may wish to clarify for your students that the issue here is *publication* in the broad sense of "making public or displaying." Neither justice denies that people have a right to own or view pornographic material in private. Burger argues that governments can enact laws to keep people from foisting such material on the public at large, but Douglas argues that the state can no more forbid such publication than it can forbid the publication of newspapers or street-corner oratory. Students need to be clear on this point: it is not the production of obscenity that got Miller into trouble but rather the public dissemination of it.

In outlining Burger's view, students should cite his statement that the First Amendment protects "all ideas having even the slightest redeeming social importance" and his assumption that obscenity does not deserve such protection. In addition, Burger points out that by general agreement some forms of free speech are not protected "because they encroach upon the limited area of more important interests"; obscenity can then be regulated on the grounds that it carries with it the danger of offending unwilling participants or of being exposed to juveniles—a danger that outweighs the value of protecting such material. Finally, students should at least consider the value of Burger's statement that "to equate the free and robust exchange of ideas and political debate with commercial exploitation of obscene material demeans the grand conception of the First Amendment and its high purpose in the historic struggle for freedom."

In outlining Douglas's view, students should note his statement that the First Amendment does not single out "obscenity" for special treatment; it does not deny sexual material the general protection given other forms of publication. They should also note his assertion that the aim of the amendment is to stave off the threat to freedom of the press brought on by a ban on publishing "offensive" material; if we start banning material because it is "offensive" to the majority of people, Burger argues, we stifle individual expression and the exchange of controversial ideas.

3. Should the California obscenity law have been struck down because of its vagueness?

This question addresses the second level of the argument, Douglas's claim that the vagueness of the law is a threat to the civil liberties of publishers. His argument is that since the court has failed to define obscenity clearly, it has put each individual court in the position of defining it *ex post facto* in each individual case. The only way for publishers or performers to find out whether their material is obscene is to present it in public, get arrested, and see whether they are convicted. There are no guidelines for judging what is obscene until a case such as Miller's arises (paragraph 10). Douglas contends that if we must censor, then we should do so by establishing an administrative agency for that purpose. Let the agency decide in advance of publication whether the material is obscene. Otherwise, the "law becomes a trap," allowing people to be prosecuted without due process. By citing *Bouie* v. *City of Columbia*, Douglas suggests that the Court is being inconsistent in its rulings, and he emphasizes the bewilderment caused by the vagueness of the law (paragraphs 13–14). "To send men to jail for violating standards they cannot understand, construe, and apply is a monstrous thing to do in a nation dedicated to fair trials and due process," he concludes (paragraph 15).

You might help your students understand the dangers of a vague law by asking them how they would feel about living in a society that had only one law: "Every citizen will conduct himself or herself at all times so as to avoid offending others. Should he or she fail to do so, the penalty will be a fine, imprisonment, or death, depending on how seriously the others are offended."

Burger believes that Douglas exaggerates the vagueness of the definition of obscenity. He seems to take the attitude once expressed by Justice Potter Stewart: you may not be able to define obscenity precisely, but "you know it when you see it." I believe that this is a central assumption behind the majority decision and behind the thinking of most Americans. In general, we Americans tend to think that publishers of sexually explicit material know perfectly well when their products are obscene—when they offend community standards. Nonetheless, Burger knows that the vagueness issue cannot be ignored. He takes care to define obscenity as clearly as he can, establishing the three-part test used in evaluating questionable materials (paragraph 3). Douglas believes that the definition remains vague and, at any rate, comes a little late for Mr. Miller.

4. Map out the arguments of both Burger and Douglas and explain how each justifies his rule with references to authority, calls for consistency, and consideration of the consequences.

The following map will give your students help in visualizing how each justice arrived at his conclusion. Notice that their dispute is less about the validity of their respective rules than about which takes precedence.

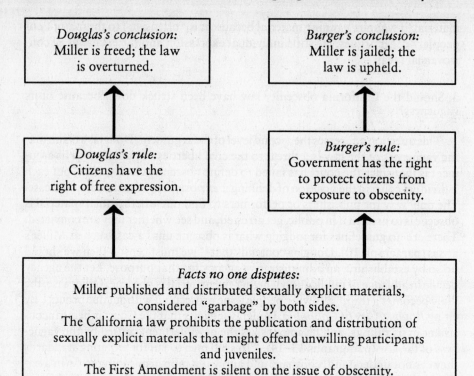

Douglas's conclusion:
Miller is freed; the law
is overturned.

Burger's conclusion:
Miller is jailed; the
law is upheld.

Douglas's rule:
Citizens have the
right of free expression.

Burger's rule:
Government has the right
to protect citzens from
exposure to obscenity.

Facts no one disputes:
Miller published and distributed sexually explicit materials,
considered "garbage" by both sides.
The California law prohibits the publication and distribution of
sexually explicit materials that might offend unwilling participants
and juveniles.
The First Amendment is silent on the issue of obscenity.
The Fourteenth Amendment prohibits states from making laws
that restrict the rights of U.S. citizens.

As you discuss the movement from facts to conclusions, you will want to evaluate how each justice arrives at and justifies his rule, focusing on how each appeals to authority, consistency, and larger consequences.

Burger appeals first to the highest authority he can, Supreme Court decisions that have allowed exceptions to the First Amendment for "classes of speech, the prevention and punishment of which have never been thought to raise any Constitutional problem" (paragraphs 1–2). He points out the consistency of the Court by citing twelve cases that support this phase of his argument. Having put the First Amendment argument to rest, he appeals to the responsibility of the government to protect its citizens, primarily by setting forth the consequences of rejecting his rule: "hard core' pornography may be exposed without limit to the juvenile, the passerby, and the consenting adult alike" (paragraph 4). Finally, Burger refutes the negative consequences his opponents associate with his rule by asserting the Court's ability to rule reasonably and fairly, scarcely endangering anyone with "state-ordered regimentation of our minds" (paragraph 7). He ends his argument, then, with an analogy seemingly intended for psychological appeal: equating the free reign of obscenity with unregulated access to heroin.

Douglas bases his argument on the highest possible authority, the U.S. Constitution, the First Amendment of which he interprets more strictly than have most justices of the Supreme Court. He construes the silence of the framers of the First

Amendment on the issue of obscene material to mean that they intended it to be treated no differently than any other material: all should be equally publishable. He appeals to consistency by citing *Bouie v. City of Columbia*, a case in which the Supreme Court forbade states the right to interpret vague laws *ex post facto* (paragraph 13). And he appeals to the consideration of unwanted consequences by suggesting that using "offensiveness" as a standard for stopping publication could stifle the expression of ideas: "That test would make it possible to ban any paper or any journal or magazine in some benighted place" (paragraph 17).

SUSAN BROWNMILLER

Let's Put Pornography Back in the Closet

Brownmiller's attack on pornography represents the direction the antiobscenity campaign has taken since *Miller v. California* (1973), being primarily led not by moralists concerned about the sensibilities of unwilling or juvenile viewers but by feminists appalled by what these viewers are seeing. Feminists like Brownmiller believe that the primary victims of pornography are women—not only those who allow themselves to pose as subjects for it, but all women equally. Pornography, feminists argue, shapes societal attitudes and actions toward women, encouraging not only the subordination of women but rape and violence as well. "Let's Put Pornography" is best discussed after teaching "*Miller v. California*" because while Brownmiller unreservedly sides with the majority opinion, her method of arguing and her motives for doing so contrast considerably with those of the justices.

QUESTIONS

1. What are the facts no one disputes in Brownmiller's argument?

Though Brownmiller's argument is not structured like a legal case, establishing the facts is still an important step in analyzing her reasoning. While she takes roughly the same side as Justice Burger in the *Miller* decision, an important difference is the location of the opposing side and the "court": her opposition is made up of the abstract "other side," and her court is us, her readers. Therefore, establishing facts that no one disputes is not as simple as getting a group of lawyers and justices to stipulate. The facts "no one disputes" must be modified to facts Brownmiller *assumes* no one will dispute.

While implying those facts stated by Burger, Brownmiller focuses on facts of her own to make her case. Her first step is to establish (or assert) the "fact" that pornography is harmful to society, not necessarily because of its displays of explicit sexuality, but because it "represents hatred of women" and its intent is "to humiliate, degrade and dehumanize the female body for the purpose of erotic stimulation and pleasure" (paragraph 9). This is the fact on which she builds the rest of her argument. Her proof for this fact is not extensive in this article but is graphic enough to convince most readers: she describes scenes from pornographic magazines that depict "the female body being stripped, bound, raped, tortured, mutilated and murdered"—and that also encourage both men and women to excuse rape and sexual masochism "in the name of commercial entertainment and free speech" (paragraph 9). By establishing as fact that hard-core pornography is harmful, Brownmiller paves the way to her larger argument, that this type of obscenity should be banned from public display.

Brownmiller also implies a fact that is important in understanding her link from the community to the law: the only way to forbid hard-core pornography is to have a well-defined community standard. An avid supporter of political rallies, demonstrations, and public communication with legislators, Brownmiller assumes that community standards are defined by such community political activity.

2. Map out Brownmiller's argument against obscenity, and explain how her argument compares with Burger's argument in the *Miller* case.

If students have not read the *Miller* decision, you will need to review, at least, Burger's argument (pages 240–242) with them before analyzing Brownmiller's. In general, Brownmiller fully agrees with Burger on the First Amendment issue, quoting his belief that "to equate the free and robust exchange of ideas and political debate with commercial exploitation of obscene material demeans the grand conception of the First Amendment and its high purposes in the historic struggle for freedom. It is a misuse of the great guarantees of free speech and free press" (paragraph 3). Notice, however, that the facts she establishes are different and the rule is modified to fit her specific argument.

> *Brownmiller's conclusion:*
> The law should prohibit hard-core pornography from public display, in order to discourage the cultural climate created by it.

↑

> *Brownmiller's rule:*
> The government has a responsibility to protect its citizens from the cultural climate created by the public display of hard-core pornography.

↑

> *Facts Brownmiller assumes to be beyond dispute:*
> Hard-core pornography, which portrays people "tortured or terrorized in the service of sex," is being publicly displayed.
> This material is obviously harmful to society.

Siding with the majority, Brownmiller believes the protection of the people is a greater concern than absolute freedom of speech and of the press. She supports her rule by appealing to consistency by way of analogy, framing the obscenity issue as a "free-speech abridgment" analogous to false advertising and shouting "fire" in a crowded movie theater (paragraph 14).

Brownmiller's argument differs somewhat from the majority ruling in the *Miller* case, however, because she is not only supporting the decision but also responding to the problems that decision has caused. She believes that the three-part test established in *Miller* confused rather than clarified the meaning of "unlawful obscenity" because it did not offer a clear means of differentiating acceptable sexually explicit material from "hard-core" obscenity, a difference she personally has little trouble defining. Therefore, she is sympathetic with Justice Douglas's concern over the vagueness of the law regulating obscenity, particularly since present-day pornography is a product of sophisticated visual technology that further blurs the line between offensive obscenity and art.

In addition, Brownmiller cares little about many of the obscenity guidelines established by the *Miller* decision, concerning herself only with "contemporary

---

Brownmiller's conclusion:
All citizens have a responsibility to show that there is a clear community standard forbidding the public display of hard-core pornography.

↑

Brownmiller's rule:
All citizens have a responsibility to stop behavior that is harmful to society.

↑

Facts Brownmiller assumes to be beyond dispute:
Hard-core pornography, which portrays people "tortured or terrorized in the service of sex," is being displayed publicly. This material is obviously harmful to society. The only way to forbid hard-core pornography is to have a well-defined community standard.

---

community standards" that feminists are attempting to redefine (paragraph 8). Because the "cultural climate" created by the public display of obscenity is that in which "a rapist feels he is merely giving in to a normal urge and a woman is encouraged to believe that sexual masochism is healthy, liberated fun" (paragraph 10), she is determined to establish and maintain community standards that find this sort of obscenity unlawful. Therefore, her argument is as much an appeal to the public as it is an affirmation of the Court decision. We can map this side of her reasoning as well, though our map will be based largely on what Brownmiller implies rather than what she states directly.

This part of Brownmiller's argument echoes Justice Douglas's statement that if we cannot live with complete freedom of speech and the press, we may need to resort to "a regime of censorship which . . . should be done by constitutional amendment after full debate by the people" (*Miller* v. *California,* paragraph 9). In effect, both Brownmiller and Douglas believe that the people should decide what obscenity is unacceptable, and the legislature should then be able to decide what can be publicly displayed—based on "realistic and humane contemporary community standards."

3.   How does Brownmiller persuade us to accept her arguments?

Another difference between Brownmiller's article and the arguments of Justices Burger and Douglas is that while their appeal is largely to logic and fair policy-making, Brownmiller depends equally on emotional appeal. The effect is a replacement of cool and careful reasoning by language intended to incite people to action. Brownmiller's presentation of her argument through a combination of psychological and logical appeals may make some students as likely to discredit her argument as to be persuaded by it.

However, Brownmiller uses rhetoric strategically throughout the essay. First, she proves her awareness of free speech concerns, siding with the Hollywood Ten who were denied First Amendment protection when suspected of Communist affiliations. She also proves her moderation by admitting that as a writer who relied on explicit sexual descriptions to prove her case against rape, she is in favor of protecting some sexually explicit material, even that not to her liking, if it has redeeming social value. Brownmiller presents herself in the first part of the essay as a reasonable and moderate person at least—and perhaps as the sort of liberal we would expect to oppose the *Miller* decision.

Likewise, she often uses valid logical appeals. Plugging her argument directly into that of the concurring justices in the *Miller* case gives it authority, as does taking on the "no one is compelled" argument of dissenting Justice Douglas. Also, making the obscenity issue analogous to false advertising, a "free-speech abridgment," is a solid appeal to consistency. Finally, Brownmiller closes with a return to reasonable pleading: she knows the production of pornography/obscenity cannot be regulated but urges that the law "get the stuff out of our sight."

On the other hand, Brownmiller's argument is not without flaws. Her reliance on graphic descriptions, for example, is not always reasonable. She claims that to "buy a paper at the corner newsstand is to subject oneself to a forcible immersion in pornography, to be demeaned by an array of dehumanized, chopped-up parts of the female anatomy, packaged like cuts of meat at the supermarket" (paragraph 13). Not only is Brownmiller's claim untrue in many parts of the country where the location and method of selling pornography are restricted, but it also pushes her emotional appeal to the limit. Readers may be swayed further in her direction or may be convinced that she is approaching the irrational at this point; either way, they should recognize that the appeal isn't to their reason. Also, she is using the description to refute a considerable authority, Justice Douglas, whose claim that we are not compelled to look at obscenity is much more logically handled by Justice Burger.

In her final paragraph, Brownmiller claims that the legislatures can decide what can be displayed "using realistic and humane contemporary community standards." Yet because standards vary so much and because she suggests that we already live in a cultural climate that accepts and possibly acts on the influence of pornography, her faith in "community standards" is rather questionable; the community in control may opt for *more* protection of obscenity. In addition, Brownmiller may be accused of encouraging subjection of the minority to the majority.

JACK HITT, et al.

Just Like Us?

While the debate over animal rights has been largely a twentieth-century phenomenon, the relationship between human beings and animals is a timeless question; as C. S. Lewis points out in "Vivisection" (page 259), consideration of the proper treatment of animals was discussed even in Shakespeare's day. Particularly when read in conjunction with Lewis's careful refutation of religious and secular arguments for vivisection, two of the positions presented in "Just Like Us?" flesh out a radical program for animal rights while the other two provide reasonable and insightful objections. In assigning this essay, you may wish to have various students outline the four positions, as well as those raised by Lewis, before you meet for discussion. Once the students are able to distinguish the various lines of thinking, they will be prepared to analyze the merits of each.

QUESTIONS

1. Summarize the position of each forum member.

From the beginning Newkirk establishes herself as the most aggressive of the four, repeatedly responding to or attacking Caplan's anti-animal rights statements. She believes that when presented with the facts and encouraged to believe the truth, people will support animal rights. Opposition to the validity of her point of view she dismisses as "speciesism," a barrier to animal rights that must be broken down. Her position is grounded in her inability to find any fundamental differences between humans and animals. She believes that the only solution is to legislate, to create laws to protect animals and change the attitudes of humans.

Francione is as firm as Newkirk in holding to his pro-animal rights position, but he tends to prefer logical appeals over emotional ones. Yet some of his statements are more controversial than Newkirk's. He immediately proposes that because treatment of animals as property is analogous to past treatment of blacks and women, animals rights will be "*the* civil rights movement of the twenty-first century" (paragraph 6). Like Newkirk, he believes that if people only understood what is happening to animals in laboratories, they would readily support animal rights (paragraph 27). Francione is in favor of legislation because he believes established rights are the only thing that keeps individuals from intruding on or exploiting others. Finally, he believes that laws shape our morals at least as much as our morals shape our laws, so the ultimate question is how to pass and enforce animal rights laws.

Although Goldman speaks relatively infrequently, he establishes himself in a very definite role, that of the utilitarian. Animal testing does not offend him at all unless it is "unnecessary or just repetitive" (paragraph 32). He believes that animals do not have rights (paragraph 73), and we are under no obligation to give them any, particularly because broadening the spectrum of rights would make our understanding of them more complicated; rights of liberty and rights of equality are very difficult to define and often overlap. But finally he proposes that if we really feel the need to protect animal rights, then an amendment should be drawn up that resembles the Fourteenth Amendment, establishing certain rights but not absolute ones.

At the heart of Caplan's argument is the distinction between humankind and animals, a distinction he has no trouble accepting and on which he bases all his other premises. His main course of argument is that for some, "biblical" and "natural law" has set humanity apart; for him, human rights are grounded in "the ability to reason, the ability to suffer," and a cluster of other characteristics (paragraphs 35, 36, and 39) including the need for society to survive (paragraph 48). Of the four panelists, he is possibly the most rhetorical, for rather than offering logical arguments for his own points, he often reframes the arguments of the others, explaining why they are not quite on target. For example, he finds Francione's property issue "too simplistic" (paragraph 13) because animals do not have the same moral worth as human beings and because different animals register differently in the human consciousness. In addition, he wants to move away from the battle of rights—since the excessive handing out of rights diminishes the meaning of them all—to a sense of fairness and duty that should shape our relationship with animals (paragraph 52); this is his preferred means of getting people to act decently (paragraph 69).

2. What rule or rules does each person present or imply?

Among the many possible rules, your students should be able to identify most of the following:

The rule at the base of Newkirk's position is that unless we can pinpoint a feature that distinguishes humans from animals, we should not assume there is a true separation between the two (paragraph 43). As people are taught to accept this rule, they will let go of the myth of separation and naturally make the right choices—which will be in favor of animal rights. Another of Newkirk's rules, and a more questionable one, is that if animals wish to live, we must let them live (paragraph 42). This rule can come into play only if we accept her assumption that because animals are alive, then they must want to be alive.

Francione's rules have a slightly different edge. He proposes that we must not exploit weaker beings for our own benefit (paragraph 20). In addition, he argues that since many of the "cluster" of human characteristics Caplan identifies are actually possessed by animals, particularly chimpanzees, then all animals have the same right to life that humans do (paragraph 41). The rule implied seems to be that all animals must be treated in a way appropriate to the single animal closest to a human being in its attributes.

Goldman sets forth only one rule: animals may be used for experimentation if the experimenter can justify it by a greater good.

Caplan, assuming that humankind is distinct from and superior to other animals, believes that humankind has an obligation to treat lower animals with care but does not have an obligation to treat them as equals (paragraphs 50–57).

3. Choose and evaluate examples of appeals to authority, consistency, or consequences.

Although Newkirk often risks credibility with her extreme position, she is sharp and occasionally catches her opponent Caplan in a logical error. For example, Caplan uses as an analogy to the human-animal relationship that of a parent and child, pointing out that just because a child decides that he or she has a need for a new car (as part of the child's pursuit of happiness), a parent is under no obligation to fulfill that need; the child doesn't have a right to that car that the parent is obligated to uphold. Newkirk quickly points out Caplan's error of false analogy: life is the issue here, so only fundamental rights are analogous. A "fundamental" case that she believes to be analogous to the right of animals to be protected from exploitation is the right of children to be protected from excessive factory work; and just as child labor laws had to be fought out in court, so will the rights of animals (paragraph 82). Newkirk uses another appeal to consistency that plays into this historical analogy. Citing the case of the slave Jonathan Strong, emancipated in England long before the law allowed a judge to free slaves (paragraph 71), Newkirk shows that when fundamental rights are recognized and supportive action is taken, these rights are gradually accepted—and laws are changed—for the greater good of all. Taking an analogy this far is obviously risky, but Newkirk must be given credit for having thought hers out carefully.

Toward the end of the discussion, Hitt asks the panelists to discuss the long-term consequences of animal rights. Newkirk begins the list with no breeding, no pet stores, and eventually no pets at all but rather humans and animals living separately in a symbiotic relationship (paragraph 111); Francione continues with a longer list: no animals used for food, no hunting, no experimenting, no zoos, and no using animals for entertainment such as in circuses (paragraphs 112, 114, 116). In addition, legislation would ensure animals the right to life, liberty, and the pursuit of happiness, and the right to kill one another or exist in whatever way is natural to their species. You may wish to have your students discuss the negative aspects of these consequences and add negative and positive consequences of their own.

4. Choose one or two specific clashes of opinion. Which arguer is more persuasive in each?

Possibly the most spirited clash is that between Caplan and Francione over the relative value of a human baby and a pig. Caplan would readily save a *healthy* child's life by giving it the heart of a healthy pig; however, he places a child born without most of its brain alongside the pig—below the threshold of a right to life (paragraph 89). In contrast, Francione does not defend the anencephalic but instead the pig, which he claims is the subject of a meaningful life (paragraph 90); he believes that a pig can "wish to have life, liberty, and the pursuit of happiness and the anencephalic baby cannot" and therefore the pig has a right to life that the baby does not. While Francione always sides with the creature he believes has a right to life, Caplan extends the argument to responsibility to society—human society: because the anencephalic child's parents are able to care for the child and because neither the pig's parents nor the child's parents care about the pig, the anencephalic should be saved over the pig.

C. S. LEWIS

Vivisection

Although Lewis is set apart from the *Harper's* panelists both culturally and intellectually, his attack on vivisection is as relevant as, and more rationally argued than, that of either Ingrid Newkirk or Gary Francione. Having been both a skeptic and a Christian in his adult life and an intellectual throughout, Lewis has the advantage of having thought out arguments from two widely differing points of view; his perspective adds credibility to his own ideas while providing an excellent contrast to the contemporary animal rights arguments.

Lewis's essay is a good example of a counterargument against a position so widely held that it is largely unquestioned. The skill with which Lewis pins down an opposing view and shows its weaknesses can serve as a model if you want your students to practice writing rebuttal arguments. Also, the essay has the virtue of sending students up the wall. Most students are what Lewis calls "naturalistic" defenders of vivisection, but few would be capable of defending their position against Lewis's argument. Out of such a vexatious situation you might get good journal entries or impromptu writings that students might later expand into essays.

QUESTIONS

1. How does Lewis establish facts on which to build his argument?

Like Brownmiller, Lewis is writing to an unknown audience and therefore cannot begin with facts beyond dispute, so he encourages his audience to accept particular facts necessary to make his argument. For example, he first establishes the fact that "pain is an evil" (paragraph 2), based on the assumption that if it were not, there would be no reason to raise the issue of vivisection at all; implied by this fact is another that he assumes we will accept, that vivisection causes pain. From this point on, Lewis does not establish facts to further his own argument but rather considers the "facts" that underlie various cases *for* vivisection.

Within the Christian argument for vivisection, Lewis identifies the "fact" that animals have no soul or moral sense. Next, Lewis proposes another "fact" accepted by Christian defenders of vivisection, that God made humans distinct from and superior to animals. In contrast, naturalists accept the "fact" that there is no separation of animals and humans, neither by possession of a soul nor by authoritarian position. These "facts" provide the basis of Lewis's refutation of the justifications for vivisection.

2. Map out Lewis's major arguments.

The Christian argument against vivsection can be mapped in two ways. The first looks something like this:

Conclusion:
"Soullessness" is an argument against vivisection
and proves that the practice of vivisection
is an unjustifiable evil.

↑

Lewis's rule:
Pain is only justified if a victim benefits
physically or morally or is compensated in
this life or another for that pain.

↑

Facts:
Animals have no souls.
Creatures with no souls cannot benefit morally by, nor be
compensated physically, for experiencing pain.
Vivisection causes pain and death.
Pain is evil.

And the second map is as follows:

```
┌─────────────────────────────────────────────┐
│                 Conclusion:                   │
│       The superiority of humans over          │
│  animals is an argument against vivisection   │
│       and proves that the practice of         │
│      vivisection is an unjustifiable evil.    │
└─────────────────────────────────────────────┘
                      ↑
┌─────────────────────────────────────────────┐
│                Lewis's rule:                  │
│  Creatures in positions of authority do not   │
│   have the right to torture those beneath     │
│                    them.                      │
└─────────────────────────────────────────────┘
                      ↑
┌─────────────────────────────────────────────┐
│                   Facts:                      │
│          Humans are superior to animals.      │
│        Vivisection causes pain and death.     │
│                 Pain is evil.                 │
└─────────────────────────────────────────────┘
```

The naturalistic argument looks something like this:

```
┌─────────────────────────────────────────────┐
│                 Conclusion:                   │
│     The sameness of humans and animals is     │
│   an argument against vivisection and proves  │
│        that the practice of vivisection       │
│          is an unjustifiable evil.            │
└─────────────────────────────────────────────┘
                      ↑
┌─────────────────────────────────────────────┐
│                Lewis's rule:                  │
│         Living creatures should not           │
│    torture or inflict pain on their own kind. │
└─────────────────────────────────────────────┘
                      ↑
┌─────────────────────────────────────────────┐
│                   Facts:                      │
│        Human beings and animals are living    │
│           creatures of the same kind.         │
│        Vivisection causes pain and death.     │
│                 Pain is evil.                 │
└─────────────────────────────────────────────┘
```

3.   What advantage does Lewis create for himself in paragraph 3? Is it an unfair advantage?

In this paragraph, Lewis introduces a rule that, if accepted, almost ensures him a victory in the argument: "On the man whom we find inflicting pain rests the burden of showing why an act which in itself would be simply bad is, in those particular circumstances, good." This rule shifts the burden of proof entirely to the vivisector. Given the enormous obstacles to developing a proof that the animal's pain is justifiable, Lewis has essentially won the argument the moment the reader accepts the rule.

But is the rule justifiable? Is it logically necessary that the vivisector should carry the burden of proof? Lewis's position here is not unassailable. Inaction as well as action can cause pain and evil. The pilot who fails to check the fuel gauge before taking a passenger up in an airplane is hardly less culpable than the pilot who decides to practice a risky maneuver without the passenger's consent. The researcher who decides not to test a promising surgical procedure on a chimpanzee may, by the omission, be inflicting suffering on thousands of people. Why *must* the burden of proof fall on the vivisector? An equally strong argument could be made that the burden falls on anyone who wants to remove a resource useful in the advance of medical technology.

4.   Discuss Lewis's use of appeals to consistency and authority.

Given the shifting of the burden of proof, it isn't surprising that Lewis uses the appeal to consistency destructively: that is, he shows inconsistencies lurking beneath his opponents' rules. When opposing the Christian argument for the superiority of humanity, Lewis claims that no one would concede that angels, in their position above mortals, have the right to torture human beings; to be logically consistent, then, we have no right to torture those beneath us. This aspect of his argument is strengthened when applied to the naturalist position. If we *do* have the right to torture animals, and an animal is essentially "one of us," what keeps us from torturing our own species (paragraph 8)? If we act consistently, horrendous consequences may follow, as his examples of Dachau and Hiroshima prove (paragraph 10). In addition, Lewis appeals to consistency by imploring us to uphold the ethical values of the past; the "victory" of vivisection, he claims, "marks a great advance in the triumph of ruthless, non-moral utilitarianism over the old world of ethical law" (paragraph 10).

Lewis uses authority not to take his argument in a new direction but to strengthen his other appeals. Hearking back to Lewis Carroll, then to Samuel Johnson, and finally to Shakespeare, Lewis demonstrates the consistency as well as the authority of the fight against vivisection.

5.   Throughout the essay, Lewis discounts emotional appeals. Is he correct in doing so? Why or why not?

In making his case against vivisection, Lewis largely depends on proving that proponents of it are irrational sentimentalists, though he admits from the first paragraph that both sides are guilty of triggering our sympathy, either for defenseless animals or children. He is also correct in stating that "neither appeal

proves anything" (paragraph1). Where Lewis may be incorrect is in assuming
that if vivisection is proven wrong in theory, we will then conform our emotions
to the established truth. Most of us will have to agree with Twain that our opinions are rarely formed by rational thinking ("We all do no end of feeling, and we
mistake it for thinking," page 167, paragraph17), particularly in highly emotional situations. Thus, all of Lewis's logical arguments do little good *without*
an effective appeal to emotion.

PART III

Professional & Academic
Applications

CHAPTER 8

Proposals

Purpose

I say in the first paragraph of this chapter that proposals "involve the writer in all the difficulties (and opportunities) mentioned in Chapters 6 and 7." The claim is true enough: proposals often involve arguments about facts and rules, and my own preference would therefore be to teach Chapters 6 and 7 before Chapter 8. But as a practical matter Chapter 8 is easier for students to deal with than the two that come before it, and it is written in a way that allows it to stand alone. Instructors who feel that Chapters 6 and 7 require too much time and attention in a single-term course could, therefore, skip directly to this chapter.

The purpose of the chapter is to help students understand and practice writing that is centered on problems and solutions. Students who anticipate careers in science, industry, or government will appreciate the pragmatic cast of this chapter. Students whose understanding of an English class is that it should involve only papers of the "The sun rose red as the smell of bacon wafted into my eager nostrils" type may be somewhat distressed to find themselves dealing with questions of feasibility and cost. I would argue, however, that these are the students who may benefit most from the discipline of proposal writing, which forces them to see the elegance of a way of thinking alien to their own.

Overview

The *chapter proper* divides into six parts, arranged to ease students gradually into the complexities of proposal writing:

1. A discussion of the advice column, a simple form of problem-centered writing
2. A discussion of problem/solution writing in science, where problems and solutions can be neatly defined and tested
3. A discussion of proposals on public affairs (e.g., letters to the editor), where problems and solutions are more difficult to define and test
4. A consideration of why proposals fail

157

5. A discussion of ways to refute proposals
6. Advice on writing proposals

Parts 1, 2, 3, and 5 are illustrated with short professional examples that could serve as models for student essays.

The *assignments* include a summary of a proposal (designed to reveal its essential parts), a summary with analysis, a refutation of a proposal, a proposal on a topic of current public interest, and a proposal involving improvement of college life.

The *readings* show the wide range of purposes that the logic of proposals can serve. They include

"*Miranda* v. *Arizona*," the Supreme Court decision that resulted in the familiar Miranda warning ("You have the right to remain silent . . ."). Though the context is law, the reading includes a straightforward, well-articulated proposal by Chief Justice Warren and a tightly reasoned refutation by Justice White.

George Orwell's "Politics and the English Language," an essay that is sometimes read simply as a defense of clear writing and speaking but is better understood as a proposal for a reformation of our linguistic habits.

Martin Luther King, Jr.'s "Letter from Birmingham Jail," an essay that accomplishes many other things while advancing the proposal that Birmingham's advocates of civil rights turn to nonviolent direct action as a solution to their grievances.

Theodore White's "Direct Elections: An Invitation to National Chaos," a refutation of a popular proposal to reform our political system.

Lewis Thomas's "How to Fix the Premedical Curriculum," a proposal with a tone that hovers between the serious and the ironic in a way that should provoke much discussion.

The King and Orwell essays are, of course, classics. My experience is that looking at them as proposals returns some of the glow they may have lost from long familiarity. It also reveals a drama that students might otherwise miss: these people are writing because they have thorny problems to solve, and the solutions they propose are both fascinating and open to challenge.

The Chapter Step-by-Step

The Advice Column (pages 262 to 266)

We start with Miss Manners partly because some students are put off by the proposal's association with things technical or commercial. Dealing with civilized behavior rather than civil engineering gives such students a "softer" entry and perhaps a sense of relief: not all proposals deal with metric measurements and cost/benefit ratios. The advice column also has the advantage of focusing students' attention on the essential elements of every proposal: a problem and a solution.

In the process of reading this section, students will learn that a "problem" implies a *goal* as well as *constraints* that make the achievement of that goal difficult. They learn that a solution generally involves some *reframing* of the problem to make it approachable. And, of course, there is much emphasis on the need to propose a solution that truly matches the problem. The aim of Exercises 1–3 is to give students some practice in dealing with goals, constraints, and reframings.

Exercise 1: Responding as Miss Manners (pages 265–266).   This is a good exercise to have students do in class or as homework and then compare results. Because the material is not particularly grave, you might even consider using this exercise (or one of the next two) as the basis for a contest. Have groups of about four students read each other's answers and decide which is best, then bring the groups together to have the "winners" read aloud, allowing the whole class to decide which answer is best.

Miss Manners's own answer delicately reframes (or reidentifies) the problem as being the attitude of the "Gentle Reader" rather than the attitude of the people with whom he or she deals:

> Gentle Reader:
>
> Nor would these people be embarrassed to put price tags on their goods or send out bills for their services. All you have to say is, "What is your budget for speakers?" or "Why, I'd love to; do you know my fee?" Remember that selling one's time is not necessarily a shameful transaction, depending on what one spends that time performing.

Exercise 2: Writing to Miss Manners (page 266).   Students who use their heads should gather that the "Gentle Reader" to whom Miss Manners is responding in this letter must have characterized herself as an *x* in a *y* world (the parallel of a "cucumber sandwich eater in a doughnut world"), and if they look at Martin's last sentence they will realize that the *x* must be "tea drinker." This should lead naturally to the antithesis "coffee drinker" for *y*. So what is this tea drinker's problem? Clearly she would like to have tea when everyone wants coffee (a goal), and clearly she also wants to "stress" her "willingness to work with other people" (another goal). A constraint clearly implied in Miss Manners's answer is that "Gentle Reader" is a woman in a setting dominated by men. The principle that the solution should help guide the problem closely should lead students in reconstructing a letter like the following:

> Dear Miss Manners:
>
> I am a tea drinker in a coffee world. Ordinarily, this poses no problem, but on occasion I must attend meetings where coffee and doughnuts— alas, no tea—are served. Although I am generally outspoken, I have not yet confronted my colleagues with my dilemma, mainly because I am the only woman in the group. Should I speak up and further distinguish or possibly alienate myself from the group?

Exercise 3: Writing to and Responding as Miss Manners (page 266).   This is clearly the most important exercise of the three, and if you are in a hurry, you could go directly to it. When it comes time to evaluate the result, you'll want to stress three things:

1. The question to Miss Manners should make clear the goal and the constraints that create an interesting problem.
2. The reply to the letter should match the problem presented and will probably involve some reframing of the problem.
3. Both letters need to have a compact, lively style.

The Problem/Solution Essay in Science (pages 266–269)

This section may give some of your fledgling scientists a welcome chance to star in an English class. Although the passage from Dethier (pronounced de-TEER) is written in a style that is both clear and amusing to nonscientists, some of the reasoning may be more obvious to those who enjoyed their biology classes than to those who dreaded them.

The marginal question in the middle of page 267 should help students see one of the keys to making writing on a difficult or specialized topic accessible to the general public: the paragraph beside which the question appears is full of homely metaphors. Scientific data are explained in terms of familiar objects—custard pies, landing gears, vacuum cleaners. Knowing that some of his readers may be put off and bewildered by laboratory language, Dethier works hard to keep them in contact with the world they know.

The questions at the top of page 268 may allow one of your scientists to explain to the rest of the class what a "control" is and how the control functions here. *The American Heritage Dictionary* defines a *control* as "a standard of comparison for checking or verifying the results of an experiment." The control on an experiment will ideally eliminate from consideration all extraneous factors that could give a false result. In this case, the experimenter wants to insure that when the fly's proboscis is extended, it is because of taste and taste alone. Therefore, he has to eliminate the possibility that it is merely the moisture in the sugar solution that is triggering the proboscis extension. By slaking the fly's thirst before exposing it to the sugar water, he "checks" the result of his experiment in advance, ensuring that the fly's response indicates not thirst but gustatory delight.

In the brief section on evaluating the quality of a proposed experiment, the question of establishing adequate controls is crucial. In the case of the fly experiment, the experimenter has solved the difficulty of distinguishing between reactions triggered by taste and reactions triggered by thirst. But he has left unsolved another difficulty inherent in the problem: that of distinguishing between reactions triggered by taste and reactions triggered by smell. He has established a control for thirst but not a control for olfaction.

Exercise 4: Proposing an Experiment (page 269).   The apparent glitch in the fly experiment gives students an opportunity to try their ingenuity at proposing solutions to a relatively simple scientific problem: how to establish a control for smell. One solution would be to build a thin landing platform very close to the surface of the water and cut a hole in the platform just a bit too small for the fly to be lowered through without its legs touching the platform's surface.

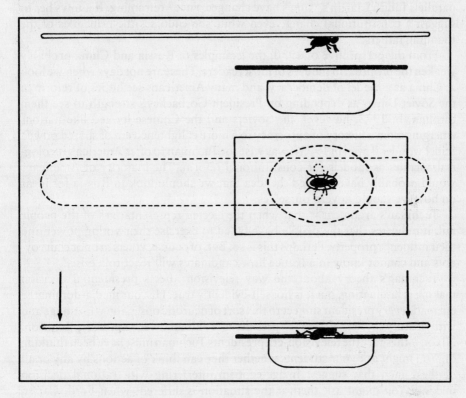

Lowered firmly onto the platform directly over the hole, the fly would be within smelling range and would have its legs in contact with a sugar-free surface. If the fly doesn't lower its proboscis in these circumstances, we can conclude that taste, not smell, accounts for the unfurling of the proboscis.

Your students may come up with other solutions, or they may be totally stumped, in which case you can propose this one. Either way, thinking about the experiment will give them some sense of the scientist's business of matching solutions to problems.

Proposals to the Public: A Letter to the Editor (pages 269–273)

This section consists almost entirely of a single example with questions and analysis. If you can get your students engaged in a discussion of the strengths and weaknesses of Tuchman's proposal, they will learn a good deal about the way proposals on matters of public policy are debated.

The questions in the margin are open to more than one answer and some may stir some debate. Here are some observations on them that may help you prepare for class:

Tuchman's mention of the Constitution is a reframing of the problem that parallels Judith Martin's "times have changed since" reframing. It allows her to suggest a constitutional change even while she endorses the principles of the founding fathers.

From the perspective of 1990, the examples of Russia and China probably weaken the proposal in the eyes of most readers. These are not days when we look at China as a model of democracy, and many Americans see hopes of reform in the Soviet Union as depending on President Gorbachev's strength to see them through. In 1973, however, the Soviets and the Chinese looked like nations emerging from a history of autocracy to a more enlightened era of shared power. Still, I wonder if even in 1973 it was wise for Tuchman to offer America's ideological enemies as models for constitutional reform. The majority of Americans would probably have resisted the idea that we should look to Russia for ideas on how we should govern ourselves.

Tuchman's argument is that when the elected representatives of the people fail, it indicates that the people have failed to exercise their voting power and their influence properly. Perhaps this is so. But, of course, voters are not clairvoyants and cannot know in advance how candidates will react to a crisis.

Tuchman's theory about the way television affects presidential decision making is fascinating, but it is not self-evidently true. Has our media-dominated era made *every* president subject to this sort of neurotic obsession with image and with history's "list of 'great' presidents"? Eisenhower, Kennedy, Johnson, Nixon—these are the television-era presidents Tuchman must have been thinking of. You might ask your students whether they can think of actions by any or all of these men that suggest image-egotism interfering with rational decision making. You might ask them if the situation is different when Ford, Carter, Reagan, and Bush are added to the picture.

Tuchman's notion that unchecked power creates personality problems in the president is controversial, of course. Students should neither dismiss it nor accept it lightly. We Americans do tend to think of power and solitude as somehow inevitably linked: "It's lonely at the top," we say; or, in President Truman's words, "The buck stops here." Perhaps our tendency to link power and isolation has some dangers attached to it.

Tuchman's discussion of feasibility may not convince everyone, but it deserves high marks for addressing precisely the question that people will find troubling: the ability to take quick, decisive actions under pressure.

Tuchman's final sentence seems to do unnecessary damage to her proposal. It seems to be a refutation of an objection to her scheme, but she doesn't take the objection seriously enough to mount a proper argument, and her tone may offend some readers because it seems an insult to millions of Americans who (as she seems to allow) feel the craving for a strong father-figure. It isn't hard to understand Tuchman's impatience with this father-figure business, and some readers may strongly share it and applaud her harsh dismissal, but others may detect intellectual arrogance in the last line.

Why Proposals Fail (pages 273–276)

Though I believe that this section is essentially self-explanatory and so won't comment on it at length, I do want to point to the list of four predictable weaknesses in proposals. Such a list can be valuable to you as a basis for commenting on student papers and valuable to your students as a way of evaluating their own work.

Refuting a Proposal (pages 276–279)

This section is essentially a study of George Will's refutation of President Reagan's school-prayer proposal. It reinforces the point made in the prior section: a proposal can succeed only if the reader accepts the goal, agrees that the problem presented is real and pressing, and sees the solution as both feasible and free of unwanted consequences that are as serious as the problem itself. Will shares the President's goal, disagrees with his identification of the problem, and questions the proposal's feasibility and consequences. Discussion of the questions in the margin should help students see what Will is up to, both logically and rhetorically. Again, there may be several answers to the questions, and again I'll give some notes that may be useful in class. In leading a discussion of the essay, one of my goals would be to help students find the balance between acceptance and resistance that makes critical reading possible.

Will's opening paragraph is an odd one. It seems to say at least two things: (1) I, George Will, share the conviction that some form of religion is necessary to a good life; and (2) I am not going to speak as a partisan of Christianity. Both of these statements help Will find common ground with his audience; they suggest that Will's goal is encouraging religion generally, on grounds that have more to do with ethics than with mysticism. Probably most Americans—clearly not all—will accept this as a goal. The quotation from the English ethicist has an odd ring to it, however. The proviso at the end ("or some substitute for it") has the sound of a backhand snub of traditional Christianity, a suggestion that Christian belief might be replaced by a more rational substitute. Will may like the double take the quotation creates, but he does not necessarily intend to incorporate the snub.

His second paragraph reveals a different framing of the problem of school prayer. Reagan seemed to see the problem as one involving the individual's right to pray. Will sees the problem as one having to do not with individual activity but with organized activity in schools where attendance is compulsory.

The sources Will chooses to quote (after the unnamed English ethicist) are ones whose sympathy with religion cannot be questioned: the Southern Baptist Convention and Senator Danforth, who is an Episcopal priest. By telling the reader that these sources oppose prayer in the schools, Will shows that opposition to school prayer is not the same as opposition to religion.

The statement that "a lowest-common-denominator prayer would offend all devout persons" needs to be examined closely by the reader—and perhaps challenged. Will supports it by quoting Danforth's eloquent statement, but one wonders if Danforth's sensibilities really represent those of "all devout persons." It could be argued that devout members of many Protestant churches with uncomplicated liturgies could live more comfortably with a bland classroom prayer than with no prayer at all.

Will's dismal picture of school prayer "perfunctorily rendered by children who have just tumbled in from a bus or playground" is at least somewhat a red herring. Are these same children that much more alert, reverent, and focused at 9:30 on a Sunday morning? The question raised by Will's scenario is not whether children should be led in organized prayer at school but whether they are capable of prayer at all.

Most students will probably agree with Will's view of the way peer pressure could turn "voluntary" prayer into an activity few students would dare resist. Will's picture of children is consistent throughout the essay: he does not see them as rational creatures who can make up their own minds—hence the analogy that suggests that leaving them "free" to pray really amounts to allowing other people to force them to pray, just as leaving nineteenth-century children "free" to work in the coal mines really meant leaving them open to exploitative contracts between parents and mine owners. Is the analogy persuasive? Some students will surely resist it because the labor in the coal mines was clearly contrary to the interests of children, but prayer in school is intended to help them.

When, in his last paragraph, Will inserts "to say no more" into his first sentence, he seems to imply that he *could* say that it is hypocritical for people who don't attend church to favor prayer in public schools. But it may not be illogical or hypocritical for people who have no strongly felt religion themselves to wish that children growing up around them be exposed to religion. They may feel that exposure to religion is important in the same way that exposure to algebra is important, for example. Some students will turn out to have a talent for the subject and will use it in later life; some will not. Such a lukewarm attitude might offend (or confound) both religious people and committed atheists, but it is not illogical. Indeed, it sounds rather like the attitude of the English ethicist Will quotes in his opening paragraph.

Advice on Writing Proposals (pages 279–280)

The simple chart on page 279 reinforces the main points of the chapter: that the proposal comprises the statement of a goal, the identification and discussion of a problem, and the presentation of a solution; that these parts create a path along which the writer must persuasively lead the reader; and that an interruption anywhere along the path can lead to a rejection of the proposal.

This chart serves as the principal basis for peer review: the writer needs to know whether the reader is being carried along the path. Additional peer-review questions are drawn from Chapter 6 and deal with the essay's persuasiveness.

The Assignments

Assignment 1: A Summary of a Proposal.   This assignment is an excellent warm-up to the assignments that follow and a good workout for students' skill in reading comprehension. You will find summaries of the Warren, King, Orwell, and Thomas proposals in the discussion of this chapter's readings.

Assignment 2: A Summary and Analysis of a Proposal. This assignment could be piggybacked with Assignment 1. That is, you could ask students to hand in a straight summary first, check its adequacy, and then have them undertake the more complete analysis.

Assignment 3: A Refutation of a Proposal. Notice that this assignment incorporates the sort of writing and thinking required in Assignment 1. I tell my students that when they summarize their opponent's proposal, they must do it justice and give it a clear form: goal, problem, and solution. If they cannot identify these parts in the argument they choose to refute, they are not dealing with it as a proposal—perhaps because it isn't a proposal.

Assignment 4: A Proposal Suitable for Publication. It is not strictly necessary, of course, to have students locate a particular newspaper or magazine in which they hope to publish, but the suggestion is a useful feature of this assignment because it forces students to see their work in a public and adult context and because it forces them to think more concretely than they might about an audience other than their instructor.

Assignment 5: A Competitive Proposal. This assignment has two considerable advantages. First, it allows for a wide range of student responses (since students are free to choose which category to compete in). Second, it puts them in a position of doing some footwork and research in their immediate environment. If you assign it, I would urge you to announce that you will follow the contest's ground rules, including the criteria for evaluation, the insistence that expenses be justified, and the strict four-page limit.

Sample papers and additional assignments are available in the package of supplementary material that accompanies the main text.

End-of-Chapter Readings

CHIEF JUSTICE WARREN AND JUSTICE WHITE

Miranda *v.* Arizona

The Miranda rule has become widely known, due largely to our oversupply of television detectives, but few students will have given much thought to its origin or effect. Before sending them off to read this decision, then, consider using the "believing/doubting" game as a class activity in order to generate a list of reasons for and against the practice of the rule. You might begin by introducing them to Mr. Ernesto Miranda, convicted by the state of Arizona on charges of kidnaping and rape. Miranda was identified in a line-up and then questioned; his written confession was obtained without his being told that he had a right to remain silent and to be represented by an attorney, and this confession was primary evidence used to obtain his conviction. Knowing these facts, students might be able to list a number of reasons that the confession should be treated as inadmissible evidence and a number of reasons that it should be admitted.

Chief Justice Warren had been concerned for some time about the methods police were using to obtain confessions and had secured the right to an attorney in the previous *Escobedo* v. *Illinois* case (1964). When Miranda's case reached the Supreme Court, the justices overturned the Arizona conviction; the 5–4 ruling in *Miranda* v. *Arizona* provided Warren an opportunity to reinforce further the privileges of the Fifth Amendment. To date, the Miranda rule continues to be debated and has been modified somewhat to make allowances for videotaping of defendant interrogations and to give police officers more leeway in their method of presenting the rights to the accused.

QUESTIONS

1.   What is Warren's goal, and is it a goal that White shares?

Stated in dry, technical language, Warren's goal is to protect the "privilege against self-incrimination" guaranteed to all Americans by the Fifth Amendment to the Constitution. Your students may detect an overtone of a more general goal that was one of Warren's trademarks on the Court: the desire to give the poor, the ignorant, and the weak-minded an equal opportunity for justice in American courts.

White is legally obliged to share the goal of protecting the Fifth Amendment privilege, and it is difficult to believe that he or the other members of the Court would disagree in principle with the goal of giving the disadvantaged an equal opportunity for justice. If there is any conflict in goals, it is a matter of how they should be balanced. White seems to place more emphasis than Warren on the goal of protecting the rights of the victims of crime (paragraph 35).

2.   What is the problem Warren presents, and does he convince us that it needs solving?

Warren states the problem indirectly in the first several paragraphs, but gives his most thorough definition of it in paragraph 16: without proper safeguards, defendants are often compelled to incriminate themselves by the coercive nature of police interrogation. Because Warren describes the problem so thoroughly in his opening paragraphs, students will probably recognize its seriousness and be convinced that it deserves attention by the time they reach his statement of it.

Several elements of Warren's strategy are worth commenting on. First, Warren recognizes that establishing the problem requires its own argument backed by substantial proof; he opens by relating the case at hand to a series of cases in which defendants had confessed to crimes without being informed of their Fifth Amendment rights. To add weight to the issue, he then attempts to prove that not only were the accused denied their rights but the admissions were made after police either physically or psychologically compelled them to confess. Basing this argument on actual police manuals—since no one can know what went on in the private interrogation sessions—Warren creates an image of the interrogation in which the police become the bad guys, well schooled in how to trick and intimidate the accused. The use of police manuals seems a logical way to gain insight into what happens in the interrogations, but one gathers that Warren has combed these manuals for passages that suit his rhetorical purpose of giving the problem presence and dramatic force.

3. Does Warren's solution solve the problem?

As Warren has defined the problem, most people would at first agree that his solution is satisfactory. If defendants are not aware of their rights, they should be made aware, and paragraphs 18–23 clearly state how. Allowing defendants to stop an interrogation at any point and to have an attorney present during interrogation seems to provide complete protection against police coercion.

However, students may not agree that the solution is adequate after they read White's argument. If interrogating police have such psychological power over defendants, then perhaps coercion is being applied from the first moment of interrogation. If this is the case, then defendants who are informed of their rights may be compelled to waive them (or possibly compelled to take the Fifth though they want to confess). White suggests that the reading of rights carries little weight given Warren's description of police interrogation; he also believes, however, that defendants are rarely the wimps Warren makes them out to be (paragraph 21).

4. How does White attack Warren's solution?

White first attacks the logic of Warren's solution and then weighs the consequences. While Warren had made a fairly strong case for using police manuals as proof of what goes on during interrogations, White discounts his proof completely, suggesting that Warren should have relied on the transcripts of the questioning instead (paragraph 27). Even though we may find transcripts as misleading as the manuals, we should agree that the mere fact that the manuals give the officers strategic advice is no proof that they take it.

White then adds weight to his argument through concession; he will grant that the nature of police questioning may be coercive, but Warren's argument remains illogical, for reasons mentioned in the answer to Question 3 (paragraphs 28–30). In addition to the difficulty of sorting the compelled statements of the defendant from the voluntary ones is the problem created by the presence of an attorney. If we believe that anything a defendant says without the presence of an attorney is the product of the will of the police, then surely anything said in an attorney's presence is prompted not by the defendant's will but by his attorney's (paragraph 30).

5. What are the negative consequences White describes and do they outweigh the strengths of the proposal?

White's most forceful attack on Warren's proposal comes from his statement of the unacceptable consequences he believes will flow from it. All of these consequences are based on the assumption that the practical effect of the Miranda rule is to eliminate *any* evidence that the accused might offer (paragraph 33). These consequences are spelled out, with some overlap, from paragraph 32 to the end of the opinion. The principal one is that law enforcement will lose what has here-tofore been one of its most convincing forms of evidence, making the jobs of prosecutors far more difficult. This difficulty will slow the pace of prosecution, since it will take longer to develop the evidence in criminal cases, and so court dockets will be even more crowded. And, of course, more perpetrators will go free. As a result, some law-abiding citizens will realize that they are not well protected and may turn to vigilantism—"violent self-help with guns, knives and the help of their neighbors similarly inclined" (paragraph 39). And criminals themselves, as White ingeniously argues, will be harmed by the loss of the oppor-tunity to confess and accept punishment.

White's argument that the consequences are unacceptable is generally offered in a very reasonable, unimpassioned, even bland way. You might point out the sentence at the end of paragraph 34 as an example of his tone: "Even if the new concept can be said to have advantages of some sort over the present law, they are far outweighed by its more likely undesirable impact on other very relevant and important interests." But his appeal is not entirely logical and factual. He presents his scenario of negative consequences with some rhetorical flair and ap-peal to emotions. Certainly the picture of the guns and knives coming out in the last sentence is intended to induce alarm.

GEORGE ORWELL
Politics and the English Language

Students may be put off by this essay because much of what Orwell says about political language in 1946 has become outdated: the clichés he identifies are not the clichés we are familiar with today, and his political allusions will mean little to students whose parents were just being born during the era he describes. Ideally, however, students will have become well acquainted with Orwell before you teach this essay, and they should be willing to bear with the voice they know from "Shooting an Elephant" and "Reflections on Gandhi." Consistent with the previous essays, this one demonstrates how Orwell's eye for politics is always directed to larger issues—to what is basic in human nature and to our fight for freedom and clarity of thought. In "Politics," the issue is language and how we allow it to imprison our minds, which in turn directly affects our personal and political actions. Chapter 8 provides you with a clear-cut way into the essay: dis-cussing it as a proposal. After students are able to analyze the problem and the proposed solution, they will benefit from a discussion of Orwell's own language and his political thinking.

QUESTIONS

1. Outline and discuss the elements of a proposal in "Politics."

Orwell states at the outset that "to think clearly is a necessary first step to-wards political regeneration" (paragraph 2), then devotes the rest of the essay to proving how our thoughts are generally muddled by language. His ultimate goal, then, is political regeneration. But clarity of thought is for him so essential to political regeneration that clearing our heads and regenerating our politics become fused as if they were a single goal.

One problem that stands between us and the goal, Orwell believes, is that we allow "the slovenliness of our language" to draw us into "foolish thoughts" (paragraph 2). Students who read the essay carelessly will assume that Orwell is considering language as a form of communication and is saying that our *discussions* of political ideas are somehow damaged by our failure to speak "good English." But this is not his main point. He is far more concerned about the way we talk to ourselves than about the way we talk to others: he believes that we strangle and mutilate our own thoughts by putting them quickly and automatically into imprecise phrases.

His solution is a reform of our linguistic habits. The reform program has several facets. It includes a simple delaying tactic: "Probably it is better to put off using words as long as possible and get one's meaning as clear as one can through pictures or sensations" (paragraph 19). It includes four questions to ask during the delay: "What am I trying to say? What words will express it? What image or idiom will make it clearer? Is this image fresh enough to have an effect?" (paragraph 12). And it includes the famous list of six rules found in paragraph 19.

2. Although this essay is ultimately a proposal, it also encapsulates Orwell's political ideal. What is this ideal?

To answer this question well, students will have to withdraw their attention from the "catalogue of swindles and perversions" with which Orwell begins the essay and focus instead on paragraphs 12 through 20. If they look closely at this section, they will see an ideal of mental freedom emerging, freedom of the sort that Winston Smith gains and loses in *1984*. It is a central Orwellian theme: "Shooting an Elephant" is partly about Orwell's struggle to stay independent of imperialist mentality; "Marrakech Ghetto" is about his discovery that he cannot be entirely free of it. For Orwell, freedom always means first the freedom to think, and the freedom to think is earned by hard labor against the prevailing political (or here, linguistic) grain. Orwell begins paragraph 17 with the observation that "if thought corrupts language, language can also corrupt thought." If your students don't see how language can be either a threat to freedom or a tool for freedom, they have missed Orwell's point entirely.

On the negative side, language as threat, I would be particularly sure that students notice these statements:

- "They will construct your sentences for you—even think your thoughts for you, to a certain extent—and at need they will perform the important service of partially concealing your meaning even from yourself" (paragraph 12). *They* in fact refers to "ready-made phrases," but when we take the sentence out of context we see how much it might refer to the makers of the Newspeak dictionary in *1984*.

- "When one watches some tired hack on the platform mechanically repeating the familiar phrases . . . one often has a curious feeling that one is not watching a live human being but some kind of dummy" (paragraph 13). And, as Orwell goes on to say, such a speaker "has gone some distance towards turning himself into a machine." The machine-man, Winston Smith with his will removed, is Orwell's constant symbol of unfreedom.

- "This invasion of one's mind by ready-made phrases . . . can only be prevented if one is constantly on guard against them, and every such phrase anesthetizes a portion of one's brain" (paragraph 17).

- "In prose, the worst thing one can do with words is to surrender to them" (paragraph 19). A seldom-noted gem of wisdom. Your students should especially note the political spin on the infinitive.

On the positive side, we have less to show (Orwell's habitual tendency to turn a subject rough side out), but there are these glimpses of the free person's use of language: the mention of the "fresh, vivid, home-made turn of speech" (paragraph 13) and the delineation of circumstances in which "one can choose—not simply *accept*—the phrases that will best cover the meaning" (paragraph 19). There are, of course, the rules listed in paragraph 19, but these are negatively stated. More positive and more important is the statement in paragraph 12: "A scrupulous writer, in every sentence that he writes, will ask himself at least four questions, thus: What am I trying to say? What words will express it? What image or idiom will make it clearer? Is this image fresh enough to have an effect?" Orwell consistently insists that freedom means the unrelenting exercise of judgment. To be free of the need to make judgments is to be a slave. *Scrupulous* is laden with meaning here. Orwell must primarily mean "very conscientious and exacting," but in so political a context he probably means "principled and responsible" as well.

3. Why does Orwell value images so highly, and where can you find examples of his effective use of them?

Orwell takes a surprisingly strong stand on the importance of images, discussed primarily in paragraph 19. Here Orwell urges the writer to do something very few composition teachers would recommend:

> Probably it is better to put off using words as long as possible and get one's meaning as clear as one can through pictures or sensations. Afterwards one can choose—not simply *accept*—the phrases that will best cover the meaning . . .

Orwell apparently believes that we can think wordlessly and that our wordless thoughts—our images—are more reliably ours than worded thoughts are. When your students realize how important Orwell believes images are to the process of thought, they will begin to understand why he makes such an issue of stale imagery throughout the essay. You might point out that he begins his criticism of the five bad examples by saying that they share a "staleness of imagery" (paragraph 4) and that his first praise of the passage from Ecclesiastes is that "the first sentence contains six vivid images" (paragraph 11). His comment on mixed metaphor is that "the writer is not seeing a mental image of the objects he is naming; in other words he is not really thinking" (paragraph 12). Notice that in the last paragraph of the essay, Orwell puts some political distance between himself and Stuart Chase, who comes "near to claiming that all abstract words are meaningless," but there appears to be little distance between the men's attitudes toward language. We think in pictures, Orwell seems to say, and we write by communicating these pictures.

Ask each of your students to come to class with a list of half a dozen examples of Orwell's images. Among my favorites are these:

- ". . . prose consists less and less of *words* chosen for the sake of their meaning, and more and more of *phrases* tacked together like the sections of a prefabricated hen-house" (paragraph 4).

- "It [modern writing] consists in gumming together long strips of words which have already been set in order by someone else" (paragraph 12).

- ". . . the writer knows more or less what he wants to say, but an accumulation of stale phrases chokes him like tea leaves blocking a sink" (paragraph 12).

- ". . . one often has a curious feeling that one is not watching a live human being but some kind of dummy: a feeling which suddenly becomes stronger at moments when the light catches the speaker's spectacles and turns them into blank discs which seem to have no eyes behind them" (paragraph 13).

- "A mass of Latin words falls upon the facts like soft snow, blurring the outlines and covering up all the details" (paragraph 16).

- ". . . one turns as it were instinctively to long words and exhausted idioms, like a cuttlefish squirting out ink" (paragraph 16).

- "Phrases like *a not unjustifiable assumption* . . . are a continuous temptation, a packet of aspirins always at one's elbow" (paragraph 17).

- ". . . his words, like cavalry horses answering the bugle, group themselves automatically into the familiar dreary pattern" (paragraph 17).

I look back at this list of images and am astonished by how Orwellian it is, how willing to embrace harshness and even pain, but not regimentation or mindlessness.

MARTIN LUTHER KING, JR.
Letter from Birmingham Jail

The American civil rights struggle of the late 1950s and early 1960s was one of the most dramatic attempts in history by a group defined by law and custom as outsiders to win full participation in a society. The brightest star in the civil rights movement's constellation was Martin Luther King, Jr. Your students will undoubtedly know something about King, but you might want to give them some background information before assigning this essay. King's civil rights activities began in 1955 when he was the pastor of a Baptist church in Montgomery,

Alabama. In that year Rosa Parks, a seventy-two-year-old black woman, made history by refusing to give up her seat on a bus to a white passenger. She was subsequently arrested for violating the city's segregation law, and black activists organized the Montgomery Improvement Association to boycott the city's transit system. King was chosen as leader of the group that, after a year, succeeded in desegregating the city's buses. Following that success, King formed the Southern Christian Leadership Conference, which championed the use of nonviolent resistance to effect desegregation. King quickly became a leader of international fame.

The events that led to "Letter from Birmingham Jail" began in the spring of 1963 with King's campaign to end segregation at Birmingham's lunch counters and in the city's hiring practices. Police responded by turning fire hoses and dogs on the demonstrators and by jailing King and hundreds of his supporters, including schoolchildren. While in jail King wrote an open letter specifically addressed to eight local clergymen who had issued a statement entreating blacks to oppose the demonstrations.

A few of your students may have seen television replays of King's most famous speeches, including his "I have a dream" speech. If so, they will know what an eloquent and powerful speaker he was. Fortunately, King's style does not depend solely on delivery. "Letter from Birmingham Jail" is an impassioned plea for justice, even if achieving that goal requires the violation of unjust laws. As King explains, "I submit that an individual who breaks a law that conscience tells him is unjust, and who willingly accepts the penalty of imprisonment in order to arouse the conscience of the community over its injustice, is in reality expressing the highest respect for law" (paragraph 20). That position should trigger strong responses, both positive and negative, from your students.

King's letter is more a justification than a proposal: that is, it looks backward to justify actions already taken (and, in this case, continuing) rather than to suggest a new course of action for the future. And, of course, it has a much broader purpose than most proposals and justifications: King knew he was writing a document with the potential to uplift the spirits of his coworkers in the civil rights cause and to win others to his side.

QUESTIONS

1. Summarize King's proposal (or justification) by explaining his goal, the problem he identifies, and his solution.

King states his goal in paragraphs 3 and 4 as the elimination of injustice—a goal difficult for anyone to reject. The particular injustice with which he is concerned is, of course, the unequal treatment of white and black citizens in Birmingham, noted briefly but forcefully in paragraph 6. How completely King's audience (narrow and broad) shared the goal of eliminating this particular injustice is unclear, but his letter seems to assume a readership at least sympathetic to it.

The problem he identifies is the white community's refusal to negotiate a surrender of its "privilege" of treating blacks as second-class citizens (see paragraphs 10–11). King sees this refusal in a broad historical perspective: "Lamentably, it is an historical fact that privileged groups seldom give up their privileges voluntarily" (paragraph 12). An aspect of this problem that he stresses in later paragraphs (23–24) is that white moderates have been "more devoted to 'order' than to justice" and so have not helped blacks overturn laws that are manifestly unjust.

The solution King proposes is "nonviolent direct action" or "civil disobedience": he and his followers will break unjust laws and will accept the consequences—including not only imprisonment but also abuse by the police—as a way of "laying our case before the conscience of the local and the national community" (paragraph 8). The campaign of civil disobedience, he says, is intended to create "a type of constructive, nonviolent tension which is necessary for growth" (paragraph 10). In effect, he hopes to bring the white community to the negotiating table by creating a level of tension that is intolerable, or (as he says in paragraph 24) by bringing "to the surface the hidden tension that is already alive."

2. Do you agree with King's statement that "one has a moral responsibility to disobey unjust laws" (paragraph 15)?

King defines an unjust law as one that is "out of harmony with the moral law," one that "degrades human personality," one that a "majority group compels a minority group to obey but does not make binding on itself," one "inflicted upon a minority that . . . had no part in enacting or devising [it]" or, in some instances, one that is "just on its face and unjust in its application" (paragraphs 16–19). If we accept that definition, few would argue that such a law should be obeyed. But a problem arises when we attempt to apply the guidelines to a specific law. To illustrate how difficult it is to agree on which laws are "out of harmony with the moral law," ask your students to assume, for example, that the United States has passed a constitutional amendment prohibiting all abortions. Then ask them to use King's definition of an unjust law to determine whether the antiabortion law should be violated. They will quickly realize that King does not formulate an objective test. In fact, some would say that his statement is in essence an assertion that we should obey the laws we like and ignore all others.

You might remind your students that King was an admirer of Gandhi and of Thoreau. In "Civil Disobedience" Thoreau asserts that when an unjust law exists, we should transgress it at once rather than obey it while we attempt to persuade the majority to alter it. Thoreau, however, makes a distinction between trivial and significant laws: "If the injustice is part of the necessary friction of the machine of government, let it go . . . but if it is of such a nature that it requires you to be the agent of injustice to another, then, I say, break the law." Thoreau undoubtedly realized that his reputation as an eccentric (that fellow who lives alone in the cabin he built on Walden Pond) might cause his critics to interpret his refusal to pay a poll tax as little more than evidence that he was a crank. He was therefore eager to explain that refusing to pay taxes used to finance the war against Mexico constitutes disobedience of a significant law. King does not distinguish between trivial and significant laws, probably because the laws he urged his followers to disobey were so obviously significant.

3.   How is King's training and experience as a preacher reflected in his writing style?

King was a fourth-generation Southern Baptist preacher. Like all good preachers, King is particularly adept at appealing to his audience by making abstract concepts concrete. We may be able to oppose the abstract notion of civil disobedience, but it is impossible to disapprove of the people King compares to the civil rights activists—the Hungarian freedom fighters and the Germans who aided Jews in Hitler's Germany (paragraph 22). In this essay King also displays his ability to create unforgettable images: "They have carved a tunnel of hope through the dark mountain of disappointment" (paragraph 43).

It is the sound of his sentences that sets his writing apart. The essay is written in language that is meant to be heard. Apparently King's legacy from his preacher father, grandfather, and great-grandfather included a remarkable ear for rolling cadences that stir the heart. I think the most amazing sentence in this amazing essay is the one in paragraph 14 that begins "But when you have seen . . ." The periodic sentence, which answers those who encourage blacks to wait for change, is 322 words long. It begins with a catalog of the abuses American blacks have suffered, and it concludes with the understatement "then you will understand why we find it difficult to wait." The 311-word catalog is organized into ten subordinate clauses. Some of those clauses are long and some short, but all open with the word *when*. The repetition of *when* ties the clauses together, creates the sonorous quality of the sentence, and contributes to the dramatic impact of the switch to *then* in the short independent clause that concludes the sentence. The length of the sentence underscores the length of time blacks had already waited—futilely, it seemed—for justice. You might want to read this one aloud to your class to demonstrate its power.

Another rhetorical device King uses effectively is the balanced sentence or sentences: "Shallow understanding from people of good will is more frustrating than absolute misunderstanding from people of ill will" (paragraph 23); "If I have said anything in this letter that overstates the truth and indicates an unreasonable impatience, I beg you to forgive me. If I have said anything that understates the truth and indicates my having a patience that allows me to settle for anything less than brotherhood, I beg God to forgive me" (paragraph 49). In his ability to present facts and ideas in clear, convincing, and attractive language, King is a rhetorician in the finest sense of the word.

4.   Who is King's audience, and how does his awareness of his audience affect what he has to say?

King's specific audience was eight white clergymen—Jewish, Catholic, and Protestant—who had issued a statement urging blacks not to support the demonstrations against segregation in Birmingham. Considerations of audience influence King's tone, the structure of his letter, and his choice of supporting examples.

His tone is consistently conciliatory. He begins by referring to the clergymen as "men of genuine good will" (paragraph 1); he tells them he is sure that each of them would want to go beyond "the superficial kind of social analysis that deals merely with effects and does not grapple with underlying causes" (paragraph 5); he emphasizes their points of agreement by stating "You are quite right in calling for negotiation" (paragraph 10); he addresses them as "my Christian and Jewish brothers" (paragraph 23); he praises each of them for taking "significant stands" on the issue of segregation (paragraph 33); he states that he does not believe they would have commended the police force for keeping order if they had observed "their ugly and inhumane treatment of Negroes here in the city jail" (paragraph 45); and he concludes with the hope that he will soon be able to meet each of them "not as an integrationist or a civil-rights leader but as a fellow clergyman and a Christian brother" (paragraph 50).

Although King wants to win the understanding and support of these religious leaders, he cannot in good conscience avoid scathing criticisms of white moderates and of the white church and its leadership. Since these clergymen are white moderate church leaders, he must have wondered how to write the truth without creating even more hostility. The simplicity of his solution is brilliant. When he refers to the clergymen he is addressing, he uses the pronoun *you*; when he criticizes moderates and church leaders, he uses the pronoun *they*. Thus he subtly encourages his audience to identify with the group of reasonable sincere people who will understand his position and not with an *ineffectual* church in danger of becoming "an irrelevant social club with no meaning for the twentieth century" (paragraph 42).

Considerations of audience also influence the structure of the essay in that it is organized to refute the criticisms these clergymen voiced in their statement opposing the demonstrations. King begins by rebutting the accusation that he and the other civil rights leaders are outsiders and then goes on to explain why demonstrations are essential, why blacks are unwilling to wait patiently for change, and why it is sometimes necessary to violate unjust laws. It is only after defending himself against their criticisms that he counters with his own attack against the white moderates and church leaders who "have remained silent behind the anesthetizing security of stained-glass windows" (paragraph 35).

Mindful that he is addressing Jews, Catholics, and Protestants, King carefully chooses examples that will appeal to all three groups. He uses the words of the Protestant theologians Reinhold Niebuhr and Paul Tillich (paragraphs 12 and 16), the Catholic saints Augustine and Thomas Aquinas (paragraphs 15 and 16), and the Jewish philosopher Martin Buber (paragraph 16) to support his argument that unjust laws should be opposed. He praises a Greek philosopher and both Old and New Testament figures for their courageous acts of civil disobedience (Socrates; Shadrach, Meshach, and Abednego; and the early Christian martyrs; paragraph 21). And in paragraph 31, he lists as extremists Jesus, the Old Testament prophet Amos, the New Testament figure Paul, Martin Luther, the Puritan minister John Bunyan, Abraham Lincoln, and Thomas Jefferson—just the sort of company these heterogeneous religious leaders would like to keep.

THEODORE H. WHITE

Direct Elections: An Invitation to National Chaos

White's brief argument opposing direct elections includes both a refutation of a proposal and a counterproposal. It has the advantage of addressing an issue that is fairly easily understood by anyone who has watched election-night coverage on one of our national television networks. Since White wrote "Direct Elections," the issue has quieted, though writers and politicians continue to question the role of the Electoral College.

QUESTIONS

1. What is the goal of the House's proposal, and how does it relate to White's own goals?

White implies in paragraph 4 that the House's goal was to allow Americans to choose a President in the most fair and responsible way. Although he does not say so directly, White implies throughout the essay that he shares this goal; his intent, then, is to prove that the present indirect state-by-state system is more fair and responsible. If we analyze the situation this way, there is no conflict in goals.

We could analyze the situation somewhat differently, saying that the House's goal is to make each vote equal to every other vote and that White's goal is to have a system that ensures that "the naked transaction in power" (paragraph 3) in a Presidential election occurs smoothly, without damage to the nation's political structure or confidence.

2. What is the problem that the bill before the House identifies, and what is the proposed solution?

Writing to an audience that he assumed would be familiar with the proposal before the House, White does not summarize it at length or explain its rationale. The headnote and common sense, however, will allow students to piece the problem together. The problem from the reformer's point of view is that the mechanics of our electoral system is too indirect. This indirectness has the practical effect of making some votes (those cast in hotly contested states, for instance) more important than others. And it could have the effect of keeping the will of the majority from being implemented: it is theoretically possible for one candidate to receive the majority of the popular vote and another to be elected.

The solution proposed is to do away with the old system that turns a national election into fifty separate state elections and that decides the Presidency by a vote of the electoral college. In place of that system, the proposal would implement a system that places all the votes into a single pool to determine the winner (paragraph 2).

3. How does White refute the proposal?

To refute the proposal, White evaluates the consequences; his point of attack is similar to Justice White's in his criticism of the *Miranda* ruling. Both Whites accuse their opponents of "metaphysics" or "high-minded theory" that will prove illogical and impractical in the face of reality.

The primary negative consequence is the counting of so many individual votes. While the present system has kept voting generally honest and fair, direct election would increase the potential for fraud. White cites several voting areas known for their manipulation of elections (paragraph 6) and contends that the Electoral College limited crooks in these places to influencing the vote of a particular state, thus diminishing the possibility that a whole national election could be stolen by fraud. Fraud would be encouraged by direct election because it would have a more widespread effect (paragraph 7), and the damage would be compounded by fear of fraud encouraging those who would not otherwise resort to it to join in. White cites the elections of 1960 and 1968 as examples of elections that were so close that nationwide ballot-stuffing could easily have reversed the outcome.

In addition, demands for recounts could become chaotic. While recounting in questionable precincts is a manageable and fair practice, when the vote of the whole country is subject to question, recounting would result in a massive waste of time and money. At the same time, if voting were funneled into one pool, national policing and uniform policy would have to be enforced so that state regulations or privileges would be forced to conform with universal standards—a practice that White believes "breaches all American tradition" (paragraph 8).

While candidates can now plan strategy for winning certain states by familiarizing themselves with the issues of a particular state or region, under the changed system "TV becomes absolutely dominant" (paragraph 10), reducing elections to a media effort dependent on the media itself to shape issues and on the ability of a candidate to raise money "to buy the best time and most 'creative' TV talent" (paragraph 10). White has always been fascinated by the effect of television on the presentation of candidates, but he views it largely as an industry of distortion that does little to contribute to the fairness and honesty of elections.

Finally, White believes that despite its democratic idealism, the proposal would have a damaging effect on minorities. Minorities need to combine forces, and this is possible only in areas where they are highly concentrated. With the direct election system, the concentration of minority populations in some areas would cease to work in their political favor; the minority vote would be lost in the enormous national vote pool. For example, while African-Americans make up a large percentage of the population in the South, they remain a vast minority of some 10 percent in the country as a whole, wielding political power only in the South and in a few isolated areas of the North. If a politician has to win a state, he or she will have to appeal to any group who could make a difference, and in the South or in states where minorities are heavily concentrated in one area, a candidate must be prepared to answer to their needs. White finds it ironic that the Southern conservatives, who would have the most to gain by the House's proposal, oppose it while the Northern liberals, with the most to lose, are all for it.

White ends his refutation by returning to a psychological appeal: "to reduce Americans to faceless digits on an enormous tote board, in a plebiscite swept by demagoguery, manipulated by TV, at the mercy of crooked counters" is an "absurdity" without redeeming merit (paragraph 13). He suggests that if we accept the proposal by the House, this is the vision we are actually embracing.

4. What is the alternative proposal White presents, and can it also be refuted?

White admits there are problems with the old system but claims that they are not related to the state-by-state system of counting votes but to the Electoral College and the anonymous electors and to the practice of allowing the House to take control of the election if no candidate obtains a majority of the electoral votes. He proposes abolishing the Electoral College but retaining the electoral vote by each state and allowing senators and congressmen alike to vote when no winner has been established by electoral votes.

White's proposal obviously takes as its strong points the weaknesses he points out in the direct election system. He argues, for instance, that the state-by-state system keeps the damage of ballot fraud to a minimum. White's argument seems somewhat illogical, though. It would seem that the effect of the traditional system of counting votes would be not to decrease the amount of voting fraud but to concentrate it in areas where a relatively few fraudulent votes might swing the election in a state.

In addition, White speaks as though the minority populations in this country, African-Americans in particular, have little power on their own. However, 10 percent is no small figure, certainly enough to swing a close election. White likewise assumes that politicians will not concern themselves with minority votes unless forced to by precincts, but the collective power of many of our special interest groups must be a concern for any candidate serious about winning an election.

It isn't clear that White's counterproposal is much stronger than the proposal before the House. It might, however, have a greater chance to succeed in the long run, if only because we seem reluctant to make major changes to a system that we have grown accustomed to.

LEWIS THOMAS

How to Fix the Premedical Curriculum

Undoubtedly the most difficult problem in teaching Thomas's essay is defining his tone: is Thomas expecting us to take his proposal seriously, or is he merely being ironic? I would guess that he is more than half-serious, for many of the essays collected with this one in *The Medusa and the Snail* share its humanistic implications. In "A Trip Abroad," for example, Thomas suggests that life on our planet has become too plastic and controlled, and we need the humanistic voice of the poet, not of the scientist, to teach us how to view the earth; similarly, in "The Youngest and Brightest Thing Around," Thomas explains what makes being human such a complex and wonderful thing. Before sending students off to read the essay, you may ask them in class to list the courses they believe are essential for a premedical curriculum. This exercise should prepare them to be surprised by Thomas's suggestions.

QUESTIONS

1. What is Thomas's goal, and what is the problem that stands in his way? Has he convinced you that it *is* a problem?

Identifying Thomas's goal may be the most difficult problem in reading his essay. Perhaps the closest he comes to a direct statement of it is in paragraph 10, where he talks about the "qualities of mind and character needed in a physician," emphasizing "tenacity and resolve," an "innate capacity for the understanding of human beings," and an "affection for the human condition." His goal is to encourage these qualities of mind and character in order to produce a generation of humanistic doctors who know much more than science, who know something "about how human beings have always lived out their lives" (paragraph 17).

The problem as Thomas sees it is that the premedical curriculum has essentially eliminated studies of "general culture" and concentrated exclusively on science. Premeds take only those humanities courses that pose no threat to their grade-point averages (paragraph 4). A curriculum that encourages students to saturate themselves with science and to focus so single-mindedly on their future as doctors has made premeds the "most detestable of all cliques eating away at the heart of the college" (paragraph 16). The premedical curriculum is, in short, anti-humanistic.

Thomas's use of strong language such as this makes us *feel* the "horror" of the present situation, and his broadening the scope to include not only the medical students but the whole of liberal arts education as well, asks us to take the problem seriously. But students will bring their own opinions to bear on this essay. Some will be members of the premed clique itself—or of a clique so similar (the business majors or engineers, for example) that they will initially reject without hesitation the value of a liberal arts education. It may be worth reminding such students that Thomas is not a Greek professor but a physician, medical researcher, and former dean of the medical school at Yale. This is not a proposal from an outside critic but a proposal by an utter insider and experienced professional.

2. Outline Thomas's solution.

First, Thomas suggests that self-labeled "premeds" be placed in the third of three stacks of applications; that anyone with membership in a "premedical society" be automatically rejected; and that any college with a "premedical curriculum" not be recognized by the medical schools (paragraph 6).

Second, he believes that in evaluating transcripts for admission to medical school grades in nonscience courses should receive as much or more weight as science grades "in order to assure the scope of intellect needed for a physician's work" (paragraph 7). Similarly, the focus of the MCAT should shift to languages, literature, and history, if the tests cannot be eliminated altogether.

Third, Thomas outlines his suggested core curriculum. At the heart of this curriculum is Greek, followed by Latin (if not taught in high schools), English, history, the literature of two foreign languages, and philosophy. Grades for these courses should count most.

Finally, concerning extracurricular activities, volunteer work in hospitals should not be considered for admission to medical school. Students should work at being "generally bright and also respected" by the faculty. This judgment "should carry the heaviest weight for admission" (paragraph 15).

3. How seriously does Thomas expect us to take his proposal?

Thomas seems serious in his goal and generally serious in his statement of the problem, but when he moves into the solution, he is clearly having fun and being deliberately outrageous. If your students look at the details of his solution one by one, they will find that his proposals are generally unfair or infeasible or fraught with unacceptable consequences. Can he really be serious when he suggests rejecting out of hand anyone who has belonged to a "premedical society"? Can he really expect us to accept his notion that *everyone* going to medical school should be required to study classical Greek?

Perhaps out of irritation with the present state of the premedical curriculum, Thomas has adopted the course of shocking his readers with an outrageous solution. The rhetoric of the essay seems to translate as follows: "The present premedical curriculum is so inconsistent with the proper goal of medical education that even requiring students to avoid science courses and concentrate on ancient Greek would be preferable."

CHAPTER 9
Evaluations

Purpose

Evaluations are difficult things for any of us to write, particularly ones that force us to examine and articulate highly subjective responses. We like something or we don't, and we have trouble saying why, let alone saying why another person should or should not like it.

But the professions—from engineering to education—require the ability to evaluate articulately and even persuasively, and the main purpose of this chapter is to help students do just that. An important prerequisite to writing effective evaluations is understanding why evaluators disagree, so the chapter also discusses the way that all evaluations—even the most technical—involve a "critical stance" derived from the writer's fundamental values.

Overview

The *chapter proper* divides into six parts and includes many internal readings:

1. An opening statement on the nature of evaluations
2. A discussion of the range of things we call evaluations
3. A section on technical evaluations
4. A section on critical notices
5. A section on interpretive evaluations
6. Advice on writing evaluations

The *assignments* include a technical evaluation, a critical review, an interpretive evaluation of an advertisement, an interpretive review, and a study of the critical reception of a book or film.

The *readings* present an array of evaluations varied in tone and purpose:

Noel Perrin's "Market Research in the General Store," a homespun account of an attempt to discover the truth about the taste of maple syrup

Gene Santoro's review of Paul Simon's *Graceland* album

John Ruskin's demonstration (from *The Stones of Venice*) that Gothic architecture is more politically correct than Greek architecture

Ellen Posner's review of Philip Johnson's famous (or notorious) AT&T building

George Will's "Well, *I* Don't Love You, E.T.," a review with an ax to grind

Three reviews of Annie Dillard's *The Writing Life*

The Chapter Step-by-Step

Statement on the Nature of Evaluations (page 316)

The opening example of the pencil sharpener contains in miniature the two themes that dominate the entire chapter. First, there is the notion that evaluators not only *will* disagree but often *ought* to disagree. They will put the subject to be evaluated in different frameworks and so will arrive at different conclusions about it: assigning values is a human activity. Second, the crucial conflicts between evaluators often have to do with deciding the priorities among *elements* of the thing evaluated. Alertness to the fact that every product offers several elements to evaluate is one key to writing effective evaluations.

The Range of Evaluations (pages 317–318)

The aim of this section is not so much to show that evaluations may range from the dry and technical to the controversial and interpretive—students know this already—but to show that there is a unity underneath this diversity. Evaluations of all sorts typically include (sometimes in truncated form) a presentation of background, an introduction of elements to be evaluated, an analysis based on these elements, and a critical stance that makes a final judgment possible.

It's doubtful that any professional reviewer or product evaluator has a list of these four parts of an evaluation thumbtacked to the wall. They seem, however, to come with the territory, consciously or unconsciously. Students will benefit from having a fully conscious understanding of how they work.

The Technical Evaluation (pages 318–324)

So-called technical evaluations are a good place for us to start because they generally follow a systematic outline. And the *Consumer Reports* article on ice cream bars is a particularly good specimen for students to study because it cranks up all the rhetorical machinery that might be used to evaluate a weapons system or a reactor design and applies it to an object familiar to all. Students can distinguish the four parts of the evaluation easily and examine how each works. And, of course, they can use the report as a model for their own technical evaluation (Assignment 1).

The key things students need to notice are the way that elements and criteria are distinguished in the second section of the report (pages 319–320) and the way that the report's final recommendations (Section 4, pages 321–324) reflect a critical stance that goes beyond the data. Exercises are included to reinforce these key concepts.

The distinction between elements and criteria is not, of course, a hard and fast one, and you should acknowledge this in your discussions with students: the two fuse, just as theme and plot fuse in a short story. But the element/criterion distinction has the same sort of usefulness that the theme/plot distinction has. When students begin to make distinctions between a feature evaluated and the qualities of that feature, they have learned to use a tool that may help clarify their thinking.

Exercise 1: Identifying Elements and Criteria (page 320).   This relatively simple exercise, which is fun to do in groups, should help your students think about evaluation in terms of discrete elements. It should also help them straighten out the relationship between elements and criteria. The first item, pencils for note taking, may be the hardest for students to deal with because they may have trouble seeing that various elements could be at work in so simple a thing. But if they think about the range of pencils on the market—from the cheapest wooden ones to the fanciest mechanical ones—then they may be able to produce a list that looks something like this:

Element 1:   Cost
  Criterion: Cheap enough to lose one a week on a student's budget
Element 2:   Convenience of use
  Criterion: Correct thickness for easy handling
  Criterion: Flattened sides or other means to prevent rolling on nonlevel surfaces
  Criterion: Cover for tip to allow carrying in pocket or purse
  Criterion: Effective eraser attached
Element 3:   Hardness of lead
  Criterion: Soft enough to make a mark legible in any reasonably well lighted room
  Criterion: Hard enough to last through two classes without sharpening

Exercise 2: Altering the Assumptions Used in an Evaluation (page 324). This exercise too can be pleasant to do in groups. Your students should quickly realize that this new set of assumptions will turn the old ranking almost exactly on its head. The leading vanilla bar might now be the Eskimo Pie Dark or even the lowly A&P ice milk bar. Dove and Haagen-Dazs land in or near the cellar because of their combination of overrich flavor and hazardous levels of fat. There is no great intellectual insight to be gained here, but the exercise should give students another warning about the danger of thinking that charts and figures and benchmarks mean objectivity. Judgments of value are rooted ultimately outside the realm of the public, quantifiable, and repeatable.

Critical Notices (pages 324–328)

This section takes students a step further in understanding the nature of conflicting evaluations, showing the way that the critical stance of the writer determines what elements of the product he or she will stress. In this case the conflict is between Pauline Kael, who admires *E. T.* and stresses its emotional impact, and Robert Asahina, who dislikes the movie and stresses its failure to raise any socially significant theme. The analysis of these two brief reviews should prepare students to analyze the three that follow as an exercise.

Exercise 3: Identifying Key Elements and Criteria (pages 326–328).   Most students will find it easier to identify elements and criteria if they look at page 329, where they will find an admittedly rather arbitrary list of terms used in film criticism. If they use the terms listed there, they may find that

- Sheila Benson stresses theme and emotional impact. She finds that the movie's theme is psychologically significant (her chosen criterion; not the one favored by Asahina) because it explores the loneliness of childhood in a broken family. In discussing emotional impact, she clearly favors strength of feeling as a criterion rather than garden-variety honesty: she isn't at all troubled by praising the "magic" of the film, by which she seems to mean its emotional uplift. On the face of it, Benson's critical stance is a bit vague: she seems to want both realistic exploration of heartbreak and magical uplift. All of us might want these things, of course, but the critic might need to point out how difficult it is to have our cake and eat it too.

- Joseph Gelmis stresses the element of characterization and places a good deal of emphasis on realism as a criterion for that element. He also stresses emotional impact: he is pleased by the movie's humor and its generally affectionate tone. But it is important to him that these good emotions be achieved with honesty (an important criterion in his assessment of emotional impact): "The three children (indistinguishable from the actors who play them) are funny and true." His critical stance is fairly clear: art should hold a mirror up to life.

- David Sterritt deals with emotional impact almost exclusively, measuring the quality of the film almost entirely by the way it affects its intended audience of children. The strength of the audience's reaction is clearly the key criterion: Sterritt seems not to care a bit about whether the emotion the film evokes comes honestly—just so it works. His only check on this reaction-centered evaluation is that the film be "goodnatured" and not "grating or snide."

The Interpretive Evaluation (pages 328–334)

At this point, I feel like a paddler in the lead canoe, shouting back a warning that there is white water ahead. The section on the interpretive evaluation creates some turbulence in class, and it ought to, since it raises some of the issues that are causing turbulence in the corridors of English departments these days. Is the evaluator free to set up a framework for evaluation that is at odds with the intent of the writer? Are there no objective criteria that can be applied to a work to establish its quality or significance?

In a brief moderating section (pages 328–329) before Phyllis Deutsch's controversial review of *E. T.*, I attempt to persuade students to be somewhat more flexible on these questions than most are inclined to be. That is, I remind students that objectivity—however desirable—is an impossible goal in most evaluations and that an open admission of the reviewer's bias may be the best we can hope for. And I argue that there is good reason—in some cases at least—for the reviewer to be more concerned about the effect of a work than about its intention.

The Deutsch review is very conventional in its structure: a one-paragraph introduction that ends in an indirect statement of the thesis, two paragraphs on stereotyping, two paragraphs on the role of the missing father, two paragraphs on the mythology that underlies the film, and a two-paragraph conclusion that echoes the introduction. It is, in this respect at least, an easily emulated model— the five-paragraph theme with a bit more elbowroom added. I've interrupted the essay to comment briefly at each joint between parts.

Having commented so much on the review in *The Riverside Guide*, I restrict my comments here to the issues raised in the questions set in the margin:

How convincing is the argument that E.T. is "male-identified"? I think Deutsch is more right than wrong about the identification: if E.T. appeared in one of our classroom buildings I would be less surprised to see him head for the men's rest room than if he made his way toward the women's. But I don't think that the single example of tossing the baseball proves much here, since E.T. seems eager (or willing) to play whatever the children want to play. He does, for instance, play dress-up with Gertie.

Who teaches E.T. to talk, and how important is the detail? Gertie gives E.T. his early language instruction. Deutsch says that this detail "is seen as far less important than the physical machinations of the boys." And indeed, Asahina's having missed it suggests that Deutsch may be right: Gertie and the language instruction seem not to have captured his attention or imagination. Does the failure to get this detail right greatly damage Asahina's review? There is no simple answer here. I think Deutsch would say so, and I would argue that his review (which does imply that the movie would have been improved by the presence of a "dominant male") reinforces a male-centered view of society.

Is the ribbing of Mary snide? Here we have a question that turns on the distinction between intention and effect. I gather that Deutsch is accusing Spielberg not of deliberate snideness but of uncritically spinning his humor out of a stereotype of the woman-housewife-incompetent. In effect, Deutsch is saying that Spielberg does with Mary what earlier moviemakers did with Stepin Fetchit. The intention is only humor; the effect is reinforcement of a damaging stereotype. Without being deliberately snide, the director may be making use of a snideness in the society.

Can you recall whether your own feelings about the mother and father match those outlined by Deutsch? I don't recall having any feelings that the father's departure was excused, and I'm not sure that Deutsch is playing fair when she says the excusing is subliminal. How can we check the accuracy of an effect that no one noticed? On the other hand, I do recall thinking that Mary came off a bit thickheaded and shrill. But I was watching the movie as an adult.

How children reacted to these characters is an interesting question, and eighteen- to twenty-year-olds are in a fair position to answer it.

Why does Deutsch link E.T. to motherhood rather than fatherhood? All evaluators are affected, positively and negatively, by the mental framework with which they work. It seems to me that the same fascination with the portrayal of women that led Deutsch to notice that Gertie was the language teacher and Mary was a buffoon may have led her to this rather stretched interpretation of Elliott as mother figure. It seems to me that Deutsch might herself be subject to an accusation of sexism here, since she seems to have trouble believing that Elliott's nurturing can be seen as his playing out the role he wished his father had played with him—a fairly obvious reading of the situation. Can't men be nurturers? Can't boys want to be?

Exercise 4: Evaluating the Assertions in an Interpretive Evaluation (page 334). The aim here is to get students to evaluate the evaluation critically, to be aware of some of its strengths and weaknesses. Here are some assertions you might want to hold up for evaluation if your students don't:

1. Gertie's teaching E.T. to talk "is seen as far less important than the physical machinations of the boys" (page 330, bottom). The evaluation is made more difficult because of the passive voice, a point worth making in a composition class.
2. Spielberg traditionally views the family "as a sex-segregated enterprise" (page 331, top). The assertion is embedded in a sentence in a way that seems to invite no examination, but it could easily be examined by looking at other Spielberg films.
3. Mary is presented as "the one at fault" in the breakup of the marriage (page 331, last complete paragraph).
4. Mike and Elliott are not angry at their dad for leaving them (page 331, near bottom).
5. If Mary marries the scientist, he won't help with the housework (page 332, top).
6. Toward the end of the film, E.T. inspires "reverence and awe" comparable to that inspired by "King Arthur, Christ, and maybe even God himself" (page 333, top).

Advice on Writing Evaluations (pages 336–337)

The checklists here are much more extensive than those in other chapters, and I would encourage students to read and use them. In my experience, the predictable pitfall for students writing evaluations is that they are uncomfortable with the middle ground between giving an unsupported opinion and merely reporting information. They are prepared to express their purely subjective feelings about a book or movie or to deliver an objective plot summary, but they have trouble staying on task when they are asked to make a case about a book or movie. The checklists are good ways of keeping them on the difficult middle ground between pure subjectiveness and safe objectivity.

The Assignments

Assignment 1: A Technical Evaluation. Reactions to this assignment have been mixed. Some of my more literary advisers have groaned at the thought that students might be doing as "meaningless" a task as evaluating hamburgers. Other advisers have been very excited, thinking about the ingenuity and discipline necessary to doing a good job. I myself am among the excited and suggest that you consider having students work in groups on conceiving ways of doing the evaluation so that they can develop some of the enthusiasm necessary to doing a thorough job. They can then produce their own reports.

Assignment 2: A Brief "Notice" Review of a Movie, Book, or Record Album. This is clearly a minor assignment, but one that exercises the student's skill at compression and clarity.

Assignment 3: An Interpretive Evaluation of an Advertisement. Students may have been asked in the past to write an analysis of the sales pitch implied in an advertisement. You need to let them know that this is *not* their job here. They are to ignore the fact that the ad is selling a particular product and to treat it instead as if it were a story, movie, poem, or play. The magazine *Messages* is interested in the social theme, not in the sell. And what we instructors are interested in is students' demonstrating an ability to take a critical stance.

The perfume advertisement, therefore, might be evaluated as an ad that tells women who see it that they should express their femininity through allure and mystery, through subterfuge and concealment—a statement that students might decide to applaud or to condemn. The AT&T advertisement associates childhood, the countryside, and friendship. It is hard to see anything sinister here, and most students would probably applaud the ad as one that praises (and so encourages) lifelong friendships between men. A few students might point out, however, that if the ad encourages us to see lifelong friendship as being *naturally* linked to childhoods in the country, it sends a rather troubling message to people who have never lived in the countryside. Are they incapable of having these deep, lifelong friendships, born in a sort of idyllic innocence? Can't these great friendships be formed at the YMCA or on an asphalt playground? Such a line of thought could result in an essay like the following:

> AT&T advertisements directed at the business audience often suggest a harsh world of split-second decisions made under enormous pressure, but the ads the company directs at the consumer market tend to be sentimental and nostalgic. Television ads will feature calls from children to grandparents or calls in which old men reminisce about events that happened half a century ago. In the domestic ads, people are off the clock, unharried, experiencing a life in which personal relationships are everything. The ads inevitably say, "Reach out and touch someone." They imply that the life they portray is the fully human life of rich emotions.
>
> It is hard to criticize AT&T's glorification of the world in which people reach out to each other, but it does sometimes seem that the

company's ads create a fairly narrow vision of our emotional world. Take, for example, an ad now running in popular magazines. It shows in the foreground two boys, too young to be troubled by the problems of adolescence, standing on a pier and fishing in an apparently unpolluted river. The opposite bank, which occupies more than half the picture frame, is dense with leafy trees. "Growing up," the advertising copy says, "meant sharing every moment. Every childhood dream." And the telephone allows childhood friends to stay in touch to "share . . . thoughts on everything from getting a raise to raising children."

Who could object to this? And yet the implication seems to be that "true" friendships are formed in an idyllic country setting that fewer and fewer children will ever know. The ad suggests that the truest friendships are formed in childhood, but in a mobile society like ours, most of us lose contact with our childhood friends. And it suggests that friendships are formed in good times and fed on pleasant experiences ("getting a raise . . . raising children of your own"). If we accept this as *the* picture of true friendship, then most of us are left on the outside, looking in at something we desire but can't have.

But friendships can be formed on asphalt playgrounds or in offices, and they can be nourished by hardship. The advertisers turn away from these less photogenic friendships, and unfortunately they may encourage us to turn away too.

In making this assignment, my preference is to discuss the advertisements in the book but then send students out to find their own advertisements. Cigarette ads and liquor ads are a treasure trove: since neither product can sell itself very well, the advertisers are constantly holding up pictures of the "good life" that they hope their products will become associated with. But is the assertion (common in Virginia Slims ads) that a life of leisure is better than a life of toil one that everyone would accept?

Assignment 4: This assignment may work best after a classroom discussion of one of the poems or stories included at the end of chapter 10. I have had good luck with Joyce Carol Oates's "Where Are You Going, Where Have You Been?," which can be interpreted either as a story about supernatural evil intervening in the world or as a "realistic" story about the emotional trauma of adolescence in unsupernatural America. By getting students arguing about which interpretation does the most justice to the story, you can put them in a position to write interpretive reviews with a clear purpose and audience.

Assignment 5: If your students seem uncertain about how to approach this assignment, point out that this chapter's treatment of various reviews of *E.T.* constitutes a reception study. Their own studies will be more compressed. Following an introduction that gives background on the book or film, they may spend a paragraph summarizing each review and another paragraph or two analyzing the review's critical stance and its use of key elements and criteria (though they will not want to follow this formula slavishly). The conclusion might speculate about the reasons that the book or movie evoked the range of responses it did.

End-of-Chapter Readings

NOEL PERRIN

Market Research in the General Store

Discussing Perrin's essay in class should be a worthwhile and amusing way to reinforce the study of evaluations. Keep in mind, however, that we can't expect of Perrin what we do of *Consumer Reports,* for like his syrup, his evaluating process is homemade. But what it lacks in precision and thoroughness it makes up for in good humor and insight. At the same time, Perrin does identify specific elements for evaluation, draw conclusions, and take a critical stance, making his evaluation a worthwhile example for students to follow.

QUESTIONS

1. What elements does Perrin use to evaluate syrup?

   While Perrin mentions the color and the sweetness of syrup, he focuses his attention on the purity and the strength of taste. In his study, the criterion for purity was absence of chemical taste; in a sense, Golden Griddle served as a benchmark, for Perrin could detect a decidedly chemical flavor in it—and knew it shouldn't be there. For strength, Perrin decided that most tasters preferred a relatively strong taste; the benchmarks had been established for him by the standard grading system for maple syrups: subtle—Grade A; less subtle—Grade B; strong—Grade C.

2. How does Perrin present himself as an evaluator?

   The first few paragraphs of Perrin's essay suggest that like the attorney general of Vermont, he's out to get Best Foods and prove them wrong—perhaps even criminally wrong—in their assessment of Vermont syrup. And his initial survey indicates that he may be right: none of the eight tasters in his first test join the Vermonters on the Golden Griddle ads in preferring Golden Griddle. But rather than accuse Best Foods of fraud, Perrin continues his testing, eventually duplicating the company's survey in order to compare results "as accurately as possible" (paragraph 9). He is even willing to give the surveyors credit for doing "a good and careful job" and to excuse Best Foods Company's misleading filming as "normal advertising technique" (paragraph 10). Perrin's fairness in handling the opposition, particularly since he has good reason to want to prove them wrong, encourages us to trust him and his results.

   But Perrin's personality plays a significantly larger role in the success of his evaluation. We know from the beginning that he is a Vermont farmer challenged by the success of a successfully competing, synthetic syrup to validate his own "hanging sap buckets, gathering, boiling, falling into snow drifts" (paragraph 2). But at the same time, he is a wise evaluator. In his search for an explanation of the discrepancy, he discovered that many people (one-fourth of those he tested) not only knew their preference but could identify it and the competing syrups exactly; he then used this information to stress in his findings that 100 percent of the people with "good palates" preferred Vermont syrup. Although he never states that Vermont syrup is somehow "better," his test implies that it is so. And in his good humor, Perrin offers plenty of options in the last two paragraphs for acquiring the "best" (since he was "hardly going to suggest" that anyone opt for imitation brands) and even offers to "pass orders on" to Vermont farmers.

3.   What critical stance is suggested by Perrin's evaluation?

In terms of pancake syrup, Perrin offers clear-cut interpretations of his findings, which he spells out at the end of the essay. If you're a gourmet ("even if you just *want* to be one"), you should use Fancy or Grade A maple syrup; if you're not ("and don't care whether you ever are"), you should save some money and go with Grade B or C, which have the hearty taste most people want (paragraph 15). And you can write to him if you don't know any farmers to get maple syrup from (paragraph 16).

Perrin's unstated critical stance seems to be that when given the choice, people should opt for the authentic rather than the artificial. His lighthearted interest in the topic of Vermont syrup doesn't call out for deeper analysis, but it may be worthwhile to discuss the broader implications of his stance. The general store that sells Golden Griddle may also sell margarine as well as butter, synthetic fabric alongside wool and cotton, or jewelry made with manmade gems instead of pearls or diamonds. Students are probably comfortable decorating their rooms with posters and prints rather than paintings or buying plastic instead of cedar Christmas trees. These examples prove what Perrin points out, that most people have "weak palates" and are just as happy with the synthetic as with the real. Why prefer the real?

Some of your students may say, not incorrectly, that Perrin recommends real maple syrup simply because he is a syrup producer himself. But they ought not draw the easy conclusion that his motives are therefore primarily economic. As the headnote to the essay suggests, Perrin has many irons in the fire, and maple sugaring is certainly more of a hobby with him than a livelihood. I suspect that the defense of real maple syrup, like the defense of many other products that depend on time-honored, labor-intensive manufacturing processes, has to do with the desire to preserve a way of life. The tone of Perrin's essay suggests his affection for a life that includes "hanging sap buckets, gathering, boiling, falling into snow drifts." He does not sound like a man who wants to be "working at a Best Foods factory in New Jersey" or who wants others to work there. He prefers the natural manufacturing process over the artificial partly because it preserves a precious link to the land.

4.   How is Perrin's evaluation related to the proposals we studied in Chapter 8?

Like the writer of a scientific proposal, Perrin begins with a well-defined problem: determining the validity and/or cause of Vermonters choosing synthetic syrup over authentic Vermont maple syrup. Like Dethier testing the tasting abilities of flies, Perrin carefully sets up his experiment, explains his procedure, and interprets the results.

By slightly modifying the experiment conducted by Best Foods—offering two types of Vermont syrup instead of one—Perrin devises what Dethier would call a control. His test results indicate that many tasters rejected Grade A syrup, but not necessarily because they like Golden Griddle itself: they merely like a strong flavor. When given a choice between Golden Griddle and Grade C, those tasters desiring this element chose Grade C almost as often as Golden Griddle. This insight allows Perrin to reframe the problem in terms of "good palates" and "weak palates." Of those tasters with palates good enough to identify the syrups, 100 percent preferred the real thing and always chose Grade A. Fifty-two percent of those without good palates also preferred real maple syrup, though almost all went for the strong taste of Grade C. So in essence, Golden Griddle only appealed to those people with a sense of taste so weak that they could not sense the chemical nature of Golden Griddle nor the purity and smoothness of Grade A. This aspect of Perrin's study suggests that Best Foods' results can be explained by assuming that many of those who chose Golden Griddle did so by default: no Vermont syrup with a strong enough taste was made available for those tasters with weak palates. Perrin's experiment is both a proposal that offers a solution to the problem of the conflicting test results and an evaluation that proves Vermont syrup superior to Golden Griddle.

GENE SANTORO

Review of Paul Simon's Graceland

Ideally, you would either play *Graceland* throughout the class hour to give your students a basis for evaluating Santoro's evaluation, or your students would be so familiar with the album that they could sing portions of the songs (complete with back-up rhythms and harmonies) to prove their own assertions about Simon or Santoro's work. Students may find this review somewhat problematic, however, since many of them will have paid little attention to Simon's album, and many who have will disregard the album's strange sounds that scarcely resemble those of Madonna or Bon Jovi. Any music review, like any book or art review, appeals to a limited, and possibly an elitist, audience since opinions about what makes music good vary so widely. Santoro's evaluation is successful because he carefully establishes his own critical stance before evaluating the product in light of it.

QUESTIONS

1. How does Santoro introduce Paul Simon's *Graceland* as a work that is worthy of evaluation?

While this question is not an essential one to ask, it may be helpful in stressing to students the benefit of establishing in the reader's mind a reason to read the evaluation.

Santoro begins by reminding us of Simon's lengthy career which began with Art Garfunkel about a quarter of a century ago. Santoro notes that it was Simon who began experimenting with new sounds, which resulted in the creation of many of the duo's hits and many hits in Simon's solo career. The list of songs included in the first paragraph tells (or reminds) the reader that any album by Paul Simon deserves some notice and consideration. Finally, Santoro introduces *Graceland* in paragraph 2 in a sort of "and if you thought *that* was good stuff" manner: those "previous dips into generic crosscurrents" were nothing compared to the "total immersion" on Simon's new album, an album surely worth discussing.

2. Identify the musical terms Santoro uses. What do they add to the evaluation?

The point here is not to clarify the types of music precisely but to give students an idea of the range of sounds Santoro is bringing to our attention. A recent music dictionary should identify quite a few of the terms; either advise your students to look up the unfamiliar ones ahead of time or bring a dictionary with you to class so you can look them up together.

From the Simon and Garfunkel era we get a broad range of cultures and instrumental sounds: Andean panpiping, traditional gospel changes as well as jubilee spirituals, salsa (distinctly Cuban, though the rhythms are based on African-American dances), and second-line soul. *Graceland* adds South African styles, American r&b (rhythm and blues), c&w (country and western), zydeco (black Cajun music), Tex-Mex-flavored rock & roll, and Tin Pan Alley tune-smithing (from New York City). The cultures represented, then, are South American, Cuban, South African, and the white and African-American cultures of the United States, ranging from New York City to the Rio Grande valley to southern Louisiana. The sounds themselves are even more multicultural: zydeco—a mixture of French Cajun, Caribbean, blues, rock and roll, and country and western—features the electric and bass guitars along with the accordion and washboard; salsa combines the sounds of trumpets and conga and bongo drums with flutes and fiddles; and Tex-Mex imitates the Mexican *mariachi* while drawing on German polkas and American country music. Working through this assortment should set students up to discuss the thematic content of the album.

3. What are the elements and criteria Santoro establishes in his review, and how does he analyze *Graceland* in light of them?

Don't be alarmed if your students have trouble distinguishing elements from criteria, but be prepared to guide them when they stumble. Though Santoro does not name his elements and criteria clearly, we could say that the key elements are sound, message, and the interaction between sound and message. His criterion for excellence in sound is a rich cultural variety ("polychromatic" sound); his key criterion for message appears to be ethical commitment; and his key criterion for the interaction between sound and message is that the two should be fused so that musicality is not sacrificed. The criteria reveal Santoro's critical stance: he is a confirmed integrationist, both on the political and the aesthetic level.

We get our first hint of Santoro's critical stance when he characterizes the way Simon blends sounds: Simon "hasn't so much fused his elements as he has created a musical space they all inhabit as neighbors" (paragraph 2). The interaction of the musical elements, Santoro believes, reflects the way various cultures and traditions throughout the world mesh—and always have—to produce something new from various attributes of each. As Santoro explains, this is "a process as old as the hills" (paragraph 2). Because cultural integration is important to music in Santoro's opinion, Simon's music is validated by integrations of sounds from a variety of cultures.

As Santoro focuses on the qualities that make Simon's album specifically applicable to our time, however, he shifts his evaluation from a focus on sound to the lyrics of the songs. Citing "The Boy in the Bubble" first, Santoro discusses the ironies of our present-day world. But our time, the album suggests, is tied to the past in a way that also involves specifics: America as it is today is linked to the Civil War and the fight against American apartheid, which is linked to the South, which includes the home of Elvis Presley. The most pervasive question implied by these connections is that of grace—has America become a land of grace where all people can know freedom, or is "graceland" confined to the world of music? That an album prompts us to ask such questions, Santoro suggests, makes it important; even if *Graceland* cannot give us answers about the political and social conditions of our world, it beyond doubt identifies music as an integral part of the universal struggle for freedom.

The lyrics, like the sounds, tie America to the rest of the world, South Africa in particular. A woman in New York City who wears "diamonds on the soles of her shoes" reminds us of the diamond industry in South Africa, while her shoes contrast with the gumboots worn by the diamond miners, her affluence with the impoverished conditions of black Africans. Yet Santoro seems to admire *Graceland* equally for reaching beyond the political and social concerns that tie people together to the personal context of everyday lives. Its songs speak of loss, of disappointment in love, of the inevitably superficial nature of our conversation at times, of fascinating people and places. Indeed, "Homeless," one of the most moving songs on the album, brings together all its threads by suggesting the need for community—somewhere in the world, and all around the world.

Santoro is also concerned with Simon's ability to teach us through the ideas he presents. Yet it is because Simon never makes any direct political statements and never sacrifices the music for his ideas that Santoro finds the album first-rate by all three criteria. The music itself holds us captive while the lyrics teach us that "apartheid—apartness—is not only racist and stupid but ultimately untenable in a shrinking world whose confluent cultures create cross-currents as rich as these" (paragraph 5). Finally, Santoro finds that as the focus of the album is as much on America as on South Africa, Simon "brings us face to face with the implications of the music"—for our world but also for ourselves.

JOHN RUSKIN

Slavery, Freedom, and Architecture

Your students may be confused by the many references made and terms used by Ruskin in this passage, so be prepared to explain. First, the earlier paragraphs in *The Stones of Venice* to which Ruskin refers (paragraphs 13 and 14 of Chapter XXI) merely introduce the ideas discussed at length in this passage. Also, the passage is part of Ruskin's chapter titled "Gothic Architecture," made famous primarily by the social criticism in this section; at the same time, Ruskin's praise of this type of architecture (attributed to the Christian era, which this passage focuses on) has been so influential that he is often blamed for the number of Gothic buildings on college campuses. Finally, note that in referring to "Servile ornament," Ruskin includes ornament of Greek, Assyrian (or Ninevite), and Egyptian construction; Constitutional ornament is that found principally in medieval and Christian architecture; and Revolutionary ornament is found in architecture of the Renaissance. The terms are not entirely synonymous with historical periods—for example, not all medieval ornament would be considered Constitutional—but Ruskin uses the terms to characterize the predominant type of ornament found in the architecture of each culture, and he tends to use them interchangeably.

QUESTIONS

1. This passage consists of a series of comparisons and contrasts. Briefly summarize each of them.

First, Ruskin breaks Servile ornament into two contrasting groups in paragraph 2. The Greeks, more advanced in knowledge and power, made no allowance for imperfection; in ornamentation, then, they only used forms that could be perfectly composed with precision tools: "balls, ridges, and perfectly symmetrical foliage." In contrast, the Assyrian and Egyptian societies did not demand complete perfection but instead lowered their standards so that what was attempted in ornamentation could be done with very little—and with legally acceptable—error. In spite of these differences, the same harsh discipline under which the workman worked assured excellence of execution, and in both systems the workman was a slave.

Ruskin then contrasts the attitudes that formed the Servile system of ornamentation with those of the Christian system. With the emergence of Christianity, no longer was the workman a slave, for Christianity recognized "the individual value of every soul" (paragraph 3). Thus, while to the Greeks or Assyrians the fallen nature of humanity was so painful it was often denied, in the Christian system imperfection was accepted as part of the fallen world and valued for augmenting the glory of the perfect, namely God. The idea was to strive for perfection always (since there is no fear of failure with an unconditionally forgiving God) while acknowledging the inevitability of failure (since there is no fear of shame, and failure ultimately glorifies God).

Later, Ruskin applies these attitudes to workers in general, who he believed could be molded into either tools or men. Since it is not man's nature to work with the accuracy of tools, to get workers to do so means to "unhumanize them." The eye and the soul, bent on "steely precision," will then be so worn down the whole person will be depleted intellectually. In contrast, if a worker is allowed to think, the precision—and the tool—are lost. If the worker is made a man, all his faults and failings will come out, but with them "comes the whole majesty of him also" (paragraph 5).

The final two paragraphs consist of two contrasts. The first holds up the "modern English mind" (as Ruskin defines it) beside the Greek, and the second contrasts the result of this mind to that of the Christian system. Now Ruskin turns specifically to the Industrial Revolution, accusing it of slavery worse than that of ancient Greece. Both systems could produce inferior works, yet the ancient slaves, "beaten, chained, tormented, yoked like cattle," were still more free than modern factory workers, who have been made into "leathern thongs to yoke machinery with" (paragraph 6).

For the end result of the modern system, Ruskin directs our attention to the ornaments of the typical English room: "all those accurate mouldings, and perfect polishings, and unerring adjustments of the seasoned wood and tempered steel." Rather than reflecting the greatness of England, these ornaments are "signs of a slavery in our England a thousand times more bitter and more degrading than that of the scourged African, or helot Greek" (paragraph 6). In contrast, the "ugly goblins, and formless monsters, and stern statues" of the old cathedrals are "signs of the life and liberty of every workman who struck the stone" (paragraph 7).

2. What does Ruskin gain by using this technical strategy?

To clarify the effect of the accumulation of contrasts, begin by defining Ruskin's thesis: the Christian system of ornamentation is the most perfect one because in acknowledging a higher authority *and* allowing the worker to act on his own imperfect will, the system liberates the worker and glorifies his humanity as well.

Through the first two contrasts, Ruskin is able to emphasize *freedom*, first by completely illustrating its opposite—the works of the Greeks, Assyrians, and Egyptians—and then by pitting the slavery of previous ornamentation against the freedom of the Constitutional, or Christian, system.

As Ruskin continues, he makes the slavery issue more relevant to his Victorian audience; any worker can be viewed as a tool or man, and this contrast should impress on readers that humanity has to be valued over the machine. But the most shocking contrast, particularly to an audience allied with Christianity, is that which links Victorian England to the Greeks and then charges England with the worst form of slavery. In this contrast, Ruskin has moved far beyond a critique of architecture to an indictment of his own industrial society, sharply clarified through the accumulation of contrasting images.

When at last Ruskin returns to a discussion of Gothic architecture in his final contrast, he is able to unite his art and social criticism: the sight of the old cathedrals should remind his audience not only of their artistic superiority, but of the "freedom of thought" they represent. Not only is the Christian system of ornamentation the greatest, but it embodies a social attitude that Ruskin believes must become "the first aim of all Europe . . . to regain for her children" (paragraph 7).

Finally, notice that over and over Ruskin uses the "divided" method of comparison/contrast. The complexity of his ideas is not the issue, so he does not need to discuss them meticulously point by point. Instead, the complete image of Christianity as liberation, the worker as tool, or the English drawing room as slavery is most effective, particularly when placed beside an equally strong, contrasting image. Ruskin's example of the power of this strategy is a fine one for students to follow.

3. Identify Ruskin's critical stance and show how it shapes his view of architecture.

Students should see that Ruskin's central and rather surprising idea here is that in evaluating a product or a work of art, we should not look exclusively at its effect on those who view it or use it but should also consider its effect on those who make it. Some may identify this framework for evaluation as simple socialism. Socialism it is, but not of an entirely simple sort, for Ruskin's concern is as much with the spiritual welfare of workers as with their physical welfare.

The spiritual dimension of his critical stance shows throughout the essay. He views Christian and Victorian ornamentation as two discrete things: this says something rather shocking about the spiritual understanding of a Christian nation like England. The notion of freedom in Christianity has been replaced by a skewed perspective of perfection: we "prefer the perfectness of the lower nature to the imperfection of the higher," while things of the earth (animals, wheat, etc.) prove that "the finer the nature, the more flaws it will show through the clearness of it" (paragraph 4). Ruskin implies that the more we aspire to godliness, the more we will fail, but this condition is justified by the glorious design of God. In their aspirations, the Victorians have made themselves like the Greeks, obsessed with the perfection of lesser things rather than risking failure and striving for the greater.

While the religious consequences of this attitude are inherent in Ruskin's discussion, he singles out as most important our assessment of human souls, particularly marred by withholding "our admiration from great excellencies, because they are mingled with rough faults" (paragraph 4). Yet the same principle applies to the common worker. When Ruskin turns specifically to England, it is with a serious indictment of the Industrial Revolution. He considers it the worst kind of slavery because the workers of England are "sent like fuel to feed the factory smoke, and the strength of them is given daily to be wasted into the fineness of a web, or racked into the exactness of a line" (paragraph 6). The flawed and noble souls of humanity are sacrificed for the monotonous perfection of the assembly line.

The various forms of ornamentation are vehicles used by Ruskin to expound on the degenerative spiritual and social climate of Victorian England; at the same time, they serve as a physical reminder of the smothering of British souls, enslaved in a way that is "a thousand times more bitter and more degrading than that of the scourged African" (paragraph 6), and an indication of the sort of freedom all of Europe must once again strive for (paragraph 7).

ELLEN POSNER

Learning to Love Ma Bell's New Building

Before asking students to read Posner's review, you may want to introduce them to postmodern architecture in general to give them a sense of the way that the postmoderns have tried to avoid producing the glass-and-steel boxes we find in most of our cities. If your students are not familiar with the Renaissance Center, the Facade of the Best Products Showroom, or the Bronx Development Center, you might bring to class a book like *The Critical Edge: Controversy in Recent American Architecture* (1985), which is filled with photographs of such controversial buildings. Also, spend some time in class discussing the reproduction of the model of the AT&T building (pages 350–351) in light of other buildings of its kind.

Posner's evaluation is strong from the beginning, for she draws us in by reminding us of the current negative assessments of the AT&T building—a building that has been compared to a grandfather clock and a Chippendale highboy and has been called not only a "Renaissance Revival pay phone" but a "postmodern joke." Her evaluation opens with a strong sense of purpose, then, particularly as Posner indicates that she will challenge the prevailing negative reviews of the building and characterize it as "dignified and exciting," with a personality all its own.

QUESTIONS

1. What elements does Posner focus on, and how does she use specific criteria to make her evaluation?

The first element Posner introduces stems from a primary concern voiced by the architectural community: the environmental responsibility of the building. For skyscrapers, a major criterion established by architects is a design that allows plenty of light to reach the streets (paragraph 3); they believe this effect is achieved by buildings set back from the street as they rise in height. By accepting the criterion but rejecting the setback as the only way to achieve it, Posner is able to give the AT&T building high marks for environmental responsibility. Because the building is narrow and allows much of the block to remain clear or be occupied merely by its four-story annex, the structure allows plenty of light to reach the streets and perhaps even enhances the side streets "by contributing visual diversity" (paragraph 4).

Next, Posner addresses the building's visual impact when viewed as a whole, demonstrated best by the model constructed long before actual building began (paragraph 5). This view of the building evoked initial criticism of it, particularly because the angle from which it was viewed drew disproportionate attention to its "Chippendale" top. Posner suggests that if we are to consider visual impact at all, then again she will give the AT&T building a high rating *when viewed from street level*. As architect Michael Graves stated, the fact that the form of the building attracted attention was a positive sign, for at least critics "meant it evoked some association with something"—and most buildings have no such power (paragraph 9). And when the building is viewed from the street, the ornamentation of the top is distinctive without being too obtrusive.

The third element under consideration is the excellence of the building's detail work (paragraph 11). Posner suggests, by her balance of positive and negative remarks, that elements evaluated should include the fine materials on the outside and the tasteful and elegant design on the inside. While the AT&T building scored extremely high on the former (due to the "sensuous qualities of the rough-cut granite, the smooth, elegant bronze and the polished marble"), it did not fare so well on the latter. Despite its "elegantly composed space" and its "glamorous urban quality" of early skyscrapers, the interior was criticized equally for its unnecessarily gilded ceilings and its grotesque statue (paragraph 12).

Finally, we might consider Posner's closing remarks indicative of one last element: the public nature of the building. Posner suggests that a building, perhaps as a representative of art, should appeal to, and be intellectually accessible to, all people. The AT&T building succeeds. It ranks as both a "classic" New York skyscraper and as a "truly public building."

2.   What does Posner's article imply about the level of agreement among experts about how architecture should be evaluated?

I ask this question because students need to remember that the selecting of valid elements to be evaluated is not a simple process, and Posner illustrates this problem throughout her essay. While she personally believes, for example, that the environmental issue is solved by the placement of the building on the block, architects like Michael Graves and Robert Stern believe the issue is a nonelement and should not even be considered. We're in New York, after all, and the dimness of the streets is "wonderfully urban," just as the dark and cavernous nature of Wall Street makes it "'the most exciting street' in the world" (paragraph 10).

Likewise, Posner herself does not believe that the structure of the building viewed in isolation should be considered as an element, for once the actual building was placed in the middle of downtown New York, no one was capable of viewing it whole. In fact, she even quotes an authority who gives the problem of misjudging a building by its model a name ("modelitis") as further proof that the element should be disqualified (paragraph 5). Yet in her fairness, Posner cited other architects who did believe the model mattered, since office space was rented—and a degree of public recognition created—on the basis of the model.

Both these examples suggest that the selection of elements depends to a great extent on the goals of the evaluators. Environmentalists and building managers may favor pragmatic elements over the more aesthetic ones architects prefer.

3.   What critical stance does Posner take?

Posner's closing comments clarify her critical stance: modern architecture should couple utility with an aesthetic pleasure for common people (as opposed to architects, professors of architecture, and commentators on architecture). She applauds the AT&T building's "simple structure, with an identifiable roof, windows, entrance, and materials that a great many people can understand," and its function as a "truly public building" (paragraph 14); this final note closes her essay with an image that matches one at the start, of people pausing to look and to "walk with obvious pleasure" through the lobby (paragraph 2).

GEORGE WILL

Well, I Don't Love You, E.T.

You and your students may be asking why, after the extensive discussion of *E.T.* in the chapter, we are including yet another review of the movie. We have two reasons: given Will's perspective and the thoroughness with which he discusses the movie, his review provides an excellent contrast to Phyllis Deutsch's; also, the analysis of Deutsch's review in the chapter outlines a means of analyzing an evaluation that students can now put into practice on their own.

QUESTIONS

1. What critical stance underlies Will's review, and how does it reveal itself?

Will's stance is very firm: movies aimed at a juvenile audience ought to teach them proper attitudes toward life (or at least avoid teaching improper attitudes). He never says this in so many words, but the demand for proper instruction runs throughout the review. Thus, although Will admits that adults are in fact "yucky," he implies that children should be taught to respect them. He probably knows that adults exist who fit the stereotypes Spielberg draws, but he sees no reason for "inoculating [children] with anti-adultism" (paragraph 2) since adults are in general no more yucky than children.

Will also finds that the film gives children a debased view of science. *E.T.* is clearly hostile to science, he claims, as it depicts the scientists as "callous vivisectionists and other unfeeling technocrats" (paragraph 15) and locates the wonder of life outside of the scientific world. What Will wants, for the sake of the children watching, is an honest view that dispels the myth that "nature is a sweet garden and science and technology are spoilsome intrusions" (paragraph 16).

In a sense, Will's whole complaint about the movie is that it denigrates the adult mind and undermines adult authority. The children in *E.T.* not only question adults but ridicule and outsmart them as well, and Will does not approve. He clearly wants children to want to grow up.

2. How does Will make use of background information?

Although Will stops in the middle of his review to summarize the movie, it is clear that he is not pausing to offer an objective report on the plot; instead, he uses the summary strategically to engage the reader while reinforcing his own opinion of *E.T.* Will's writing is at its cleverest in these few paragraphs, when E.T.

is described as a "stump with a secret sorrow" (paragraph 14), a "little critter" (paragraph 15), and a "brilliant, doe-eyed, soulful space elf who waddles into the hearts" of the children (paragraph 14). Likewise, adults are depicted as, for instance, a "horde of scary scientists" (paragraph 14) who, acting like "Watergate understudies," "pounce" on E.T. (paragraph 15). And E.T. is rescued from their "fell clutches," of course, by a "posse of kid bicyclists" (paragraph 15). Will's summary is very likely as delightfully amusing for those who have seen the movie as for those who haven't.

But not everyone will agree. Ardent defenders of *E.T.*, already put off by Will's criticism of it, may find that the particular slant that the summary takes does little more than reiterate Will's agenda. The belittling characterizations of E.T., for example, diminish his symbolic importance about as much as Deutsch's review inflates it. Likewise, the words chosen to depict the adults and children highlight the film's comic effect to a degree that makes any discussion of its meaning seem rather silly. The primary effect of the summary, then, is to make light of the film in general—Will's purpose from the outset.

3. How does Will's review of *E.T.* compare with Phyllis Deutsch's?

Students will probably see first the differences between the two, and they are likely to defend Will because of his reasonableness and sense of humor while dismissing Deutsch as a cranky, off-the-wall feminist—and be confident that Deutsch and Will would not like each other much at all. You might pause here to look closely at the language each reviewer uses, for Will seems to be working at appeasing the reader with his style, while Deutsch has an argument to make and is going to make it. Will and Deutsch part company primarily over their definitions of harmful stereotyping and mythologies. Deutsch is concerned that the stereotyping in the movie is teaching children to understand male and female roles according to sexist stereotyping; Will is concerned that children will be persuaded to mistrust authority. Oddly enough, the very mythology Deutsch attacks, particularly that of the Eternal Father, Will seems to have little trouble accepting, although he would hardly find it operating in a movie like *E.T.*, where the "space elf," for all his wisdom, scarcely rises to the level of God. Will never singles out male or female roles but sees children as children and adults as adults, and the only myth that concerns him is that which distorts science, of no concern to Deutsch except as creating a role for the male to play. Ask your students to decide which is the more correct view of the film and of the society we live in, and you will probably get some interesting discussion.

But students may be surprised at how much the two reviewers have in common: both have taken the risk of attacking a very popular movie from an angle alien to the thinking of most Americans. Both reviewers are motivated by a concern about the effect of the movie on the minds of children, as well as by their desire to dispel harmful myths that the movie, and our society, willingly buy into. For all their differences, both reviewers share a sense of moral responsibility: they believe adults have considerable power to shape the minds of children, a responsibility that cannot be taken lightly.

Reviews of The Writing Life

These three reviews appear in *The Riverside Guide* partly because they serve as models for writing thoughtful reviews, but also because the way that they contrast with each other reinforces the idea that reasonable people can (and even should) disagree in their evaluation of some things.

While you may want to have your class examine each essay separately, I think the most productive way to use this essay is to ask a single question that requires students to see the differences in the stances taken by the three reviewers.

QUESTION

1. What do these reviews reveal about the reviewers, especially about the differences in their critical stances?

Sara Maitland, writing for the *New York Times Book Review*, presents herself as a person who values honesty and associates it with modesty. We see this in her own statement about the writing life: "Does no one else [but me] write because it is the most agreeable way of earning a modest living without having to dress up and go out at crack of dawn?" Maitland dislikes the inflated, the pompous, the self-important, and enjoys *not* taking herself too seriously. Notice the humor at her own expense in paragraph 5, where she portrays herself as a reader driven to dislike Dillard's book because it makes her feel "frivolous and worldly, guilty even."

Maitland's persona—and, one assumes, her true personality—are consistent with her criticism of the book. She finds it self-important, pompous, and perhaps dishonest (paragraph 6). She finds the prose "mauve" if not "royal purple" (paragraph 5). And though Dillard is one of Maitland's favorite authors, her review is finally a pan.

Michael Edens is also disappointed with the book, but he is not Sara Maitland, and so his reasons for being disappointed are slightly different. If Maitland's persona is that of a plain speaker, Edens's appears at first to be that of a hard-nosed realist, one who is prepared to blow the whistle when a writer has wandered into silliness and self-delusion. His irritated comment about Dillard's self-pity at doing a job "so worthless to the world" is typical: "Ten minutes at a job that really is meaningless might change her mind" (paragraph 2). If your students read *The Nation* (few do), they will realize how fitting for its pages is Edens's suggestion that Dillard's privileged position has given her a warped view of reality.

Maitland, the plain speaker, is disappointed that the book does not speak plainly and honestly enough. Edens, the realist and writer for a magazine with socialist leanings, is disappointed with Dillard's "whining" and self-absorption. In effect, he wants her to cut that stuff out and get back to work, and he sees her work as the construction of a "spiritual autobiography" (paragraph 6). For him, "spiritual autobiography" does not mean writing "merely about the inside of her head." It means writing about the world outside in a way that is illuminated or transformed by personal perception (paragraph 6).

Both Maitland and Edens are filled with praise for Dillard's other works, and both acknowledge that her special gift for language has not abandoned her in *The Writing Life*. But ultimately their reviews are pans, and students need to realize this.

B. Jill Carroll's review is not a pan. Carroll, writing for *The Christian Century*, brings a framework to the book that is distinct from Maitland's or Edens's. From her first paragraph, she emphasizes the religious dimension of Dillard's work, describing her as "an unapologetic mystic." One gathers, therefore, that Carroll is writing as a Christian and as one who believes that mystics have much to tell us about our spiritual life. From this perspective, Carroll can find redeeming significance in what Edens calls "whining" and what the plain-speaking Maitland fears may be dishonesty. Carroll interprets Dillard's struggles with writing as yet another example of the mystic's pursuit of perfection: "the underlying idea of the book is that writing and all that it involves is a sign and possibly even a part of the substance of Dillard's spiritual life" (paragraph 4). Ultimately Carroll, speaking as a believer, sees this book as a successful metaphor for life "in the pursuit of God" (paragraph 5).

CHAPTER 10
Writing About Literature

Purpose

This chapter, which is fairly traditional in its content and approach, requires less commentary than most of the assignment-centered chapters. My one warning to the unwary is that it is a literature chapter in the spirit of the book as a whole. That is, even while it exposes students to the traditional terms of literary analysis, it reinforces the idea that equally qualified and intelligent analysts may disagree about such matters as what the theme of a story is or even who the protagonist is. In a nutshell, the purpose of this chapter is to help students understand how to locate problems of interpretation in a narrative and how to make a case for an interpretation.

The other side of that warning is an invitation. Some instructors are uneasy with the introduction of literature into the composition class because they fear that the literature will dominate the rhetoric and composition instruction. Such instructors may too hastily decide to omit this chapter from their syllabus. In fact, the emphasis on persuasion in the chapter makes it a natural follow-up to the material in Chapters 5, 6, and 7. Like Chapters 8 and 9 ("Proposals" and "Evaluations"), this is essentially a chapter in applied argument.

Overview

Following the prologue on the purposes and nature of writing about literature (pages 358–359), the bulk of the *chapter proper* divides into two parts: one focused on a short story by Isak Dinesen, the other focused on a narrative poem by Sharon Olds. Both halves include an analysis of six key elements: setting, character, point of view, plot, theme, and symbolism. The second also includes an example of a short interpretive essay. The chapter ends with a checklist for analyzing a narrative and advice on writing an interpretive essay.

The *assignments* include an analysis of a narrative by elements, a problem-centered interpretive essay, and a similar essay using secondary sources. For curious or ambitious students, there is a fourth assignment that asks them to reinterpret Dinesen's "The Blue Eyes" in the context of the longer story in which it originally appeared.

The *readings* include three poems, four short stories, and two critical essays:

Robert Browning, "My Last Duchess"

Edwin Arlington Robinson, "Richard Cory"

Gwendolyn Brooks, "The Chicago Defender Sends a Man to Little Rock"

Joyce Carol Oates, "Where Are You Going, Where Have You Been?"

Toni Cade Bambara, "The Hammer Man"

Alice Munro, "Day of the Butterfly"

Ethan Canin, "Star Food"

Robert Keith Miller, "Mark Twain's Jim"

Charles Woodard, "Wilbur's 'Still, Citizen Sparrow'"

All the literary works are narratives analyzable according to the six elements discussed in the chapter. The short stories are all initiation stories and so are easily compared with each other and with the student's own experience.

The Chapter Step-by-Step

The Prologue (pages 358–359)

The key paragraphs here are the second and the fourth. The second paragraph states that a principal purpose of writing about literature is to arrive at a fully conscious understanding of what might otherwise be only dimly perceived: this statement links the chapter to Chapters 2 and 5. The fourth links the essay about literature with the view of interpretation and argument that runs throughout the text. More explicitly, it urges students to locate genuine problems of interpretation in the narrative and to propose solutions to them.

Since some students are accustomed to writing essays about literature that are essentially plot summaries and vague statements that the work is great, you may want to point these paragraphs out in class as a corrective.

Analysis of a Short Story (pages 359–370)

"The Blue Eyes" was chosen for analysis because it is very short and very accessible. Some of your more sophisticated students may at first be offended by its simplicity, but the simplicity of the narrative leaves so much room for interpretation that we think even they will find opportunities to exercise their minds and imaginations.

The discussion of the literary elements is very straightforward and needs no review here. If any section contains any surprise for those who have taken introductory literature classes, it is the treatment of point of view. Students are often confused by the assertion that they should be able to name the (one) point of view in a story. They can see perfectly well that the point of view shifts from part to part, sometimes from sentence to sentence. *The Riverside Guide* attempts to teach point of view in a way that acknowledges this fact.

Exercise 1: Identifying Point of View (page 364).   It should be fairly clear to students that the first passage is told from an omniscient point of view: it summarizes action no particular witness claims to have seen. The second passage is dramatic: it is straight dialogue, without comment by the narrator or author. The third passage is limited: it gives the thoughts of the wife and suggests, at least, her visual perceptions. This exercise should help students see that most stories mix points of view.

Exercise 2: Summarizing the Plot from Another Perspective (page 365).   If we assume that the skipper is the protagonist, then the plot might be summarized as follows:

> A skipper wanted to create an expression of his love for his wife [the goal], so he named his ship after her and had its figurehead carved in her image. He explained that the figurehead *was* her, but she did not understand [the conflict]. He acquired precious blue stones and made them the eyes of the figurehead. The wife did not understand, and she cut the gems out of the ship to keep them for herself [a heightened reoccurrence of the conflict]. She went blind and he shipwrecked on a rock in broad daylight. Then she understood the meaning of the figurehead.

You may not find this plot summary very convincing, however, because the story lacks evidence to support the summary's conjecture about the skipper's goal. The story's point of view, as we have seen, prevents our entering the skipper's mind, and he never tells his wife or anyone else precisely what his motives are. But in order to be alert and flexible readers, students should give some thought to the possibility that more than one character might be seen as the protagonist.

Exercise 3: Evaluating Arguments About Theme (page 366).   The aim of this exercise is to create a discussion during which students will discover (under your guidance) some general principles about making effective literary arguments. By my standards, both the first and third argument represent good student work. The second is interesting and deserves to be treated with respect, but it is not as convincing. Here are some things you may want to bring out in class discussion:

Argument 1 seems at first idiosyncratic in its identification of the theme. A great many readers would likely see the story as being primarily about jealousy and trust, and very few would say that it is primarily about mystery and belief. Most would probably say that the element of mystery in the story is merely a means to an end, a way of building an interesting plot around the trust theme. Still, the essay makes its case well, tying theme to character with a simple contrast between the skipper and his wife that few would deny to begin with, and using details from the story (like the way the wife "tucks her hair respectably under her cap") to demonstrate and clarify the contrast. Then the essay ties theme and character to plot, showing that by failing to trust in mystery, the "ordinary" or "average" person in the story does, in plain fact, cause the catastrophe. Most students will probably see this as a strong paper that makes a plausible argument, albeit not the argument they would make themselves.

Argument 2 is made up of conviction, error, and insight in about equal parts. Here is a writer who brings a framework to the story—something we want to encourage. Determined to read "The Blue Eyes" as a story about the inferiority of women to men, the writer argues with energy and ingenuity, using not only evidence from the story but also evidence from Dinesen's life—which the writer has taken the trouble to research. Some kudos is due here.

On the other hand, the student has let her knowledge of Dinesen's biography and psychology dominate the paper and almost drive the story out of consideration. One gets the impression that this writer would find the theme of male superiority the key to almost any Dinesen story. Literary critics are less inclined today than they were twenty years ago to insist that every story must be read as a freestanding structure, independent of biography or history. Still, students need to be warned that information that comes from outside the story must be used with care. When literature professors assign a paper about a story, they continue to expect essays that are primarily about the story rather than about the author. An indicator that this student has let biography get out of hand is that in the first sentence, she gives as the theme a statement about Karen Blixen rather than a universal statement about the human condition.

On the third hand, so to speak, the student's "reading" of the story works well enough that it stops me in my tracks every time I read it. Isn't there some unexpected truth here?

The third argument is the most conventionally "correct." One might wish for a clearer and more graceful first sentence, one that wasn't so anxious to outline the whole essay. But the outline is accurate. The essay does make its case about theme by pointing to aspects of character, setting, and symbolism. The case would be stronger with the addition of a few details that the writer implies: the exact deception that the wife resorts to, for example, and the skipper's statement about the figurehead that justifies the interpreter's comment about its being "a symbol of the wife as she might be."

Be prepared to have your students ask what grade you would assign each of these essays. I won't presume to give you advice on this point, since grades must necessarily reflect your own standards and the level of expectation reasonable for students in your particular class.

Exercise 4: Writing Short Arguments for an Interpretation of a Symbol (page 370).   Having students write such short essays should put you in a position to allow them to compare their arguments. You might have them do so in small groups, perhaps having each group pick its favorite response to read to the whole class. Or you could duplicate a few paragraphs for the class to discuss.

Analysis of a Poem (pages 370–376)

You'll note a brief disclaimer on page 370, which states that we are not in a position in this brief chapter to deal with nonnarrative elements of poetry—metrics, for example, or other aspects of sound. This was a hard decision, but

I think a correct one. Those of you teaching a course that prepares students to enter a literature class in a subsequent term will probably agree that trying to pre-teach this whole class really is a fool's errand.

The analysis of "Summer Solstice" therefore proceeds almost as if it were a prose work. The analysis is briefer than the one done on "The Blue Eyes" because the earlier analysis has laid the groundwork. The interpretive essay on pages 375–376, I must acknowledge, is mine. Oddly enough, I couldn't find among the student essays I have collected any traditional enough in their approach to serve as safe models.

General Advice on Writing About Literature (pages 376–378)

There are obviously two agendas here. The first is to give students a guide to the traditional analysis by elements; this agenda is reflected in the checklist on pages 376–377. The second is to push students toward problem solving and persuasion in their literature papers; this agenda is reflected in the checklist on page 378.

The Assignments

Assignment 1: An Analysis of a Narrative. Our only comment on this assignment is that both students and teachers need to set aside any preconception they may have about such an analysis producing a shapely paper. The analysis has six parts, and to attempt to impose one thesis on these parts is probably a mistake if the students are to use the analysis as a method of exploring the work. If, therefore, you give this assignment for a grade, you should be prepared to abandon organization as a major element in the grading. You will probably want to give special weight to thoroughness and to insight.

Assignment 2: An Essay on a Problem of Interpretation. I believe this assignment speaks clearly enough for itself.

Assignment 3: A Problem Essay with Sources. Your students will do better on this assignment if you assign and discuss the Miller and Woodard essays first.

Assignment 4: A Study of the Effect of Context. It is probably unwise to assign this essay to the entire class. It involves a good deal of extra reading and your library is not likely to have enough copies of *Winter's Tales*. I suspect that some individual students who found "The Blue Eyes" intriguing will want to undertake the assignment, however. What they will find is that Peter tells this story to Rosa as the two young lovers are considering running off to sea to be together. Peter apparently understands this to be a story about the wonders of the sea and the life of adventure. Rosa apparently understands it to be a story about the sea taking men away from the women they love. Eventually Rosa betrays Peter in an attempt to keep him ashore, and both of them perish as a result.

I will not presume to forecast what a bright student will say about how the larger story affects the reading of the smaller, but it surely has an effect.

End-of-Chapter Readings

I should preface this section with a general observation about the use of these readings. My own practice is to use them strictly as the chapter suggests, asking students to do analyses of the elements in one or more of the selections and eventually to produce an essay centered on the problem of interpretation in one of them. That is, I would curb the tendency to talk about literature in general or the particular authors or elements of literature that go beyond our simple list of six narrative elements. Such talk is better saved, on our campus at least, for the first course in the literature sequence proper.

We have, nonetheless, provided you with two or three questions on each work that you could use if you wanted to approach it in a way not so closely tied to the type of analysis outlined in the chapter.

ROBERT BROWNING

My Last Duchess

Some of your students will find Browning difficult to read, so it is best to come to class equipped to admit gracefully that he *is* difficult and that readers have always found him so. A famous statement on this issue comes from an anonymous wit who said that Browning's translation of Aeschylus' *Agamemnon* (1877) could be understood quite easily by referring to the Greek.

While Browning is also known for his lyric poetry, his fame will always be secured by his dramatic monologues, such as "My Last Duchess," which continue to intrigue readers because they follow the movement of alert minds that shuttle quickly between honesty and sophistry, between special pleading and large philosophical statements. Unfriendly critics say that the philosophy of Browning's characters is never very deep, but this criticism misses the point. It is always deep enough that we can imagine a person living by it. Browning can take us into the maze of a character's thinking and show us every twist and turn. Mazes are never simple, of course, but they are what we must expect if we accept the unstated premise of the dramatic monologue—that everybody is constantly composing a justification for his or her life. This dramatic monologue is particularly useful because it allows students to sift through the words of the Duke to reconstruct not only his character but that of his former Duchess as well.

QUESTIONS

1. Explain the implied setting and circumstances of Browning's "My Last Duchess." How do these details affect our reading of the poem?

"My Last Duchess" is an excellent introduction to the dramatic monologue because it is so extraordinarily compressed. Studying it, your students will discover how much work Browning leaves to the reader, but they will also see how much help he offers in this work. The single word "Ferrara" after the title gives your students a place and gives anyone with a background in Renaissance history an atmosphere. (Browning does assume such background in his readers. Most of us learn to rely on an encyclopedia.) Ferrara was one of the little Italian Renaissance city-states grown prosperous by trade. It flourished in a period of political intrigue—think of Machiavelli's *The Prince*—and its wealth, concentrated in the hands of the Duke, was lavished in conspicuous consumption. In Browning's century and even more in our own, art is often confused with effeteness or civic-mindedness. Browning enjoys writing poems that put art in a hot-blooded context, and a Renaissance Duke can plausibly be presented as avaricious, dangerous, double-dealing, and passionate about art. (Perhaps museum curators can be so characterized, but not in fifty-six lines.)

City and period established, you can turn to the question of who is addressing whom and under what circumstances. The Duke (that much is established in the first line) addresses a stranger (line 7), who is in the service of a Count (line 49) whose daughter (line 52) the Duke intends to marry. That much is clear, but I would push further and ask your students *why* he is talking to this man. Students who have read the poem attentively will realize from lines 48–53 that the Duke and the Count's man have been arranging a marriage: "as I avowed / at starting" is the giveaway. At starting of what? At starting, apparently, of a part of the negotiation of a marriage contract.

And now I like to ask my class to tell me as precisely as possible what the physical situation is, where in the palace the two men are talking (the gallery?), and in what posture (the Duke standing, having just drawn the curtain aside; the Count's underling seated). Once all this is settled, we are ready to discuss what the Duke reveals about himself, both deliberately and unintentionally. The astonishing arrogance of the man shows most clearly only to students who realize that he is deliberately revealing the murder of one wife to a man who represents the interests of the next. The odd combination of pride and groveling is only apparent to students who know that the Duke is revealing his secrets to, and employing his unctuousness on, a man who is not only a stranger but also his social inferior. "I choose / Never to stoop," the Duke says (lines 41–42), while he attempts simultaneously to bully and to butter up a functionary who may help him squeeze a greater dowry out of the Count.

2.   How would you characterize both the Duke and his late Duchess? What make each character ambiguous or complex?

As mentioned in the previous question, the most prominent characteristic of the Duke is his extreme arrogance. He is concerned only with his own impressiveness, his "nine-hundred-years-old name," and his possessions—including his Duchess. It is easy to focus on the Duke's pride because of the incredible jealousy it produces; so jealous that he could not bear to see the Duchess smile at anyone but him, so proud that he could not stoop to stop the "insults" these smiles cast on him, the Duke opts for killing his wife. The fact that he keeps the portrait of the late Duchess hung behind a curtain that he alone controls (line 10) reflects the attitude he held toward her during her life as well as after. It is easy to focus on this outrageous aspect of the Duke, but his character is complicated by the tone of the poem; behind his voice we have the influence of Browning, shaping our interpretation of the Duke through what the poet has him say and do. The irony of the Duke simultaneously standing over the Count's agent and groveling before him is lost on the Duke himself, but not on us nor on Browning. The Duke is as witless as he is full of pride.

Any analysis of the Duchess is complicated by the fact that all we know of her comes directly from the Duke. *He* believes that she was easily flattered (lines 16–23) and that she was also flirtatious (lines 24–25). *He* thought she was frivolous and lacked respect, ranking his "gift of a nine-hundred-years-old name" (line 33) with any other gift. But from our perspective, it is very possible to view the Duchess as merely a beautiful, passionate, and compassionate woman and to interpret her heart, "too soon made glad" (line 22), merely as one that went out to those drawn to her. Her joy of life extended far beyond love for her husband, to include "The dropping of the daylight in the West, / The bough of cherries some officious fool / Broke in the orchard for her, the white mule / She rode with round the terrace" (lines 26–29). We may see in the late Duchess a young, innocently and perhaps foolishly happy woman, but the Duke's comments about her encourage us to overlook any faults she may have and see only the best in her. She serves as a foil to the Duke doubly, for both the person he perceives her to be and the person we see in her emphasize the ugliness of his own character.

3. How does the poem function as a narrative?

Once students can see the action of the poem clearly—the Duke entering the gallery with the Count's agent, instructing him to sit as he pulls the curtain aside and offers his commentary on his late wife, and then leading the man down the stairs to rejoin the rest of the party—they can then discuss the poem *as* a narrative. In addition to this primary plot line is a complete past, constructed through our imaginations in conjunction with the Duke's speech, and an implied future as well. Actions of the past are very briefly and subtly alluded to, but so completely that we can almost re-create the past daily lives of the Duke and the Duchess. The Duke is clearly the protagonist, and the primary conflict is his inability to manage his wife as he would like to. The climax of the narrative undoubtedly involves the execution of the Duchess, but it is ironically understated in the poem: "I gave commands; / Then all smiles stopped together" (lines 45–46). The conflict is resolved as the Duke transforms his wife into art, leaving the Duchess's smile frozen within the portrait.

Another conflict emerges in the confrontation with the Count's agent, however, for the Duke now must find some means of making sure his new wife does not make the same mistakes as the old one. While we may not be able to predict the events in the future of the Duke and his new Duchess, we can anticipate the ominous tone it will take.

4. What does the closing image contribute to the poem?

Without endowing the statue of Neptune with a great deal of symbolic meaning, we can still see in its characteristics a reflection of the overall tenor of the poem. The statue is a rarity; it was made specifically for the Duke; it is a representation of the god, Neptune, taming a sea-horse; and it is cast in bronze. Like the character of the Duke, the presentation of the statue is couched in irony; while it portrays the brute force of the god over a beautiful but untamed creature, it is also a scene forever frozen in time through the medium of art. Thus, it echos the two other art-captures in the poem: the portrait that captures the Duchess and (in an irony Browning must have enjoyed) the monologue that captures the Duke.

EDWIN ARLINGTON ROBINSON
Richard Cory

Robinson once defined poetry as "a language that tells us, through more or less emotional reaction, what cannot be said." I'm afraid that many readers today, seeing Robinson's rhymed stanzas and willingness to point to a moral, will conclude too hastily that they *know* what the man is saying, that he is a simple poet. "Richard Cory," they will conclude, says that even the fortunate can be unhappy, just as "Miniver Cheevy" suggests that we should live in the real world rather than in dreams. When students get beyond these simple formulas, they will find that Robinson is much deeper and much sadder than this, and they will learn a valuable lesson about the difference between the paraphrasable content of a poem and its meaning. In addition, students should recognize the mastery with which Robinson chooses each of his words; in four short stanzas, he has given us remarkably complete portraits of Richard Cory and of the poem's speaker.

QUESTIONS

1. Characterize Richard Cory and the speaker.

In characterizing Richard Cory, we must keep in mind that the way we view him is shaped largely by the point of view of the speaker. From the beginning of the poem, we get a sense of this perspective as the speaker emphasizes the separation and contrast between "Richard Cory" and "we people." From the speaker's perspective, Cory may as well have been a king, his wealth set him so far above the rest of the townspeople. Robinson evokes this image of Cory by his careful word choice: Cory went "down" into the town, he was "a gentleman from sole to crown," and he was "imperially slim" (stanza 1). Cory was further set apart by his style, for he was obviously a perfectly educated and cultured man whom the people could not help but envy. At the same time, although Cory "glittered when he walked" (a suggestion that he wore gold, or that he *was* gold) he was "quietly arrayed" (stanza 2); but Cory did not set out to lord his wealth over people. He was "human when he talked" (line 6), not an arrogant man, and perhaps even shy.

To emphasize the perspective of the speaker, you may wish to encourage your students to imagine another framework in which to view Cory. For example, that the people "on the pavement" (line 2) stop to look at him possibly implies that Cory's coming to town was not an everyday occurrence and that he spent most of his time apart from the community. Also, he is thin, possibly not as physically or emotionally healthy as the speaker himself. Likewise, the wishing to be "in his place" (line 12) emphasizes separation, for although the "we" work too hard and enjoy too little in life, they know a sense of togetherness seemingly foreign to Cory. The complete portrait of Cory, then, turns out to be rather complex and evokes some sympathy for him as well as some envy.

2. What is the tone of the poem?

The tone of "Richard Cory" is complicated by Robinson's use of sound. The consistent use of rhyme—emphasized by the poem's lack of enjambment, which forces us to pause on each rhymed word—and Robinson's play on words make the poem seem almost humorous; its brevity also undermines the poem's seriousness, for it reads so quickly we almost overlook its dark side. As for the effect of Robinson's humor, no one could describe it better than Robert Frost, who said that "style is the way the man takes himself; and to be at all charming or even bearable, the way is almost rigidly prescribed. If it is with outer seriousness, it must be with inner humor. If it is with outer humor, it must be with inner seriousness." Robinson's charm—and his courage—show in his ability to express grief and humor simultaneously.

Merely one line is devoted to the startling and grievous outcome of the poem, and it is reserved for the end, when Richard Cory "Went home and put a bullet through his head." Again, the action is stated only indirectly and depends on a careful consideration of Cory's character to achieve its complete effect. Once we view the person in the proper light and see that he *is* a person not so different from the speaker in the poem, the "inner seriousness" is clear.

GWENDOLYN BROOKS

The Chicago Defender Sends a Man to Little Rock

It will be interesting to see what becomes of Gwendolyn Brooks's reputation over the next few years, as it is hard to name a poet of comparable ability who has presented both academic critics and appreciative readers with such a conundrum. Brooks began writing poetry when she was seven years old and had her first poem published when she was eleven. She won a Pulitzer Prize in 1950, and she published steadily with Harper and Row through 1968. Throughout these years, Brooks was comfortable using in her poetry essentially the same technical tools used by the most traditional poets. That is, she wrote sonnets; invented her own stanzaic forms; adopted, varied, or abandoned the iambic pentameter line; and mixed meters inventively within poems. She was, as Clara Clairborne Park pointed out in *The Nation* (September 26, 1987), "intellectual, disconcerting, subtle to the point of obscurity, all the things whites like and blacks [in the turbulence of the late 1960s] found unusable."

Since about 1972, Brooks has been less comfortable using poetic tools that seem so irrelevant to her African-American heritage and has worked on developing a new poetic voice. At the same time, her early poetry has been undergoing a reappraisal, and critics are expressing increasing admiration for its fusion of technical skill and concern with the psychology and politics of race relations in the United States. "The Chicago Defender Sends a Man to Little Rock" is a good example of this fusion.

QUESTIONS

1. How does the tone shape our interpretation of "The Chicago Defender"?

"The Chicago Defender" is a poem that shows the virtues that won Brooks her wide audience in the fifties and sixties. In tone, it is objective and compassionate. Apparently the newspaper would prefer a report full of rhetorical fire, a condemnation of Little Rock and its people. Instead the speaker finds that the "biggest News" is that the people of Little Rock "are like people everywhere" (lines 46 and 48), even though they spit at black schoolgirls and beat black schoolboys, even though they are filled with the "lariat lynch-wish." In this poem, Brooks is clearly writing as an "integrationist," someone whose deep impulse is to minimize the differences between the races. The term would later be leveled against Brooks as a criticism by more radical African-American writers.

The speaker (and presumably Brooks) can't work himself up into a glowing hate. He even admires some things about the people of Little Rock: their culture (high and low), their sense of community ("it is our business to be bothered, it is our business / To cherish bores or boredom"; lines 39–40). Yes, they do horrible things, but they are not the first or last: "The loveliest lynchee was our Lord." Because the tone is somewhat unexpected, more sympathetic and reasonable than we would expect from a reporter for a highly political African-American newspaper, it allows us to place the event in a fresh and unusual framework.

2. How does Brooks use contrasting views of Little Rock to clarify the event?

The poem sets a historical framework by providing the date—"Fall, 1957"—and mentioning Little Rock in the first line. The setting *should* incite a host of feelings in readers familiar with the desegregation of Central High. The atmosphere created initially by the 270 armed guardsmen who barred the nine African-American students from entering the building, the heightened tension brought on by the self-appointed mob that forced the students to withdraw from school a few weeks later, and the strained order kept by over 10,000 troops that descended on Little Rock immediately afterward certainly cast a huge shadow over the pleasant portrait Brooks presents in her poem. Writing shortly after the event, Brooks very likely assumed that her audience would have this framework in mind as they read the opening lines.

By inserting a competing framework forty-one lines long, then, Brooks fixes a very different picture in our minds, one that reminds us that people in Little Rock are "like people everywhere." She does not make reference to the desegregation at any time in these lines. Nor she does not focus on the negative ways that people are all alike; instead she fills the lines with images of various traditions, pleasant forms of relaxation, and universal passions. By presenting the people in this way, Brooks invites us to feel comfortable with them, to feel that they are just like us.

By closing the poem with a return to the initial framework, however, Brooks invites us to view the ugly incident itself through a new pair of eyes. We have been set up to see these people sympathetically, but then Brooks turns the poem to depict the event ("I saw a bleeding brownish boy . . . . / The lariat lynch-wish I deplored"), and we are all the more shocked to discover that even very likable people are capable of brutal behavior. While we may leave the poem with a greater understanding of the offenders, we cannot help seeing that if these people are "just like us," then we too are capable of such brutality. By structuring the poem around contrasting frameworks, Brooks makes her message clear.

JOYCE CAROL OATES
Where Are You Going, Where Have You Been?

You might wish to inform your students that Oates's story appears to be based on a true incident. Arnold Friend is probably based on Charles Schmid of Tucson, Arizona, who was convicted of killing three teen-age girls. An article in *Life* magazine (March 4, 1966) describes Schmid's habits of stuffing "three or four inches of old rags and tin cans into the bottoms of his high-topped boots to make himself taller" and of making up his face: "the hair dyed raven black, the skin darkened to a deep tan with pancake make-up, the lips whitened, the whole effect heightened by a mole he has painted on one cheek" (23–24). The effect of knowing the "truth" of the story and its outcome may provide the basis for an interesting discussion of Oates's social commentary as well as of the layers of meaning she gives the story through her careful manipulation of the elements of fiction.

QUESTIONS

1. What is the point of view in the story, and what does Oates gain from using the point of view she does?

The story mixes points of view generously, so the principal thing you want to do in class discussion is to force students to rethink simple answers. Since the most gripping parts of the story are told from Connie's perspective, students may be inclined to remember the story as being told from a limited point of view. Sometimes, however, the narration is omniscient, and both the limited passages and the omniscient serve their purposes.

The limited point of view allows us both to understand Connie's impressions and to distrust them. Connie lives a life of fantasies and daydreams to such an extent that it is even possible to view her whole encounter with Arnold Friend as unreal, as the result of hormones acting on drowsiness one Sunday afternoon.

On the other hand, Oates uses a good deal of omniscient narration, especially in the early parts of the story. She begins with the simple statement "Her name was Connie," as if presenting to us the subject to be observed. This extreme objectivity allows the narrator to show us much about Connie that she herself was never aware of, such as her "high, breathless, amused voice" (paragraph 3) and the dual nature of her life—at home and at the mall. The tension in the story depends on Connie's innocence and ignorance, and these traits are probably easier to reveal from outside the character's own consciousness.

It is worth noting that a first-person narrator, such as in "Star Food" or "The Hammer Man," would not work in this story because it would announce from the beginning that the protagonist has survived and is at least sane enough to tell her story. In this respect, the omniscience of Oates's narrator contributes to our anxiety as we read the story. We've no reason to believe that Connie survived.

2. What about the story supports an interpretation of it as a religious parable?

First, the contemporary setting and situation strongly suggest such a reading. While the family seems typical, the father is generally absent and unable to communicate with his wife and daughters. His absence parallels the lack of God in their home (the entire family views Sunday as a day like any other). Also, the story is set in the summer, and constant references to the heat, and somewhat ironically to the barbecue that the family attends, suggest an affinity with hell.

Without the religious tradition to guide Connie, she makes music her god and the drive-in the "sacred building" that endows her with a "blessing" and provides that eternal rock 'n' roll music, "always in the background like music at a church service" (paragraph 6). (The reader may be more inclined to associate the bottle-shaped and "fly-infested" restaurant with hell than with heaven.) In addition, with nothing external or spiritual to worship, Connie listens to music and worships her own image in the mirror, always attempting to make herself more attractive. Similarly, her expectations for life come not from religious teachings but from what is "promised in songs" (paragraph 12).

Of course the most obvious link with a religious parable is the characterization of Arnold Friend. His face is like a mask, and his boots seem not to have proper feet in them (one twists awkwardly to the side, and he has trouble walking). He "had come from nowhere" (paragraph 94), he knows everything about Connie and her family, and he is acquainted with people long dead. When he comes for Connie, the music playing in his car is the same she has been listening to, and it pulses constantly in the background as Arnold Friend slowly convinces her to leave with him. Finally, as Connie finds herself unable to resist Friend's beckoning, her world becomes less and less real. On one level, Friend convinces her that her home is no more than a cardboard box that he could easily destroy; at the same time, as she looks around the kitchen, "she could not remember what it was, this room" (paragraph 130), as if his hypnotic power has already gained physical and psychological control over her. By the time he takes her away, Connie has already lost her soul: she watched "this body and this head of long hair moving out into the sunlight where Arnold Friend waited" (paragraph 160).

Oates has carefully put the story together to suggest, but not insist on, this level of religious meaning. You may want to ask your students for the "natural" explanation of the supernatural elements mentioned in this answer.

TONI CADE BAMBARA
The Hammer Man

Ask almost anyone who has read "The Hammer Man" what is most memorable about the story, and the reply will undoubtedly be "The voice." As in many of her stories, Bambara has created a voice that is refreshingly frank, good-humored, and full of determination and resilience. According to one of Bambara's contemporaries, it is tinged with "bite and verve" and "comes close to poetry." If your students have read the other literature selections, ask them which first-person narrator Bambara's most reminds them of; while Canin's Dade and Munro's Helen share youth and coming of age with this narrator, Browning's Duke, oddly enough, may also be a fair choice, since his personality comes across with force comparable to that of Bambara's narrator. If you haven't assigned the other stories and poems, a general discussion of the use of narrative voice to reveal a character or establish the tone of a work should make students more aware of Bambara's technique as they study this story.

QUESTIONS

1. How do the voices of the adult narrator and younger self fit together in "The Hammer Man"?

Perhaps the best way to draw the distinction between the two is to have students look for statements that would not have been made by the child narrator and for those that illustrate a child's view of the world. A few statements that sound more like an adult interpreting than a child observing include:

- "Miss Rose went back to her dream books and Manny's mother went back to her tumbled-down kitchen of dirty clothes and bundles and bundles of rags and children" (paragraph 5).

- "He carried on like this for days till I thought I would scream if the yellow fever didn't have me so weak" (paragraph 6).

- "I ran [the word *deviant*] into the ground till one day my father got the strap just to show how deviant he could get. So I gave up trying to improve my vocabulary" (paragraph 11).

In these examples, the narrator has added irony or insight that we would not expect from a child. In contrast, some statements capture perfectly the types of observations only a child would make:

- "He must've gone to the bathroom right there cause every time I looked out the kitchen window, there he was" (paragraph 2).

- "That really got me. The 'little girl' was bad enough but that 'boyfriend' was too much" (paragraph 27).

- "... Oh God here I am trying to change my ways, and not talk back in school, and do like my mother wants, but just have this last fling, and now this— getting shot in the stomach and bleeding to death in Douglas Street park" (paragraph 31).

The interest in bodily functions, the embarrassment of being intimately linked with another, and the melodramatic account of her life all reflect the child's perspective. Students may object, with cause, that they cannot hear a distinction in the two voices; Bambara's voice so naturally blends the two that we never completely leave the mind of the child, but we gain the adult's insight and sense of humor at the same time.

The question then becomes, what are we to make of this voice? Although we may sense at times that the narrator is making statements no child would make, we almost believe that Bambara has created an extremely precocious child in this narrator who *is*, nevertheless. When the policemen approach Manny—at the climax of the story—the narrative voice blends images natural to a child's mind with a thematic emphasis that distinctly belongs to an adult.

> I'll be damned if I ever knew one of them rosy-cheeked cops that smiled and helped you get to school without neither you or your little raggedy dog getting hit by a truck that had a smile on its face, too. . . . And I wished Manny had fallen off the damn roof and died right then and there and saved me all this aggravation of being killed with him by these cops who surely didn't come out of no fifth-grade reader (paragraphs 30, 32).

By creating this particular narrative voice, Bambara is able to draw us into her political message while keeping us fully entertained at the same time.

2. What are the major themes of the story, and how does the plot reinforce them?

Students should see that this is a story about growing up. They need to see that the story connects growing up with learning to identify with others, with learning about group solidarity—its inevitability, its value, and its boundaries.

The narrator establishes herself as the protagonist, and her most immediate conflict is that she created with Manny by calling him "what [she] called him" and saying "a few choice things about his mother" (paragraph 2). Getting herself into fights with neighborhood children, and in trouble generally, is part of the narrator's character, but a part she decides to give up in the course of the story. Her conflict with Manny feeds into the larger one of making the choice to "grow up"—to fix her hair right, to start wearing skirts, and to begin doing things her mother's way. At the beginning of the story, the narrator suggests that saving herself from Manny and making the transition to her new behavior are her goals.

Bambara develops and resolves these conflicts in surprising ways, however, and it is the course the action takes that directly establishes the themes of "The Hammer Man." First, given the chaos that surrounds the lives of the characters, the narrator demonstrates a surprising amount of control over her life; provided that she does not end up dead during her "last fling with boy things" (paragraph 12), she will begin to identify herself with the girls who spend their time at the center. At the end of the story we know that this transition has been successful, for "then it was spring finally, and [she] and Violet was in this very boss fashion show at the center" (paragraph 33), and she is quite proud of her first corsage and yellow shoes.

The resolution of her conflict with Manny dominates the story, but not through any direct confrontation; the narrator's actions get her father in a fight with Manny's brother and Miss Rose in a fight with Manny's mother, but the narrator herself never comes to blows with anyone. Manny's fall from the roof resolves the immediate conflict while introducing another: understanding the relationship of the narrator and Manny. Throughout most of the story, if the narrator thinks of Manny at all, it is as her enemy. She steals his hammer and taunts him to impress her friends, and when she sees him playing basketball in the dark, she cannot pass up the opportunity to poke fun at him once again; having been warned that Manny is both mean and crazy, we may well be expecting a fight before the story is over. But at the climax of the story, the narrator realizes that when pitted with Manny against outsiders, "crazy or no crazy, Manny was [her] brother at that moment and the cop was the enemy" (paragraph 22). Immediately, then, the narrator is able to see Manny in a way she never had before—she finds beauty in his "swooshing" the basketball through the hoop that is lost on the policeman, who cannot see that Manny has "just done about the most beautiful thing a man can do and not be a fag" (paragraph 30). At least momentarily, before she begins to fear for her own safety, the narrator has understood that commitment expressed earlier by her father and Miss Rose.

We naturally identify themes and the plot from the point of view of the narrator; in order to give students a broader understanding of the way plot and theme interact, ask them to describe the story as if Manny were the protagonist and then analyze the plot and the themes.

3. How would you describe the tone of "The Hammer Man," and what does it contribute to the story?

"I was glad to hear that Manny had fallen off the roof," the story begins, and this opening line encapsulates the tone because it is shocking in its humor while revealing the atmosphere the narrator lives in at the same time. Certainly the details of the environment are not humorous in themselves and belong at least as much to a harshly realistic story as to Bambara's: the narrator spends her time "hitting off the little girls" and raising "some kind of hell" (paragraph 3), the women in the neighborhood fight each other with "scissor blades and bicycle chains" (paragraph 5), and the entire neighborhood is classified by the center as "deviant" (paragraph 11). The home Manny lives in, with its "tumbled-down kitchen of dirty clothes and bundles and bundles of rags and children" (paragraph 5), seems typical of the depressed and run-down neighborhood.

But the tone with which Bambara presents these details keeps the focus off the setting and on the dynamic characters that inhabit it, particularly the narrator herself. We cannot help but be amused by a young girl who takes on the craziest boy in the neighborhood, who fakes yellow fever so well it makes her weak, who delights in words like "deviant" (even when they are applied to her), and who, in the midst of danger, instantly transforms her limited experience into melodrama. In addition, that the young girl *has* a father who stands by her, that her mother sends her to the center because she "needed to be be'd with" (paragraph 11) and taught social behavior, and that the narrator can comprehend how she is bound to the Hammer Man all focus our attention on the rightness of the people who live in these troubling circumstances.

The humorous tone Bambara maintains to the end of the story may lead the students to various conclusions. Some may be troubled that the tone remains constant while Manny is taken away by brutal policemen and forced into a home for the mentally handicapped, and that the narrator continues to entertain us with her elaborate imagination throughout the scene. Although we have enjoyed the characters and the story Bambara created here, we may not believe that the narrator learned something—that in effect she missed the epiphany inherent in her experience with Manny. And that may be Bambara's point. Regardless of the narrator's consciousness, *we* will not leave the story without understanding the importance of solidarity and that the policemen in fifth-grade readers have little in common with those who patrol the streets of the narrator's neighborhood. The story is a success because the tone captures and holds our attention while introducing us to serious themes at the same time.

ALICE MUNRO

Day of the Butterfly

Alice Munro frequently writes stories that focus on those everyday-life events that force us to see ourselves in a new way. The event may involve traumatic change or may be quite commonplace, but for Munro the way we make sense of our lives comes less from startling epiphanies and more from thoughtful recollection. And what that sense translates into in Munro's stories is always wonderfully surprising for the reader because it so perfectly captures what is true about our lives. In "Day of the Butterfly," the event is commonplace—a narrator visits a "friend" in the hospital; the perspective of the narrator, however, looking back and interpreting this stage of growing up, seeing for the first time the "treachery of her own heart," offers a fascinating variation on the traditional initiation theme.

QUESTIONS

1. What does Munro gain by having the story told by Helen in retrospect?

First, the double perspective created by an older narrator allows Munro to incorporate interpretation into the telling of the story. We hear the two voices in the brief statement, "Our teacher, a cold gentle girl . . . resembled a giraffe" (paragraph 2), where the older Helen can call her teacher a "girl" while the child likens her to a giraffe. But more significant is the contrast between the young Helen's realization that Myra is different as she stands with her little brother alone on the school porch and the way the older Helen portrays them: "They were like children in a medieval painting, they were like small figures carved of wood, for worship or magic, with faces smooth and aged, and meekly, cryptically uncommunicative" (paragraph 3). The older Helen sees in the Saylas exotic and pathetic qualities that the child could not have seen and so broadens our perspective of the children.

In addition, the older narrator provides the point of view most appropriate for the initiation story. She can see, much better than Helen the subject, that she *was* bound to Myra more than she may have liked to have been. Helen *should* be an outsider as well, being a country girl, the only one "who carried a lunch pail" and the only one "who had to wear rubber boots in the spring" (paragraph 12)—and yet she feels only slightly uneasy and never completely excluded.

The perceptions of the younger Helen give the story immediacy, but some of the poignancy of the story depends on the perspective created by looking back on an event that has gathered meaning over the years.

2.   Analyze the character of Myra.

What makes this story different from Bambara's "The Hammer Man" is that the psychology of the outsider (Manny and Myra) is scrutinized in addition to that of the narrator. We know that Myra is used to being excluded; she scarcely even watches other children playing as she stands alone with her brother (paragraph 3), and when Helen first approaches her, she waits in a "withdrawn and rigid attitude," suggesting that she expected Helen to be "playing a trick on her" (paragraph 14). Myra is also vulnerable; she does want friends and is willing to trust Helen the minute she treats her with kindness. Her illness gives her singularity a mysterious and elevated quality, however, so that we may expect Munro to portray her, in the final analysis, as a type of suffering and all-knowing saint whose humility and goodness ultimately change the lives of those around her. But this role is only fulfilled in part. Through getting to know Myra, Helen comes to see aspects of her own personality that make her uncomfortable and ashamed but that do not essentially change her attitude toward Myra.

In addition, Myra is portrayed as a much more complex character than the typical suffering saint. While in the hospital, she plays her role well, sitting "in her high bed, her delicate brown neck rising out of a hospital gown too big for her" (paragraph 89), discussing her trip to London, opening each gift "with an air that not even Gladys could have bettered" (paragraph 77), and presiding over the conversation and excitement of the party. Singling out Helen to bestow a gift on her seems almost as much a part of Myra's act as the "bows of fine satin ribbon" (paragraph 72) were part of the display the other girls put on. We see in Myra a faint reflection of her mother, who plays a similar role as she presides over the fruit store, daring customers to challenge her and handing over fruit "with open mockery in her eyes" (paragraph 11). Yet Myra is only half-aware of the feigned sincerity of the girls, and only half-aware of her own desire to play up her newly acquired stature. These characteristics are crucial for proving that she is not merely a symbol in this story but a fully rounded character.

ETHAN CANIN
Star Food

Like "The Hammer Man" and "Day of the Butterfly," this story reads very much like a memoir and so may strike a responsive chord in students who have earlier worked with Chapter 3. Your students may take a special interest in the story because the author wrote it when he was a student in medical school, much older than the typical undergraduate.

QUESTIONS

1. How is "Star Food" an initiation story?

The first line of the story suggests that "Star Food" will take the form of an initiation story and perhaps resemble a psychological memoir as well. The narrator first introduces an event that marks a turning point in his life: when he is eighteen years old he disappoints both his parents for the first time while, presumably, learning something significant about becoming his own person. The story also contains just enough of an ironic tone to establish the double perspective of a memoir, as it is the older Dade who hints at the humor in his mother's "theory" that sky gazing makes a man great, and who is equally aware of his father's wisdom in attributing his gazing to Dade's attempts "to avoid stock work" (paragraph 2). The story's narrative voice indicates that he will look back on his life to arrive "at some sort of sign" (paragraph 57) that gives reason for why he is the person he has become.

The plot of the story, then, fleshes out the initiation process, with Dade's decision about what he wanted to do with his life at its center. Dade finally does experience an epiphany while watching the sky; the air force planes that fly over his head from the west are enough of a sign to give his life direction. Once they pass, it seems to him that he has "turned a corner" and now he feels "the world dictating its course" (paragraph 99), a course that follows in his father's footsteps. Life now seems to make sense, and accordingly, Dade becomes obsessed with catching the woman shoplifter.

But where this discovery takes us is not so clear, partly because throughout the story our attention is focused on the events recounted, never on an interpretation of them as is often the case in memoirs. And just as a strong interpretive voice is missing in "Star Food," so is a sense of resolution. Dade's epiphany—that his father's life is the one laid out before him—proves a false one, and the story ends not with his discovery of what his life will be but with a more painful and complex discovery about the human condition. It may seem that in rejecting his father's values and letting the woman escape from the store Dade will reach some conclusion about himself. Instead, he merely follows the woman down the street and finds that he is unable to communicate with her. "This moment has always amazed me" (paragraph 120), he comments, but what does the comment explain? Rather than coming to an understanding of what kind of person he is or what he wants to do with his life, Dade discovers in the end that "you could never really know another person" and that he now knows what it is to feel "alone in the world" (paragraph 121). Perhaps the most important aspect of Dade's initiation is that he comes to understand the complexity of "knowing," which is far more elusive and frustrating than figuring out goals for one's life.

2. How do the characters of Dade's mother and father help us understand Dade's character?

The first paragraph of the story sets up a dichotomy that is reiterated throughout the story: Dade's mother, the romantic, longs for her son to pursue wisdom and ideas, while his father, the pragmatist, sees business success as his son's only viable option. Also, because Dade spends so much of his time on the roof of the store gazing at the sky, his mother has constructed a theory that her son is destined to become "a man of limited fame" (paragraph 12), and she waits expectantly for his great discovery; she spends her time dreaming about her son's future and listening to "melodies of operas" (paragraph 104) in the stockroom of the store. Dade's father, in contrast, knows his son is "no fool" (paragraph 16) and will eventually see the value of the two things "God rewarded"—courtesy and hard work (paragraph 14); he spends his time atomizing the cabbage and pointing Dade's gaze to the reality that lies on the "other side of the roof," the alley where "rusted, wheel-less cars lay on blocks in the yards" (paragraph 4).

It appears through most of the story that Dade will be forced to choose between these two starkly opposed views, but the ending of the story suggests that this is not quite so. His apparent epiphany on the roof encourages him to pursue his father's route, to apprehend the shoplifter and live a limited, realistic life. But when he acts on this new impulse, the result is not satisfactory. In the end we feel that he is no closer to knowing what he wants from life but that he has escaped from the simple dichotomy.

In the closing scene, Dade is aware of the movie theater, the alley, and the rain, all reminders of Dade's attempts at discovering what sort of person he will become. The distant sound of "other people's voices" suggests his sense of isolation, the isolation of someone who has become, in a sense, parentless.

3. Which image carries the most symbolic meaning in "Star Food," and what is the most plausible interpretation of it?

Titles, names, and places generally attract symbol hunters because we assume they have been chosen with greater care than the individual words that make up the story. Various meanings can be attached to "Star Food," "Arcade," and the "New Jerusalem River," for example, and you may wish to begin questioning students about these. In addition, images and objects, while posing as the natural things that are what they are, often take on additional meanings as a story progresses. The star positioned on the roof of the grocery store and the sky that Dade studies day and night, for example, provide an interesting pair of symbols with potentially contrasting meanings. Moving from the most narrow to the most interpretive, your students might list these meanings, among others:

The star:
1. The grocery store
2. The uncertain future of the store (drooping points)
3. The father
4. The father's view of the world
5. Artificiality
6. Commercial success
7. Desire, which attracts but also destroys (the insects flying into the star)

The sky/clouds/stars:
1. The mystery of the infinite universe
2. Dade's mind and imagination
3. The mother
4. The mother's view of the world
5. Natural beauty and an attraction to it
6. Intellectual success
7. Inspiration, particularly poetic

In general, the primary function of each of these symbols is to emphasize the dichotomous nature of life as Dade sees it, encompassed by the differences in his parents. Dade's problem may be rooted in his belief that the world can be neatly divided into two ways of viewing the world—his father's and mother's. From Dade's perspective, all the other meanings fit inside of this one, making his decision symbolic because it means not only following either his father's or his mother's dreams but also choosing between two opposing identities for himself. But much of the meaning of the story depends on the combination of the two symbols. The star on top of the store, while it tends to be associated with the orderly and perhaps limited world of business, courtesy, and success, cannot be separated from its source, the sky and the stars beyond it, which is limitless and romantic; likewise, Dade is the son of his father as well as of his mother, and he feels drawn to both aspects of life.

4. What do the details of the setting contribute to "Star Food"?

The actual setting is not essential, since the story could have taken place in almost any town—large or small—in this country; wealthy and poor sections of town and a view of the sky are all that are required. The setting serves the story much as Canin's delineation of characters does, however, for the east/west division merely emphasizes the broader dichotomy that runs throughout the story. When Dade sits on the roof, he looks west—to the clouds of barbecue smoke and the hills and to the direction that in this country is associated with adventure and discovery; Dade's father (and his mother, with some coaxing) had made the choice for the east (paragraph 56), to the traditional means of success, before opening the grocery store. Likewise, Dade's father makes him look to the east from his perch on the roof, to the poverty and decay of the more realistic world.

ROBERT KEITH MILLER

Mark Twain's Jim

This excerpt from Miller's book on Twain provides an excellent model for students: it demonstrates one way of using critical sources to introduce and establish the significance of a topic without letting them control the analysis. Miller is also an inspiration as a critic himself, for he discusses a sophisticated problem with such directness and clarity that students should have no trouble following his argument.

Obviously, they will follow the argument better if they have read *Huckleberry Finn*, but Miller's analysis is so clear and the issues of racial stereotyping are so frequently discussed that students should be able to read and appreciate this selection without knowing the novel directly.

QUESTIONS

1. How does Miller use statements by other critics to strengthen his argument?

Miller's use of critics in the first paragraph establishes one popular view of Jim: that he is "a larger-than-life figure" who represents everything from the spiritual "conscience of the novel" to "the great residue of primitive, fertile force." By directly quoting a variety of writers and by choosing his quotations carefully, Miller shows that the case has been made for a view other than his own. He shows us, in short, that he is dealing with a question on which reasonable people can disagree.

Miller questions the exalted view of Jim in the body of his argument. By asserting his own interpretation of Jim's superstition—for example, that "there is nothing admirable about believing in witchcraft and turning one's delusions into a source of pride" (paragraph 7)—Miller directly challenges the value Walter Blair places on Jim's superstition. Likewise, the vital force that critics Salomon and Cox attribute to Jim is undermined by Miller's proof of Jim's passive acceptance of his position. In fact, the manly, mythic figure drawn for us in the opening paragraph quickly fades when Miller reminds us of Jim in women's clothing learning that his freedom is due not to his own strength but to Miss Watson's generosity. By establishing a contrasting interpretation and then gradually dismantling it, Miller makes his own more persuasive.

Miller implies that the critics have been guilty of a kind of liberal racism in their view of Jim. They have tended to view him as the incarnation of virtue because he is black. But Miller understands Twain to be an equal-opportunity misanthrope (or skeptic, at least) who would not have separate standards for white and black. All would be part of "the damned human race."

2. What is the purpose of paragraphs 2–5?

In addition to playing off other critics to gain our trust, Miller demonstrates his reasonable position through a number of concessions. He believes strongly ("there can be no question") that we should feel sympathy for Jim, that Jim is good at protecting Huck, and that Jim is a loyal and kind person. But even these strengths contribute to Miller's argument: by focusing on Jim's mothering Huck, blindly giving his loyalty to the scheming and injurious Tom Sawyer, and weeping over his separation from his children, Miller praises Jim for attributes that are far more human—and specifically feminine—than godlike. Certainly we appreciate, with Huck, Jim's innate goodness, but such goodness does not make him the lofty figure other critics have made him out to be.

CHARLES R. WOODARD
Wilbur's "Still, Citizen Sparrow"

Before having your students read Woodard's essay, you will want to spend time in class analyzing Wilbur's poem. Have your students consider carefully the denotations as well as the connotations of any ambiguous words and encourage them to interpret the poem for themselves. Once students are fairly certain of their own understanding of the poem, as well as of the ambiguities they cannot explain, they will be ready to read Woodard's essay.

QUESTIONS

1. Summarize "Still, Citizen Sparrow."

Before having your students write a summary of the poem, you may wish to discuss the following words:

1. *Still*: quiet, motionless, or "now as before"
2. *citizen*: connotations of the average person in society, a part of the state and taking responsibility, but the underdog compared to the powerful politician
3. *sparrow*: smallest bird, but singled out in the Bible as an example of God's watching over all creatures
4. *vulture*: a large, predatory bird, associated with death and rot
5. *office*: bureaucratic, or at least businesslike; notice that it is a "rotten" office, relates to *vulture*; consider also the meanings of the word—can mean a "beneficial duty or service"
6. *orchard*: full of life in the form of fruits and nuts
7. *childheart*: the immaturity, or innocence, of the sparrow
8. *bedlam*: uproar and confusion; the sound of Noah's saw and the building of the ark, in contrast to the song of birds
9. *gnaw*: not usually a noun—but the sound of eroding
10. *keel*: the principal structure of a ship; relates also to the backbone of a bird

11. *Ararat*: the mountain on which Noah landed; the highest mountain in Turkey

The following summary is one possible reading of the poem:

> In "Still, Citizen Sparrow," the poet admonishes the sparrow, a "citizen" of rather limited perspective, to stop concentrating on what he finds disgusting about the vulture—his association with dead things and decay—and look to the good the vulture does; by relieving nature of the decaying things, the vulture performs a noble function which "mocks mutability" and "keeps nature new." His flight across the sky should remind the sparrow of Noah, who spent much of his time amidst the decay of humanity building his ark and, having done so, sailed over the ruins of the earth with whatever life he could save—including the sparrow. All that remains on earth owes its life to Noah and that "slam of his hammer" that provided the means of preserving life, and perhaps it owes much to the vulture as well.

2. How does Woodard establish his argument as one worth making?

In the opening paragraph Woodard briefly summarizes the standard interpretation of the poem, which views the poem as chiefly about politicians. The "however" in Woodard's third sentence should alert us to his own position: the common reading is problematic, and although he understands the source of confusion, he cannot let the interpretation stand. His combined sensitivity to alternative readings and then his delineation of the problem in paragraph 2 proves that he has an argument that is worth making.

Woodard's opening can be used as an example of how to set up a problem in interpreting literature, challenging a point made by a critic. A similar technique might, of course, be used by students who "challenge" their own first understanding of the poem or the understanding that is revealed by class discussion. The important thing for students to notice is that Woodard uses his introduction to show that the question he addresses is one on which reasonable people can disagree.

CHAPTER 11

Some Advice on Research

Purpose

This chapter is not designed to be "taught" in the ordinary sense of being the subject of class discussion. Indeed, as I stated in the third paragraph of page 418, it is not even designed to be read completely at a sitting. It is designed to be skimmed at some point during the term and then consulted in greater detail when students confront particular research problems.

If you are doing a unit on the research paper, you would do well to assign this chapter and the next very early on, so that students can get an idea of the nature and magnitude of the task they are undertaking. The task will then begin to focus their attention, and they will learn about the process of doing research as all of us do, by rolling up our sleeves and getting to work.

In some classes, I have found it useful to set up "consulting groups" during the research unit. These groups of three or four students discuss their research progress and difficulties for a very few minutes during each class period, offering each other advice and support. Not much can be done in these few minutes, of course, but I encourage the students to exchange phone numbers and to consult outside of class as well. A fair number seem to do this: "consulting buddies" are soetimes seen working together at the library and many of the students review each other's drafts-in-progress without my asking them to do so.

An Exercise

Most teachers will probably simply assign Chapter 11 as background reading and not take much class time working with it. But if you are teaching a research-oriented composition class, you may want to link this chapter to a practical exercise in finding information.

If so, you might consider the following exercise or some variation of it. Divide your students into small groups (these might become the consulting groups mentioned above) and have them, during class time, plan a research path for each of the following tasks:

1. Find five recently published articles on the effectiveness of the anti-cholesterol campaign in improving the nation's health.
2. Identify the five national issues that are of greatest concern to students at your college.
3. Find the width of the English Channel at its narrowest point.
4. Decide whether there are enough sources in the library to allow someone to write a good research paper on Preston Sturges's movie *Sullivan's Travels*.
5. Find the titles of the two or three leading biographies of Martin Luther King, Jr.
6. Find out what President Lyndon Johnson said when he was criticized for pulling his dog's ears.
7. Find a recently published bibliography on the spread of AIDS.

When you bring the class together for discussion, students should have decided that item 2 is not a library problem. Have them discuss in some detail their plan for gathering the information from interviews or questionnaires. See Hint 4, pages 422–424.

The other six are potential library questions, great or small. Economical routes for each might be:

1. A look in *Readers' Guide to Periodical Literature* or *New York Times Index*.
3. A look in any general encyclopedia.
4. A look in a standard encyclopedia to see who Sturges was. Examination of the card catalog (by subject) for books and for bibliographies. Examination of the *Essay and General Literature Index*. Examination of *Readers' Guide* and *New York Times Index* for appropriate years. Students could dig further, but if these leads have not given them a few titles that they can locate in the library, they can probably conclude that the library won't provide adequate material without their taking extraordinary measures.
5. A look at *Encyclopaedia Britannica* or a card-catalog search for an annotated bibliography.
6. A trip to the card catalog to find biographies, then a look through indexes in the biographies, or else an examination of entries in *New York Times Index* during the Johnson years.
7. The card catalog, perhaps, but also *Bibliographic Index*.

You could then send the students to the library to complete each of the tasks, either in teams or individually.

CHAPTER 12
Writing the Research Paper

Purpose

Like Chapter 11, this chapter is designed less for class discussion than for out-of-class reading and reference, so my commentary here is limited. If I were assigning a research paper for a freshman class, I would have students read these two chapters to prepare for our first serious discussion of the research paper assignment. If students come to class imagining themselves producing an essay like Carolyn Douglas's "Changing Theories of Darwin's Illness," they will be prepared to listen attentively to your description of the exact assignment, the schedule, and so forth. They will probably have questions on their mind as well.

They may want to know, for instance, if you expect them to do as extensive a research job as Douglas did, often giving several citations per paragraph, or whether it will be enough for them to use a few sources just to set up their own thinking. They may want to know if you feel that the amount of quotation in Douglas's paper is about right. They may want to discuss what they can do if they find that the library is not yielding for them the number and quality of sources it did for her. They may want to know if you object to their using encyclopedia sources the way that she did.

Ideally, you will clarify some of these issues in an assignment sheet. If you have never assigned a research paper before, I would advise you to think about your own experience doing such papers and remember that they do involve a tremendous time commitment. An essay like "Changing Theories of Darwin's Illness" might represent forty to sixty hours of work, which at my university is about half the homework hours expected for a three credit-hour course. You may want to consider a shorter assignment with fewer sources if you must do your research paper unit in a two- or three-week period.

Practical Considerations in
Assigning Research Papers

If you've not assigned research papers before, I would encourage you to talk to someone else who has done so at your college. Your colleague may be able to tell you what topics are so overused locally that students may be tempted to recycle old essays, what difficulties he or she has experienced with limited holdings in the library, and other practical matters that pertain to your particular teaching situation.

My own best luck with term papers has been in semesters when I set a common, very broad topic (e.g., "Twenty-five Years of Change") and then let students propose topics that would fit within it. The first day of such proposing happens in class and usually produces broad areas of interest (e.g., advances in computers in the last twenty-five years, changes in relationships between blacks and whites in the last twenty-five years, the decline of sportsmanship in baseball in the last twenty-five years). After the broad areas are roughed out, I give students a chance to do some preliminary research and propose three topics narrow enough to be covered in the time and space allowed. Ideally, I pick one of these from each student's list. Sometimes all three create problems too serious for the student to overcome and we meet to renegotiate.

The advantage to this plan is that the students are working on analogous writing assignments and using comparable sources, so they are in a position to consult with each other. The consultation does not raise questions of plagiarism, however, since no two topics are identical. And the range of topics is wide enough that the students don't end up in a cutthroat competition for sources.

An alternative is to have all students work on the same topic, using a sourcebook I provide. (Usually the "sourcebook" is merely a folder containing a dozen or so articles.) Two or three copies of the sourcebook are kept at the reserve desk of the library, where students can check them out to read or to photocopy. In order to give students some practice in research without creating an impossible strain on library resources, I require students to write their essay using the sources in the sourcebook (cited as they would be if students had found them themselves) and at least two additional sources. The difficulties with this system are (1) it gives the students a narrower opportunity to practice research skills, (2) the students invariably find fault with my choice of sources, (3) on some topics, the requirement of two additional sources *does* lead to a strain on library resources, (4) I work long and hard on putting the sourcebook together, and (5) some students dislike the topic they are forced to work with. The advantage of the system is that because you know so many of the potential sources so well, you are in a good position to know whether they are being used properly.

Another practical consideration in assigning a research paper is that students need a chance to submit a preliminary draft well before the final essay is due. No matter how clear the model that is set before students, some of the least experienced will produce papers that don't come near to fulfilling the assignment's requirements. An opportunity for these students to correct their understanding of the assignment in the *early* drafting stage will save both them and you a good deal of heartbreak. If the first draft of an ambitious research paper comes to you a week before the final draft is due, you may find that some students have already sunk twenty or thirty hours into a project that hasn't a chance of coming out satisfactorily.

But on the bright side, if you make a good research paper assignment and track your students' progress by looking at drafts and holding short conferences, you may well find the whole business invigorating. Indeed, some of your best moments in this course will come from coaching students through the production of papers that both they and you can be proud of.

PART IV

Matters of Form and Style

CHAPTER 13

Organizing the Expository Essay

Purpose

The purpose of this chapter is to give students both a way of organizing an essay and a way of thinking about organization. That is, the chapter gives students enough information about the relatively rigid thesis-statement-topic-sentence system of organization for them to see its virtues and be able to apply it to their own work. At the same time, the chapter attempts to show them that this very "firm" approach is not the only game in town and that a more flexible approach is sometimes more effective. The hope is that by helping students see organization less as a matter of mechanics and more as a matter of revealing a structure of ideas, we can decrease the number of papers whose "organization" is no more than a *pro forma* following of a fixed pattern.

The emphasis in this chapter is on the body of an essay. Introductions and conclusions are treated in the next chapter.

Overview

The chapter includes a section contrasting firm and flexible approaches to organization, a section on the traditional patterns of organization (illustration, comparison or contrast, classification, and division), and a section on outlining.

The Chapter Step-by-Step

Firm and Flexible Approaches to Organization (pages 476–480)

This section holds up for inspection two contrasting passages. The Theodore White paragraph follows the firm, topic-sentence-based pattern. The Annie

235

Dillard passage does not announce its intentions in a clear, conspicuously placed topic sentence, but instead requires readers to discover for themselves the framework that holds the passage together.

The text does not, of course, contrast these two passages in order to praise one at the other's expense. Both are excellent, but their excellences are of very different sorts. White's rather boxlike paragraph on the grammar school has the advantage of making its intention clear from the outset and working always inside that intention: the first sentence announces the framework. Like all such paragraphs or passages, it runs the danger of being boring because its direction is so firmly set that it seems almost impossible to surprise the reader. But White does manage to get in an element of surprise by introducing details and figures of speech we wouldn't have anticipated. His energy as a writer carries him through.

Dillard's passage, though broken into several paragraphs, is comparable to White's in length and in its feeling of self-containment. The reader feels at the end of the passage that something has been rounded off, completed; some idea has been explored here about as thoroughly as White explored the idea that "the Latin School taught the mechanics of learning with very little pretense of culture, enrichment or enlargement of horizons." But because the idea is not articulated in an obvious topic sentence placed at or near the beginning of the paragraph, each reader has the experience of discovering for himself or herself what framework holds these details and images together. Dillard's approach (like her prose) can create interest, but it runs the danger of leaving the reader confused. In this passage, however, she seems to overcome that danger, largely by the strength of her controlling images.

Textbooks tend to recommend an organizational pattern like White's without giving students much sense of the reason for the recommendation or the alternatives that are available. By inspecting these two passages in *The Riverside Guide*, students should be in a position to see their options and also to appreciate the common-sense recommendation on page 480: for most college writing the organization should be basically firm, with some conscious deviations from a too-mechanical firmness.

Exercise 1: Converting a Passage to a Firmer Organization (page 479).   This rather demanding exercise produces excellent papers for a workshop on paragraphing. Such a workshop could be done with the class divided into groups, but this particular exercise might work better if you keep the class together and help students focus their discussion. The best approach might be to duplicate two or three solutions to this paragraphing problem and discuss the strengths and weaknesses of each. The main things to emphasize at this point are unity and coherence: has the writer included only information that fits under the topic sentence, and does one sentence seem logically connected to the next?

The following solution is 263 words long:

> The main fact and difficulty of China is its millions of square miles
> of terrible soil, soil that all the will and cooperation in the world cannot
> alter. Although there is good soil in the river valleys of China, and
> 2,000-acre fields, and John Deere tractors, most of the nation is barely

arable, and the methods are labor-intensive. Driving to a meeting with Chinese writers, we saw fields on the outskirts of the city and patches of agriculture. In an eggplant field, the clay was so hard that the peasants squeezed it into mud walls for shade to protect the shoots and stems of the young plants from the drying wind. In a nearby field, two men were pulling a plow through the baked ground by ropes lashed across their chests. A third man guided the plow's tongue. Consciousness of the problem of working this terrible soil is so great, even among Chinese intellectuals, that one of the men at the meeting, speaking of his goals as a writer, said, "I believe that after several decades we will be able to lead a good life on our soil." Even this elegant intellectual, erect and relaxed in his trim gray jacket, could not speak of the future without thinking of the soil and could not speak of the soil without seeming to keep a great passion under great control. "The old planet," Maxine Hong Kingston calls China. It is the oldest enduring civilization on earth, and its life from ancient times has been a continual struggle to lead "a good life *on our soil.*"

Something is gained by the rewrite. As a report on the role of the soil in China, it is clearer. Details are subordinated to the main idea in a way that is logical: "Even this elegant intellectual . . . ," for instance, tells the reader that the man's elegance and intellectuality are pertinent because elegant intellectuals in most countries aren't inclined to speak of the soil with such passion.

But much is also lost. For the cooperative and attentive reader, Dillard's more flexible pattern of organization creates pleasing surprises and suspense, and it opens up the possibility of larger meanings than the one neatly framed by the topic sentence. When I first read the passage, I looked into the palm of my right hand to see the map of China and found myself thinking about the soiled hands of farmers everywhere and the ancient link of all humankind to the earth. The rewritten version would not have given me that thought.

Four Common Patterns of Organization (pages 480–486)

The patterns of organization discussed here have been a mainstay of composition instruction for decades. If the treatment in *The Riverside Guide* differs from the traditional, it is only in confessing what every experienced composition teacher will have already noticed—that the patterns of organization are actually patterns of thought, and they are just as likely to control the organization of a paragraph or a pair of sentences as they are to control the organization of a whole essay.

The box diagrams used to illustrate the organizational patterns reflect the sort of *ad hoc* diagramming many composition teachers do on the chalkboard as they discuss the organization of essays and passages, a method of diagramming that seems to help students see the connection between the abstract intellectual framework and the physical framing (by sectioning, paragraphing, etc.) of the words on the page.

Exercise 2: Drawing Box Diagrams to Reveal Organization (pages 485–486). Precision and detail in the diagram are not what counts here, of course. Students should not have great trouble roughing out some of the frames in this well-organized essay, and the rough sketch is what we are after.

As an example of comparison/contrast, your students might use the opening paragraph's picture of Darwin before and after the voyage:

During voyage he was in robust health: 400-mile horse-back journey, hunting with gauchos, thriving on irregular diet.	After voyage he was an invalid: living in secluded country house, capable of only a few hours' work, exhausted even by visit from friends.

The state of Darwin's health changed drastically after the voyage.

As an example of illustration, they might point to the long paragraph that begins on page 4 of Douglas's paper (book page 450) and ends on page 6 (book page 454):

George Gaylord Simpson: theory of undiagnosed disease such as brucellosis	Saul Adler: theory of Chagas's disease	Gavin de Beer: uses Adler's theory in biography and in *Britannica* article	John H. Winslow: theory of arsenic poisoning

Some of Darwin's admirers were irritated by psychoanalytic theories (and argued for theories of the disease's physical causation).

Students might characterize the bulk of the paper as being organized by a loose chronological division:

Theories in Darwin's own time	First theory of psychological cause: neurasthenia	Psychoanalytic theories	Theories reacting to psychoanalytic theories	Today's theories of psychological causation

Theories about the causes of Darwin's illness have changed over the years.

Outlining (pages 486–489)

Conventions of outlining vary, and if you have strong opinions about such things, you will need to make them clear to your students. The example in the text uses full sentences for the Roman-numeral level entries and fragments or even words for other levels. You may want to instruct your students to use full sentences down to the capital-letter level or even at every level.

From our perspective, the conventions are less important than the clarity with which students identify the major and minor framing of the essay.

Exercise 3: A Formal Outline (page 488). The outline below follows most of the conventions governing the example in the text, but it differs in two respects. Like many outlines used for term papers, it simply lists the introduction and conclusion without giving details, and it specifies the thesis.

Changing Theories of Darwin's Illness

INTRODUCTION

Thesis statement: The precise cause of Darwin's illness remains a mystery, but the best evidence now available suggests that it was caused by the psychological stress of advocating the theory of evolution. The persistent attempt to find a physical cause reveals at least as much about society's reluctance to consider mental disease "real" as it does about what was wrong with Charles Darwin.

I. The breakdown in Darwin's health after his return from the voyage of the *Beagle* was dramatic and mysterious.
   A. Darwin's vigorous life on the *Beagle* expedition
   B. His semi-invalid state from 1842 on

II. In Darwin's own time, physical explanations of the disease were suggested, but they are inconsistent with present-day knowledge of medicine.
   A. Darwin's inability to identify a physical cause
   B. His theory of seasickness
   C. His son's theory of gout
   D. Modern medicine's rejection of these theories

III. Serious speculations about psychological causes of the disease began in this century.
   A. Johnston's 1901 theory of neurasthenia
      1. The meaning of neurasthenia in early twentieth-century medicine
      2. Rejection of neurasthenia later in the century
   B. Psychoanalytic theories
      1. Kempf's 1918 theory of anxiety neurosis
         a. Resentment of tyrannical father
         b. Mask of conscious kindness
         c. Stress of repressed emotion causes illness
      2. Good's 1954 Oedipal theory
         a. Resentment of tyrannical father
         b. "Reaction formation'
         c. Murder of Heavenly Father by evolution theory
         d. Oedipal remorse

IV. These speculations were challenged in the second half of the century by re-
searchers who were uncomfortable with the idea of psychosomatic illness
and who proposed physical causes consistent with present-day medical
knowledge.
   A. Simpson's 1958 suggestion of brucellosis
   B. Adler's 1959 theory of Chagas's disease
   C. De Beer's influential acceptance of Adler's theory
      1. Attack on psychoanalytic theories in biography
      2. *Encyclopaedia Britannica* article
   D. Winslow's 1971 theory of arsenic poisoning

V. The most recent research indicates that Darwin's illness must have been at
least partly psychological in origin, and scholars now accept the idea that
Darwin may have been simultaneously a great man and the victim of a neu-
rotic illness.
   A. Woodruff's questioning of Adler's theory and Adler's reply
   B. Colp's disproof of Winslow's theory
   C. Colp's *To Be an Invalid* (1977)
      1. Correlation of disease to work on theory
      2. Conclusion that emotions related to theory were a major cause of
         illness
   D. State of opinion since Colp
      1. Stress on psychology in Clark's 1984 biography
      2. 1989 *Encyclopedia Americana*
         a. Advocacy of Chagas's disease
         b. Failure to revise since at least 1972
      3. Repetition of Colp's ideas in 1990 *Encyclopaedia Britannica*

CONCLUSION

WORKS CITED

Exercise 4: Re-Paragraphing an Essay (pages 488–489).   For the record,
Goodman's own paragraph breaks come at the beginning of sentences 4, 6, 8 12,
15, 17, 20, 23, 27, 30, 33, 38, 41, and 45. Obviously, such paragraphing would
look odd on a standard page, but there may be considerable disagreement about
where the "standard-sized" paragraphs fall.

This exercise works well in groups, especially because when the groups come
together at the end of the class hour, they tend to be surprised by how much they
agree. They will tend to find the thesis embedded in sentence 18: "many of us
have transferred a chunk of our friendships, a major portion of our everyday
social lives, from home to office." And they will tend to agree that paragraph
breaks should occur at the beginning of sentences 12, 17, 30, and 41—though
they may suggest additional breaks elsewhere. When groups disagree, the discussion of their reasoning should be productive.

CHAPTER 14

Introductions and Conclusions

Purpose

Chapter 14 is simply a lesson in writing the parts of the essay that some students find most troublesome. Its approach is to look at the introductions and conclusions of four essays included elsewhere in the book and to show how they work. The essays chosen are varied in their tone, purpose, and audience so that they give students some sense of the range of possibilities open to the writer.

Overview

The chapter divides into five parts:

1. An examination of Annie Dillard's introduction and conclusion to "Singing with the Fundamentalists"—an example of an essay that begins with a scene and ends with a parallel scene.
2. An examination of George Orwell's "Reflections on Gandhi," which begins with a "funnel-shaped" introduction and ends with a "web" conclusion.
3. An examination of Maya Angelou's "My Sojourn in the Lands of My Ancestors," which has an introduction stressing the author's mood or attitude and a conclusion stressing her changed attitude.
4. An examination of Eileen O'Brien's "What Was the Acheulean Hand Ax?"—which begins by developing a question and ends by discussing an answer.
5. A list of six generalizations about introductions and conclusions based on the cases examined above.

So straightforward is the chapter that we can forgo a step-by-step review of it. If there is anything novel in it, it is the treatment of introductions and conclusions as pairs. The tendency of textbooks to treat introductions and conclusions in isolation from each other has, I think, kept students from seeing the way that they work together to shape the reader's perceptions.

CHAPTER 15

Assisting the Reader: Connection, Imagery, Simplicity

Purpose

The aim of this chapter is to focus students' attention on the issue of clarity in prose, to get them to appreciate the virtues of a "windowpane" style, and to give them some practical help in achieving such a style.

Overview

After an introductory section intended to get students thinking about the difficulties readers have understanding even a simple text, the chapter divides into three sections, each dealing with an aspect of style that can assist the reader: connection, imagery, and simplicity.

The Chapter Step-by-Step

The Daneman-Carpenter "Bat" Study (pages 500–501)

The chapter begins with a discussion of Daneman and Carpenter's experiment primarily because it helps students see the need for the sections that follow. Understanding that readers *are* easy to confuse helps students understand the importance of connection, imagery, and simplicity. The experiment also recalls one of the themes of *The Riverside Guide: everyone* plays the game of verbal communication with a fairly weak hand. Thus this chapter connects with the discussion of fogginess in Chapter 2 and of being "blocked by openness" in Chapter 5.

Connection (pages 502–506)

The lesson here is quite straightforward and will be familiar to anyone who has taught composition before. You might note particularly the box on page 503: students could probably benefit from charting one of their own paragraphs in the way that the White paragraph is charted there.

Exercise 1: Inserting Transitional Markers (page 506).   Logical markers might be:

For the start of sentence 2, *For instance*

For the start of sentence 3, *Furthermore*

For the start of sentence 4, *Moreover*

For the start of sentence 6, *Finally*

For the start of sentence 7, *In short*

For the start of sentence 8, *And* or *Therefore*

For the start of sentence 9, *To take a second example*

For the start of sentence 10, *To take a third example*

For the start of sentence 11, *In this instance*

Inserting these transitions will make your students more conscious of them in their own prose and will remind them that they are not interchangeable. (I have had students sprinkle *thus* and *therefore* through their essays almost at random, apparently on the theory that they sound impressive.) Adding the transitions will also create a hideous paragraph that should stand as a warning not to use transitions excessively, which some students are inclined to do.

While you may not be convinced that any of these markers necessarily improve this paragraph, students may make a good case for one or two additions.

Exercise 2: Unscrambling a Scrambled Paragraph (page 506).   The original sentence order of Mead's paragraph is 2, 8, 5, 6, 4, 1, 9, 3, 7. It is possible to rearrange the order slightly and still arrive at a coherent paragraph—but only slightly. The important thing is not that students simply unscramble the paragraph but that they articulate the reasons why one sentence must follow another.

One way I have done these unscrambling exercises is to tape each sentence to the back of a shirt cardboard and write the first two and last two words of the sentences with a felt-tip pen on the front. The shirt cardboards are then handed out to students in random order, and the students with cardboards stand at the front of the class and read their sentences aloud, from left to right, in whatever order they find themselves standing. The rest of the class then rearranges the students at the front, giving reasons why Fred's sentence must come after Mary's, etc. After our initial reshuffling we read through the sentences again and shuffle again until we finally arrive at an order everyone approves of.

If your students have used copies of *The Riverside Guide*, this exercise may be so marked over that it no longer works in class. A good paragraph to substitute for Mead's is the third in George Orwell's "Marrakech Ghetto," an essay that is not included in the *Guide* but is widely anthologized and should be easy to locate.

Imagery (pages 507–509)

The object here is to counteract the tendency of some students to see imagery as purely a matter of decoration. The example is, therefore, provided by the businesslike George Orwell and is from an expository essay rather than a descriptive one. The exercise also stresses the pragmatic use of imagery.

Exercise 3: An Experiment with Imagery (pages 508–509). You may want your students to develop hypotheses about the passages by White, Dillard, and Dowden whether they undertake the experiment or not. A sensible hypothesis is that White's passage would be the most thoroughly remembered because of its clear organization and its series of graphic images; that the Dillard passage would leave clear images in the reader's mind, though the memory of how those images fit in the passage might be unclear and the exact words might tend to be forgotten; and that the Dowden passage would create the greatest problems for memory, partly because of the unfamiliar terms and partly because there are so few images to cling to.

Actually testing the passages will to some degree confirm these hypotheses and to some degree remind students that the reader's mind really does move in mysterious ways.

Simplicity (pages 509–513)

Twain's criticism of Professor Dowden adds some humor and some edge to the recommendation of Orwell's model of "windowpane" prose. The real work of this section, however, is done in the exercises.

Exercise 4: Active and Passive Voice (page 510). Students would benefit by giving some thought to the reasons that sentences are active or passive as they work with this exercise.

- Sentence 1 is from the *Encyclopaedia Britannica* article on Shakespeare quoted in Chapter 6 (page 174). It is passive, one assumes, because the authors don't wish to name the cranks who made this search. A possible active version would be "In the later 19th century ingenious and energetic investigators searched for messages embedded in the dramatic text."

- Sentence 2 is from Maya Angelou's "My Sojourn in the Lands of My Ancestors" (page 37). It is active. A possible passive version would be "Leftovers from the last night feast were eaten, and a sad goodbye was said to my hosts." The effect of the change is so horrible that no one will try to defend it.

- Sentence 3 is from Annie Dillard's "Singing with the Fundamentalists" (page 44). It is passive because Dillard's focus is on the hymns rather than on the hymnists and also because an active-voice sentence would not have the kick that comes from having the comment about the greeting cards come behind as a stinger: "The same people who put out lyrical Christian greeting cards and bookmarks apparently wrote these hymns, and wrote them just yesterday."

• Sentence 4 is from Maya Angelou's "Powhitetrash" (page 110). It is active. Possible passive versions would be "My uncle was called by his first name and ordered around the store" (okay if the focus were on Uncle Willie) or "My uncle was called by his first name by them and ordered around the store by them" (a mess).

• Sentence 5 is from Barbara Tuchman's "Chivalry" (page 42). It is basically in the active voice, though it has a passive participle phrase ("on being again raped"). A possible passive-voice version would shift this phrase to an active-voice clause: "The Countess was revisited by the King and, when she again rejected him, she was raped villainously." This passive sentence might do if the focus were on the Countess, but there is something odd and evasive sounding about reporting a rape in the passive voice.

Exercise 5: Effective and Ineffective Figures of Speech. (page 512).   Though students doing this exercise may get some pleasure from recognizing passages they have read, they needn't know the context to have an intelligent opinion about the effectiveness of the figures of speech.

• Example 1 is from Annie Dillard's "Singing with the Fundamentalists" (page 48). Students who have not read the essay should recognize that the simile "as if pulled on strings" is both a description of movement and a suggestion that the boys and girls are puppets being moved by a power above them. Students who have read the essay will know the implication is appropriate, since the gesture accompanies prayer.

• Example 2 is from Barbara Tuchman's "Chivalry," but it is altered. The metaphor "heart and soul" is one of those automatic phrases Orwell warns us about. Tuchman's actual choice is "fulcrum" (page 39). The word accomplishes much more, suggesting that loyalty was the fixed point on which chivalry could pivot in order to do its work.

• Example 3 is from Annie Dillard's "Cover Your Tracks" (page 70). Its metaphors are exuberant, but they may seem to be too mixed and confusing. The line of words is compared to three things. If we keep the first of these, the miner's pick, in mind, we can make visual sense of the next sentence about the line of words digging a path for the writer to follow. But who (outside of science fiction) ever "followed" a surgeon's probe? And whether we take the pick, the gouge, or the probe, the notion of a dead end may give us trouble. Every mine is eventually a dead end, and it is hard to know just what a dead end would mean to a carpenter with a gouge in hand.

• Example 4 is from Eileen O'Brien's "What Was the Acheulean Hand Ax?" (page 197) and contains two fine similes, the almond and the teardrop comparisons. Among so many rather technical and perhaps unfamiliar words these similes create a clear visual picture of the ax's shape.

- Example 5 is from Sissela Bok's "White Lies" (page 202) and is perhaps adequate, though not much more. The tipping scale is a familiar metaphor and therefore one Orwell would have us view with suspicion, but it is so useful when the writer wants to talk about balancing two sides of an issue that it may be unavoidable. It may also be a dead metaphor rather than a dying one.

- Example 6 is from Chief Justice Burger's argument in the Miller case (page 242). It's not clear that Burger is paying close attention to the images in the first sentence: one may strike layers of *something* from *something* to improve ventilation, but it's not clear what that thing would be. The comparison in the last sentence, however, has clearly been thought out. Strictly speaking, it is an analogy rather than a metaphor, so that some people would not consider it a figure of speech, but it is worth considering. It is effective, at least, in making an argument that differences in degree, when they are great enough, can be treated as differences in kind. Morphine is addictive, but not so quickly or so powerfully as opium; therefore we treat the drugs differently. Likewise, pornography and simple openness about it are both "explicit," and the explicitness in both cases can sometimes include some degree of shock or titillation, but the differences in the aim and effect of the explicitness are great enough that we can treat the two things differently.

Exercise 6: Editing Professor Dowden (pages 512–513). The Dowden passage, 232 words long, is a bit puffy by today's standards. The following version has less "cakewalk" to it and weighs in at a slimmer 175 words:

The charm of Oxford for Shelley lay in the freedom of his student's life. He could pursue his own studies without interruption and, in his rooms, be poet, natural philosopher, and metaphysician by turns. If he wanted the company of a friend, the afternoon was free for country rambles, the evening and night for discussion and debate.

Shelley found one such friend, and only one, during the months at Oxford. Thomas Jefferson Hogg of Stockton-on-Tees, born into an old family and high Tory politics, had entered University College in 1810, shortly before Shelley. They met early in Michaelmas Term and quickly formed a friendship that for a time excluded all others and that had momentous consequences for them both. There was little resemblance between the friends. Hogg had a powerful intellect and was a lover of literature throughout his life but he lacked Shelley's appetite for revolutionary doctrines and abstract principles, and his interest in literature was that of a man of the world who finds in poetry a refuge from the tedium of life.

Exercise 7: Editing Inflated Prose (page 513). Fourteen changes have been made in the Orwell passage, some more glaring than others. The bogus stretches appear in boldface type below:

What I have most wanted to do throughout the past ten years is to make political writing into something somehow
1
more ineffable, more artlike in nature. My *point d'appui* is
2
always a feeling of partisanship, a sense of what we might
3
call, for lack of a better word, injustice. When I embark
4
upon the adventure of a book, I do not ruminate to myself,
5
"I am going to produce a work of art." I write it because
6
there is some prevarication I want to expose, some fact
7
to which I want to draw attention, and my initial concern is
8
to get a hearing. But I could not do the onerous labor of
writing a book, or even a protracted magazine article, if it
were not also an aesthetic experience. Anyone who cares to
9
put my work under a microscope will see that even when it is
10
downright propaganda it contains much that a full-time
11
politician would consider irrelevant. I am not able, and I do
not want, completely to abandon the world view that I
acquired in the dreamy, golden-domed years of childhood. So
12
long as I remain sentient and disease-free I shall continue
to feel strongly about the manner in which articles, books
and other materials are written, to love the surface of the

earth, and to take a pleasure in solid objects and scraps of

useless information. It is no use trying to suppress that

13

side of myself. **The task at hand is to find an equilibrium**

point between my ingrained likes and dislikes and the

essentially public, non-individual activities that this age

14

of man forces on us all.

The ability of students to identify—and groan over—the clumsy substitutions is more important than their ability to guess what Orwell would have written. Here, however, are the changes or resubstitutions needed to return the passage to its pristine state:

1. an art
2. starting point
3. [delete]
4. sit down to write
5. say
6. lie
7. work
8. long
9. examine my work
10. [delete]
11. alive and well
12. prose style
13. the job is to reconcile
14. [delete]

CHAPTER 16

Engaging the Reader: Texture and Tone

This chapter is intended to serve as a counterweight ~~.~~ ~~....~~ ~~er~~ 15. In effect, Chapter 15 is devoted to efficiency and good manners in prose. Chapter 16 is a reminder that efficiency and good manners are not enough, that writers must keep their readers' attention. All the stylistic helpfulness in the world is useless if the reader refuses to turn the page.

Overview

The chapter divides into three parts: a preliminary look at the problem of "limpness," a discussion of texture in prose, and a discussion of tone in prose. The use of the words *texture* and *tone* may make the chapter seem more exotic or difficult than it actually is. Texture is presented as a matter of unexpected detail, sentence variety, and sharp diction; tone is presented in terms of choices between earnestness and humor, distance and familiarity, deference and edge. Students don't seem to find this material difficult to understand. Many do find it difficult to apply skillfully, and one way of looking at the chapter is as an introduction to the sort of intense attention to style that students might experience in an advanced composition course.

The Chapter Step-by-Step

The Problem of Limpness (pages 514–515)

"Seat Belts" serves as a point of reference for the rest of the chapter, defining what a colleague of mine once called "dead-end competence" in writing. It is dangerous, of course, to use a student essay as a negative example, since fear of being criticized may cause some students great anxiety and induce writer's block. But my experience with this particular essay has been good. It belongs to no one in the class, so no individual is embarrassed, but students recognize in the paper a little devil that seems to stand near them as they write, whispering "Play it safe; follow the form; don't press your luck." I have used the paper in class as a way of telling students that playing it *this* safe is in fact very dangerous.

Texture (pages 516–522)

Texture is being used here as a catchall term for everything that can enrich the bland uniformity of prose written in the textbook manner. One phrase that comes to mind as a definition of texture is from Hopkins's "Pied Beauty": "All things counter, original, spare, strange." The chapter focuses on unexpected details, sentence variety, and strong verb forms because these three areas are particularly productive sources of texture for novice writers.

Exercise 1: A Paragraph with Unexpected Details (page 518).   The best luck I've had with exercises like this one is to use the results as the basis for small-group workshops. A good pattern for this particular exercise would be to put the students into groups of four or five and provide each group with paragraphs written by members of the other groups. Ask each group to read through the papers that come to it and choose the one they feel best fulfills the assignment. Have the spokesperson for the group read the paper aloud to the class and give the group's reason for choosing it.

Exercise 2: Revising for Sentence Variety (page 520). Here are two possible solutions, fairly typical of what you might expect from your students:

> Nixon is a television creation, a sort of gesturing phantom, uncomfortable with the old-fashioned world of printer's type, where facts can be checked and verified. His aversion to the press is understandable, since the Watergate story did not lend itself to the fugitive images of television but to the durable columns of newsprint. This is not an accident: printer's ink and domestic liberty have an old association. Television, a mass medium, can be controlled and manipulated, but total control of the printed word (as has been shown in the Soviet Union) seems to be all but impossible. If newspapers are censored or suppressed, broadsides and leaflets can still be circulated and passed from hand to hand. The revival of the press under Nixon is an essential part of the Watergate phenomenon . . .

> Nixon, that television creation, that gesturing phantom, had an understandable aversion to the press. He was uncomfortable with the old-fashioned world of printer's type, where facts can be checked and verified. The Watergate story did not lend itself to the fugitive images of television as well as it did to the durable columns of newsprint; this is not an accident. Printer's ink and domestic liberty have an old association. Television is a mass medium that can be controlled and manipulated, but total control of the printed word seems to be all but impossible, as has been demonstated in the Soviet Union. If newspapers

are censored or suppressed, broadsides and leaflets can still circulate, passing from hand to hand. The revival of the press under Nixon is an essential part of the Watergate phenomenon . . .

The first of these passages closely resembles what McCarthy actually wrote. The second develops a voice rather different from McCarthy's, particularly in the opening sentences. Putting such responses to the assignment side by side and asking students to discuss the strengths and weaknesses of each is a good follow-up to the exercise.

Exercise 3: Strengthening Verbs (page 522).   A good way to use this exercise is to list the substitutes that your students suggest on the chalkboard and discuss the merits of each—perhaps trying to reach consensus on which will serve best. The orginal verbs are:

1. *carpeted*—a choice that suggests complete coverage and also brings to mind (for contrast's s͟   ͟he neater carpet we might find in well-kept houses.
2. *stunned*—a choice so exac͟. proaching it. The word sugges͟t quite at odds with the picture of the ͟ busy ͟.
3. *crammed* [in both places]—a deliberately unpleasant word choice, typical of Orwell, who doesn't mind pointing to unpleasantness. Your students may come up with different verbs for the two replacements, but their ears will likely encourage a repetition.
4. *squared* and *aligned*—the gesture seems to be a clue to Laski's character, compulsive and somewhat rigid. It expresses neatly Didion's view of the left-wing ideologue.

Tone (pages 523–530)

Most English majors of the last generation grew up on a definition of tone as "the author's attitude toward the work and the audience." This definition has limited usefulness, however, and so *The Riverside Guide* offers one that concentrates exclusively on audience and stresses the social dimension of writing. Even students who are not particularly skillful critics and readers recognize the difference between the earnestness and deference of writers who are on their good behavior and the humor and/or edge that can take the frost off an essay. The concept of psychological distance is new to most students in my classes, but they are quick to understand it and are able to apply it in discussions of readings or of their own essays.

The text contains no exercises on the three aspects of tone because the addition of more passages for analysis would be superfluous and because the best experience with establishing or varying tone comes to students while they are writing complete essays.

Exercise 4: A Rewrite of "Seat Belts" (page 530).   This is obviously quite a difficult exercise, since the topic lends itself to dullness. If you are a committed and skillful user of collaborative writing groups in your class, you might consider assigning this exercise as a collaborative essay. If you have students work on it individually, you should give them an opportunity to see or hear the best efforts of their classmates. In giving such assignments in the past, I've always had a few students who rise to the occasion. Some produce ironic essays:

> Nobody should be allowed to use seat belts. Fatal automobile accidents serve two valuable functions in our society. They diminish the surplus population selectively, eliminating those with slow reflexes or bad vision, and so help to improve the species. They also save gas, since many people would rather walk than put themselves, unprotected, into a fast-moving box of glass and steel.

Some produce essays filled with unexpected details and data (in this case, grim details and data). Some develop ingenious arguments: "Nobody should be content with the protection of a seat belt alone. Every car should be equipped with air bags."

It is true that the best answers to this assignment will often have a garish, showy quality. But as Blake says, "You never know what is enough until you know what is more than enough."

PART V

Handbook of Grammar and Usage

Answer Key

Section 1: Grammar and Sentence Structure

1.1 *Parts of Speech*

Exercise 1: Using Pronouns in Writing (page 539)
  Answers will vary.

Exercise 2: Verbs (page 542)

1. was—Linking, Intransitive;
   was—Linking, Intransitive

2. wrote—Action, Transitive;
   started—Action, Transitive

3. was—Linking, Intransitive;
   did join—Action, Intransitive

4. disagreed—Action, Intransitive

5. rejected—Action, Transitive;
   would have brought—Action,
   Transitive

6. took—Action, Transitive;
   joined—Action, Transitive

7. replaced—Action, Transitive

Exercise 3: Prepositional Phrases (page 550)

1. Throughout history;
   in harmony;
   with one another;
   with nature.

2. in ancient Athens;
   of the ideal society

3. In Plato's perfect <u>society</u>;
   between the three <u>classes</u>;
   for <u>government</u>;
   in the <u>land</u>

5. Since Plato's <u>era</u>;
   by the <u>idea</u>;
   of utopian <u>communities</u>

4. According to <u>Plato</u>;
   in the <u>society</u>;
   in their <u>roles</u>;
   despite the <u>divisions</u>;
   among the <u>classes</u>

Exercise 4:   Conjunctions and Conjunctive Adverbs (pages 553–54)
              Answers will vary.

1.2   Sentence Structure

Exercise 1:   Subject and Predicate (pages 557–58)

1. The <u>population</u> of the world in the year 1650 <u>was</u> five hundred million

   <u>people</u>.

2. Between 1650 and 1850, the world's <u>population</u> <u>doubled</u>.

3. <u>Will</u> the rapid <u>growth</u> in population, now 2 percent a year, <u>continue</u>?

4. Because medical advances allow people to live longer, the birth <u>rate</u>

   <u>exceeds</u> the death rate in many countries.

5. Population <u>experts</u> <u>expect</u> continued growth and believe that the increasing

   population will put a strain on the world's resources, particularly food and

   energy.

Exercise 2:   Complements (page 561)
1. setbacks—Direct object;
   him—Direct object
2. undistinguished—Predicate adjective;
   him—Direct object;
   student—Objective complement
3. direction—Direct object;
   him—Direct object
4. Churchill—Indirect object;
   training—Direct object;
   student—Predicate nominative
5. adventure—Direct object;
   him—Indirect object;
   opportunity—Direct object

1.3   Phrases and Clauses

Exercise 1:   Prepositional and Appositive Phrases (page 564)
              Answers will vary.

Exercise 2:   Participial Phrases (page 566)
              Answers will vary.

Exercise 3:   Gerunds and Infinitives (pages 569–70)
              Answers will vary.

Exercise 4:   Adjective Clauses (page 572)
              Answers will vary.

Exercise 5:   Adverb Clauses (page 574)
              Answers will vary.

Exercise 6:   Noun Clauses (page 576)
              Answers will vary.

Exercise 7:   Eliminating Fragments (pages 580–81)
              Answers will vary.

Exercise 8:   Eliminating Run-on Sentences (page 582)
              Answers will vary.

Section 2:   Usage and Diction

2.1   The Scope of Usage

Exercise: Scope of Usage (page 585)
              Answers will vary.

2.2   *Correct Use of Verbs*

Exercise 1:   Choosing the Correct Form and Tense of Verbs (page 593)

1. Correct
2. <u>Having fought</u> the New York legislature for permission to <u>start</u> a school, Emma Willard went on to <u>make</u> educational history.
3. Public opinion about education for girls <u>shifted</u> back and forth until after the Civil War.
4. Correct
5. Correct

Exercise 2:   Correct Use of Tense (page 595)
Answers will vary.

Exercise 3:   Active and Passive Voice (pages 596–97)

1. wrote—Active;
   remained—Active—Intransitive
2. satirizes—Active
3. disappeared—Active—Intransitive;
   was conducted—Passive
4. lost—Active;
   produced—Active
5. were borrowed—Passive
6. wrote—Active;
   was—Active—Intransitive
7. were published—Passive
8. is based—Passive

Exercise 4:   Mood (page 599)

1. Hitch—Imperative
2. made—Indicative
3. Did know—Indicative
4. Give—Imperative
5. Would lend—Indicative

Exercise 5:   Active and Passive Voice (page 599)
Answers will vary.

Exercise 6:   Mood (page 599)
Answers will vary.

2.3   *Subject-Verb Agreement*

Exercise 1:   Locating Subjects and Verbs (page 601)

1. have constructed—Plural
2. measures—Singular
3. have—Plural

 4. have been—Plural
 5. includes—Singular

Exercise 2:   Subject-Verb Agreement (page 605)

 1. is
 2. was
 3. provide
 4. is
 5. is

Exercise 3:   Subject-Verb Agreement (page 607)

 1. stand
 2. make
 3. have, house
 4. seems
 5. is, looks

2.4   Correct Use of Pronouns

Exercise 1:   Pronoun Antecedents (page 611)

 1. his or her
 2. she
 3. it
 4. its
 5. her, her

Exercise 2:   Pronoun Case (page 614–15)

 1. We—Subject
 2. I—Appositive to subject
 3. he—Predicate nominative
 4. Your—Possessive pronoun;
    us—Object of preposition
 5. they—Predicate nominative

Exercise 3:   *Who* and *Whom* (page 616)

 1. who—Subject of adjective clause
 2. who—Subject of noun clause
 3. who—Subject of noun clause
 4. whom—Object of verb <u>saw</u> in adjective clause
 5. who—Subject of adjective clause;
    whom—Object of preposition <u>for</u>

Exercise 4:   Other Uses of Pronoun Case (page 617)

 1. I
 2. they
 3. they
 4. me (*or* I)
 5. us

Exercise 5:   Pronoun Reference (pages 618–19)
              Answers will vary.

  1. Correct
  5. Correct

2.5   Correct Use of Modifiers

Exercise 1:   Correct Use of Comparison (page 622)

  1. most engrossing—Superlative
  2. better—Comparative
  3. least lifelike—Superlative
  4. greater—Comparative
  5. shortest—Superlative

Exercise 2:   Placement of Modifiers (page 624)
              Answers will vary.

Exercise 3:   Use of Modifiers (page 624)
              Answers will vary.

Section 3:   Punctuation and Mechanics

3.1   Capitalization

Exercise: Capitalization (page 637)
              Answers will vary.

3.2   Punctuation

Exercise 1:   End Punctuation and Abbreviations (page 639)

  1. Wait! That flashlight needs new batteries.
  2. The postcard mailed from San Antonio, Texas, had a picture of La Villita, a restoration of a small city.
  3. The architect said, "That house is the best example of the Colonial period in this region."
  4. Oh! Don't forget the symbol for iron, Fe, in the equation.
  5. Mrs. Knudson, will you please repeat the last statistic?

Exercise 2:   Commas (page 643)

  1. Lyndon B. Johnson was a United States representative, a senator, and the Vice President before he became President.
  2. Sam borrowed the library book, he read the first chapter, and he copied some information for his research.
  3. Ms. Slade, a noted historian, lectured about the events leading up to the Civil War, the war itself, and the Reconstruction.

4. We can try either Indonesian, Chinese, or Vietnamese cuisine in this city.
5. After his death in 1792, the naval hero John Paul Jones was buried in the chapel at the United States Naval Academy.
6. The Dobson family has purchased a new, time-saving lawnmower.
7. Whatever caused it, it had a disruptive effect on the whole community.
8. The outcome of their experiment, unfortunately, was rather disappointing.
9. Signing the contract in the presence of a witness, the partners were ready to begin their business venture.
10. The architect who won the prize for the best design received the award on June 11, 1975, at a small ceremony.

Exercise 3:   Semicolons (page 644)

1. Rhode Island is the smallest state in the country; it measures forty-eight miles north to south and thirty-seven miles east to west.
2. The poinsettia grows outdoors in southern states; but, because of its vibrant red and green coloring, it is also a popular indoor plant during the winter months in cold climates.
3. Neptune was the god of the sea in Roman mythology; he resembled the Greek sea god Poseidon.
4. Edgar Allan Poe published "The Raven" in 1845; as a result, the poem brought him great recognition, and it is still read widely today.
5. Sara had been expecting an important call all afternoon; therefore, she dashed to the telephone and picked up the receiver after the first ring.

Exercise 4:   Colons (page 645–46)

1. John Paul Jones's response to the British commander's demand for surrender is famous: "I have not yet begun to fight."
2. A golfer might use the following clubs: woods, irons, and a putter.
3. For my course in traditions of Western literature, I read Genesis 2:15.
4. Before moving to her new home, Barbara read an informative book entitled Florida: Ponce de Leon to the Present.
5. Dear Mr. Saunders:
   Thank you very much for your helpful letter that suggests people to contact in the area, information to include with my application, and possible employment opportunities in the Midwest.

Exercise 5:   Quotation Marks (page 648)

1. "Do you know the lyrics to the song 'Give My Regards to Broadway'?" asked Mr. Rodgers.
2. The great Charlie "Bird" Parker was noted for playing the alto saxophone.
3. Scholars have searched for years to find the actual urn described in John Keats's poem "Ode on a Grecian Urn."
4. "How does sleet differ from hail?" asked Warren.
   "Although sleet and hail are formed nearly the same way, sleet occurs only in the winter," replied Mrs. Hartwick.
5. The artist explained that intaglio means "engraving."

Exercise 6:   Apostrophes (page 650–51)

1. The men's track teams at the University of Southern California held state championships throughout the 1960s.
2. How many s's and i's are there in <u>Mississippi</u>?
3. Lewis and Clark's expedition to the Pacific Ocean strengthened the claims of the United States to the northwestern territory.
4. The Gianellis' collie wound his chain around the chestnut tree in their back yard.
5. Correct

Exercise 7:   Hyphens, Dashes, Ellipsis Points (pages 654)

1. Muriel was obviously self-conscious as she practiced her acceptance speech.
2. Please take that package—if you haven't already done so—to the post office this afternoon.
3. Steven wrote down the beginning of the Preamble to the Constitution of the United States: "We the People of the United States, in order to form a more perfect Union . . . ."
4. The grocery bill for one week amounted to forty-three dollars.
5. I found <u>Robinson Crusoe</u> so fascinating that I read 175 pages in a single evening—one third of Defoe's novel!